The Real
Prison Diaries

Judy Frisby

Higher Ground Books & Media
Springfield, Ohio.
http://www.highergroundbooksandmedia.com

Printed in the United States of America 2019

The Real
Prison Diaries

Judy Frisby

Acknowledgments:

This book is for my faithful prison diary readers, for Kendra and Judy Young who believed in me even after I failed, for Mike and Bonnie for saving my child's life when she had lost all hope, for my soul mate RDF, for my children, and last but not least this book is for my little brown bear Isiah....Someday you will know how much of a gift from God you are, my sweet boy.

TABLE OF CONTENTS

Year One

The Sentencing

I had my Xanax in my purse ready for this day. This was the day I had been nervously dreading for the past month. Brown bear was staying with my nephew. He had no idea what would be happening that day, or how it was going to affect the rest of his life. I parked across the street from the courthouse as if the one-minute walk would put this off longer. While walking up the sidewalk I see a group of family members gathered outside the courthouse doors. My stomach began to feel like a washing machine. How could these people be here because of one of my children? I was holding my 18-year-old son's arm, which honestly was keeping me on my feet at that point. I suddenly stopped; I could not take another step. Cole said, "Mom you're going to be OK", but I was not.... I was definitely not going to be OK. I started to forget how to breathe. My body was in paralysis from anxiety. I started to sob right there on Main Street in the middle of the day on a Thursday. I want my child, they took her from me. I was scared and sad. This was harder than any funeral visitation I had ever been to, and those I hated more than anything else in the world. I told my son that I could not walk inside. I just could not see her. It was not the embarrassment of the whole ordeal, or the looks I was going to get from the "public workers" inside that courthouse. It was that this was the last time I was going to see my little girl for a very long time. My little girl was not little in physical stature...she was little mentally, and little to me. She was 19 years old and had just ruined her life. She was about to stand up in front of a judge and attorneys and a stupid local news camera crew and plead guilty for a spree of crimes that had happened over three months before that. I was about to watch my first-born hit rock bottom in front of a courtroom full of people. I was not prepared for this, I must have not taken this class in high school. I absolutely forced myself to put one foot in front of the other so that Mackenzie could see my face inside that courtroom. I know her, I created this human. I also knew she was scared to death. She did not have any idea this would be the result of trying some drugs for the first time at 14. It was. I hate drugs, they have made me do many things I do not want to do either directly or indirectly. My daughter had just hit the brick wall at the bottom of a spiraling downward tunnel.... a spiral that lasted five years long. To top off my parenting failures, it was about to be publicized. Of course, it had to be the big story in the news did I expect anything less of Mackenzie? My child has an intensity that is like no other.

People love it, the problem is she has no shut off switch to it. When she was on the softball field that intense power made very big plays and won many many games. When you place her in with a group of drug addicts or drug dealers her intense personality can be very very bad. My daughter has always wanted to fit in so bad, with whatever group will recognize her. The last group she found played off that intense personality and acted like they were her "friends".... that is how I ended up here...... writing The Real Prison Diaries.

From: Mackenzie Basham
Date: 09/16/2014
To: Judy Frisby

Hi to my beautiful mother...

writing to you to tell you that I love you very much and miss you more than ever.

can't wait to see you again, hope you're having a good day and you relax your mind and know that everything is okay.

smile mom you deserve it !!!!!!!!!!!!!!

LLOOOVVVVVVEEEEEEEEEEE
YYYYYYYYYYOOOUUUUUUUUUUU

From: Judy
Frisby Date:
09/16/2014
To: Mackenzie Basham

Hey Mack! It's Gracie. Mom and I are sharing this thing or
whatever lol I miss you! I'm coming with mom on October
1st to see you! So we can eat junk food together lol.
Mom's doing good since the surgery, I'm taking good care
of her so I'm always busy now (haha). I love you and will
send you more pictures and letters soon!

From: Judy Frisby
Date: 09/21/2014
To: Mackenzie Basham

Mack, I got your letter! I miss you so much, having a rough
day today because I am home by myself and that makes
me start missing my girl. I scheduled a video visit for
October 5th a Sunday night at 7:00 so Isiah and Gracie can
see you too. I hope you are coping with your situation right
now, it feels like a movie or a bad dream to me right now.
It's like it cannot be real, then I go to work and yep, it's real.
I still cannot go in public right now, I grocery shop at 3 or 4
am so I don't run into anyone staring, whispering, trying to
be fake and talk to me when they don't give a shit....they
want to know where you are and what really happened! I
have come to have a REAL appreciation for my home and
yard and what I have. I am sobbing now, a mother is
connected to her children and I can feel when you are not
at ease and the torture is that I cannot go to you and make
it all better. I have to beg God to watch over my little girl
and wipe her tears when she cries at night because she
misses her mom or her baby. It is ok to feel weak and
scared I feel it all the time, I also feel a little crazy but

whatever. My best conversations are with myself and I guess that's not normal but our life right now is not normal. Isiah is perfect, he loves his mommy just as much as when you were here. He is also hysterical just like you, all your good traits you passed to him. Ritchie and I love it, it's like we have our big Mack here, haha. See you soon T, love you more than chocolate my sweet girl....Mama

From: Judy Frisby
Date: 09/29/2014
To: Mackenzie Basham

Whew, I was getting nervous when I didn't hear from you girl! I'm glad to see that inbox have a reply haha. The more people talk around here, they say you will not have to do even half the time so let's just keep that in mind. It is your own thoughts and fears that are keeping you in this depression you have to keep an open mind and focus on your one goal which is to come home. Show them you do not belong there by volunteering for any work or group that you can. Do not allow yourself to get into a fight or not follow their rules, it is only going to set you back, and we do not need any more setbacks! One day gone is one day closer to you coming home, don't think about the sentence hanging over your head, think about the small accomplishments like another day you served your time. You cannot change the past or what you did, move on and you will still be able to lead a normal life with Isiah and your family.
Depression is getting you nowhere or me, I try to say to God a few things I'm thankful for every day instead of begging for you to come home. It's a way more positive feeling. Look how you and I have become so much closer like when you were younger! There were about 4 years that were just fighting, and you had no respect for me, you would cuss me out and talk terrible like I was a piece of crap and that hurt me and Ritchie and Gracie so bad. It was not you, that is not my Mackenzie that was the drugs and people you were with! Now you are clean and not with them and I absolutely love talking to you and Ritchie and I can't wait until

you get out and can move back in and we can enjoy our daughter instead of avoiding the drama. Ritchie and his brothers are going to open a Bait shop and sell fishing stuff and hunting stuff and you can work in the bait shop until you get back on your feet. It is so nice to feel like we can trust you instead of scared for you to be in our home or jobs like when you stole from my shop or stole all of our stuff from our house and what hurt was that you would deny that you took it. We love you and knew that eventually, we would get the REAL Mackenzie back we had until you were 16. Well I gotta go take Cole to the dr he has strep throat and he starts college next Monday so we have to get his books and uniforms! I'm so proud of him for taking this step just like I was of you when you tried it... It's not for everyone so even if he fails at least he tried, good enough for me. Ok talk soon, love you more than chocolate sis, MOM

From: Mackenzie Basham
Date: 09/30/2014
To: Judy Frisby

Hey, mom so I got your email, I hope you guys had fun fishing. I tried to call you but it says global telling has your number blocked. So, call them back and tell them that it won't let me call. I can't wait until Wednesday, and aw I love that picture of Zay! I added Ritchie to my phone list he just Has to accept it. I'm missing you guys a lot, it's a hard struggle in here especially right now that I don't have anything. Have you seen my grandma? When will you guys be able to buy my box? I'm really needing clothes and a TV; I'm missing all the football games!!! All I do is set on my bed; I start working in the cafeteria this week. So that should be interesting, a lot of girls get caught stealing food from there, lol cuz they starve us...!!! But I'm not stealing anything, ever again in my life. I've learned my lesson. I'm listening to 2pac: Dear Mama, it makes me think of you (other than you're not black or a crack fiend lol), Just the part that says, "thru all the drama I can depend on my mama!" There's no way I can pay you back for everything, all I can do is do everything you ask for and that's my plan... I don't know what I'd do without you mom. you are my rock, you've never left me hanging when I needed you the most, you've never just forgotten about me. I went to church this Sunday and it felt like Jesus was right next to me, I cried the whole time. I feel so beautiful inside and out, I feel no hate inside me and it feels so good. I think it's called being sober. Well, I'm going to go to sleep, I got to be up early for blood work they are checking my thyroid to see if it chemically imbalanced. See you on Wednesday!!! LOVE YOU SOOOOOOO VERY MUCH! Tell Zay I love him and I can't wait to see him. Love you all tell Ritchie hello and I love him, I'll call him this week sometime! Tell my brother I love and miss him and want his phone number so I can put it on my list since he doesn't write me at least I can talk to him. Well goodnight sweet dreams, love you.

From: Mackenzie Basham
Date: 10/2/2014
To: Judy Frisby

Hey mom, how's your day going? I hope better than mine, I've been depressed and all I want to do is sleep... I need to shake this off, it's just so hard to realize that I'm going to be here for a while... I can't forgive myself for this. I just think why was I so stupid? I have crazy feelings like death would be better than this, I don't want to get out of bed or even wake up some days... I feel so hurt, like this nightmare will never end, I feel like I've lost everything, but the truth is I just see the only thing I've ever had, and that's family... I'm so thankful for my family, if I didn't have you mom, I'd of already tried to kill myself, the only reason I care about life is to come home to my family and zay. Please forgive me, I worry about you and your health.
You've got to stay strong and healthy, without you I can't get

thru this... I love you mom, miss you so much!! Stay strong and SMILE you deserve it!

From: Mackenzie Basham
Date: 10/06/2014
To: Judy Frisby

Mom I haven't talked to you... I hope you are doing ok. I love and miss you... I'm missing you really bad...

From: Judy Frisby
Date: 10/16/2014
To: Mackenzie Basham

Hi Kenzie, video visit was a huge fail! I will get it down but Zay was sick, just cold and flu and now I have it. I called the phone place and unblocked my number so you can call me there are 25 dollars on my phone account. Love you..... Cole shot a deer and I have to go pick him up, I don't even have any time to be sick!!! Call us tonight, love you..., Mom

From: Judy Frisby
Date: 10/10/2014
To; Mackenzie Basham

Hi Kenzie, how did work go tonight? I am very proud of you for staying busy to stay out of trouble! I know what you mean when you said, "Mom, I'm going through it". I am too. Today I got sad and was pissed off at you. I felt good you're doing better, then I hit your name in my phone to see what would happen. Too many emotions in one freaking day, then I got home and baby Zay snapped me out of it, I was then on "Nana Duty". I told you how many messages I have got and encouragement from Facebook friends and family so this one got to me, you played ball against her when you were young. She writes the following message......

"I'm super horrible at expressing my feelings! so I'm going to try my best! I constantly stalk your page. lol not to be creepy haha. I just like to see updates on Kenzie! I don't know if you know, not something I'm proud of or many people do know. I am addicted to opiates. I have been in recovery for quite a while now. I've done things I am ashamed of and carry around so much guilt, some days it's unbearable. if it wasn't for my daughter and supportive family I truly do not know where I would be today! reading your posts does something powerful to me... being a mother myself I cannot fathom what you or Kenzie are going through. for her to be away from her beautiful little boy. and the letters she writes to you bring tears to my eyes every single time. I have felt those feelings she feels. and I'm proud of her for being honest about how she feels. it is the worst sickness you can go through, to physically be healthy. but mentally disabled basically. is like being trapped inside your own mind and bad decisions. addiction takes over your life and before you know it.. you don't have one anymore. she, just like I am. is so lucky to have a strong and supportive mother. from what I read you do so many amazing things for her! and I'm positive she appreciates you more than she can express. the main reason I am writing you is because you have put some much into perspective for me. I already know I have put my parents through hell and back, repeatedly. but for you to express your feelings and share what you are going through makes me realize the effect it's had on my mom and appreciate my mom so much more than I already do. when you are using you don't realize your addiction affects so many people. Kenzie and I are so lucky to not have burnt the most important bridge we have, our momma's. the guilt and shame we feel will never compare to the sleepless nights, stress, panic, pain, and hurt we have caused the most important people in our lives. she sounds like a strong girl who can overcome her addiction. if I can, she can too. especially with your support and most importantly unconditional love. just want you to know I am always willing to talk to anyone about my story. it's important to addicts to know the grass is truly greener on the other side. she will have to learn to live life sober again, just like I did. she will be such a better and stronger person because of her mistakes. and facing them head-on. just know, reading your post help me on my bad days, because someone always has it worse. just like her, its something ill struggle with the rest of my life. but being inspired by someone is what helps you wake up every day and choose to be sober rather than choosing to give in to the devil. I pray for Kenzie, you and your family!! and truly wish her the absolute best on her journey! if you ever need to talk ask questions or vent, I'm always here"

I feel like your "story" may just have helped someone, so see Kenz, you are just like other people. You are not alone in this big world and you are going to find this out. I'll talk to you soon, baby boy is feeling better and getting very spoiled, we need to work on that too... Love you more than chocolate sweet girl..... Mama

From: Judy Frisby
Date: 10/13/2014
To: Mackenzie Basham

Hey Kenz, how was today? Yesterday was rough. I am sorry about how I was on the phone. Tough day for us here too. When I asked you if you thought of Zay during those last days of April, I was not trying to make you feel bad or worse or go do the unthinkable. Honey, I am your number one fan and you have to know that, but I get angry at you just like you get angry at me. We don't have time to sugar coat things, we have shit to do. You told me it hurt you when Zay cried and said he wanted me; I get it but what an awesome thing for your child to have a close bond with your mom? Do you know how many women are in there with tears running down their pillows because their babies are with strangers like in foster homes? Isiah has it made, so instead of getting all sad when he lashes out at you put yourself in HIS SHOES for just one second and stop thinking about how it is hurting you. There is only one thing you can do for Isiah, and that is to stay on track to get out. He doesn't care about all the words and the promises until you are out and staying clean and away from that low life trash you associated with. I always refer back to your so-called friends....do they write you now? Did any go up to that nasty county jail and go up in the elevator that smelled like human throw-up just to see you through a glass and chat on the phone for 20 minutes? I love that you appreciate the power of family now but you still not there yet with the "friends" thing. Your beautiful and smart and funny as hell and giant- hearted and you should not let anyone into your life that is not worthy of that. I do not tolerate ignorance or fakeness or to show people because I learned honey that they don't deserve all this, haha. Watch out for "jail friends" and do not fall for peer pressure in there, those kinds of people love that place.

You just let them be the top dogs in prison, it will be very cool when their butts die in there and nobody remembers their name. You make people remember you sister!! Well, I have to get back to my exhilarating life of cooking and washing everything again because it smells like pee. You freaking owe me big time for having to potty train chubbs. I feel like we have a new puppy, I sniff everything to see if it has pee on it......Chin up, remember no matter where we are, we'll always be together. Start every day with an attitude that you will own it! I miss you so very much that it physically hurts me......write back soon. Love you more than chocolate.......Mom

From: Judy Frisby
Date: 10/25/2014
To: Mackenzie Basham

Hi Mackenzie,

I haven't talked to you in a while, just hoping your hanging in there. Isiah is doing great in school and we are getting ready for trick or treat. He is going to be a shark.... he says a BIG HUGE SHARK! Your grandparents are all doing good, no one is sick, I know you worry a lot about their health. It's starting to be fall, it feels like football weather finally and I sure am missing that number #16 play out on the field. I was looking at pictures from last year's season how much fun we all had going to Cole's games.... hard to believe how much has happened in a year. Are you going to get on the softball team in there? That would be awesome. Look up the movie " the longest yard" in your library....it reminds me of you playing on the inside haha!. I hope your crazy Indian roommate didn't hurt you with her "Indian cooking" she was going to make you. I went to Gracie Jo's choir concert and it was so nice, she is such a sweet girl and she worries about you so much. I hate that she can't be a normal 13-year-old. She worries about Isiah first then herself just like she is a little mother. I would trust Grace to take care of Zay more than Cole.....he still loses his driver's license every week imagine him handling a child!

He is good with Zay but he gets him to wound up wrestling and in football stances then leaves and I am left with this crazed adrenaline pumped up 3 years old. Isiah loves it here, he is having a bit of separation anxiety right now, always asking me, "Nana, are you coming right back to pick me up?" I always tell him, yes but we have to go over this about 10 times before I leave him at preschool or a family members house.

He has just been traumatized and needs to make sure I do not leave him, for him to relax and feel safe. He is sleeping in his own big boy bed (when he sleeps) and that is a great forward step. After 5 months of what felt like sleeping with a wild animal, I bought him Monsters Inc. sheets and pillow, and he loves his room.... the Tv and DVD player helps too! I miss you so much. At least now I can talk about you now without sending myself into a panic and getting a sick feeling in my stomach. To be honest, when you first went away, I grieved you as if you have died. You may not understand that, but it was actually easier to deal with you being in heaven then the gut-wrenching horrifying thoughts of you in a jail cell or a prison. I still try to block out where you actually are, if I think about the things that happen in a prison it eats me alive and I just close up and can't speak or function on a day to day basis. This thing with your new "roommate" is bothering the hell out of me. As a mother, you are only as content as your most troubled child, and to think of my sweet baby girl sleeping in a close quarter room with a convicted murderer makes it hard to swallow my own saliva, I'm not going to lie. When I first looked her up and found out her charges of murder and abuse of a corpse, I slept about 30 minutes that night. Ritchie says, "Mack can take her, she's tough". That does not put my mind at ease. Pray, Jesus is my very best friend right now, and my faith in knowing you have his protection is what I am desperately clinching onto. Sorry, I can not write you letters, it is too hard to see my thoughts and fears wrote down on a piece of paper, when I email them to you, I don't have to see it again. Someday I can write a letter, just not now. Grammy Shepherd lives for your letters. You are on her mind 24 hours a day, and she calls me to see if I have heard from you every day. I lie to her all the time, but only to tell her you are fine and doing good. Those lies I will be forgiven for, I have to protect my mom she cannot handle it. I know I have help, but I understand when you tell me you feel alone. I do to honey, nobody gets it. The emptiness caves my heart, especially at night. I have your clothes in my closet and I have to touch and smell them sometimes, Gracie even sleeps in your clothes when she is having a tough night. Well, I cannot wait to see you again, 3 hours a month sucks but I cherish that time and it sometimes helps me get out of bed in the morning. I know it does you too. Stay focused, positive attitude, stay working and going to church and your group.....do not eat the Indian food! I love you so much. I put money on your phone account, we have to hear your voice soon, I'm getting in a funk again. Love you more than chocolate, Mom.

From: Mackenzie Basham
Date: 10/31/2014
To: Judy Frisby

So today is Friday and I woke up went to the case manager to get in programs and he wasn't there, so I took a deep breath said," ok God we'll try again Monday"... then I walked over to the school, began talking to the teachers begging them to put me into some kind of schooling (anything they have opened) they told me because of my out date I have to wait until I'm 5-7 years into my sentence!!! I began to get frustrated like why would you make someone wait that long, hopefully, I'll be on my way home in that time!!! So, they said since I'm already on the waiting list there's nothing else I can do... I took a deep breath told God to keep me strong because I feel the devil trying to break me... I then walked over to the public defender's office and began, asking questions about my case and what I could do to get home as soon as possible, he had the nerve to say "I've seen many young women come in here that end up doing their full sentence" "you will eventually get fed up and end up seeing the hole", I told him thanks for the advice and got up and walked out.... I got back to my room and fell to my knees begging God to hold me the devil is all over this place..... I couldn't hold my tears in so I cried and cried, then I realized that these "people" that are telling me these negative things are only "human" ..... I KNOW what I'm capable of and I KNOW I want more in life than a prison number ..... I've got a baby boy to come home to and a wonderful family and support that so many people don't have, I know I've got God on my side and I won't give up, nothing can stop me from coming home... I've got to keep

on pushing no matter how hard it is, some days I feel so low and alone but I know God's with me
..... I just picture myself holding Zay and it makes me so motivated... I will do ANYTHING to get home to him and won't stop until I am. it's us against the world!

I LOVE YOU MOM!!!

"ONLY THROUGH EXPERIENCE OF TRIAL AND SUFFERING, CAN THE SOUL BE STRENGTHENED, VISION CLEARED, AMBITION INSPIRED, AND SUCCESS ACHIEVED"

Give bubby kisses for me, see you soon!!!!

From: Judy Frisby
Date: 11/5/2014
To: Mackenzie Basham

Hi Kenz,

How are you holding up? I am excited I get to visit you on Thursday! I have had a very exhaustive week here on the home front. Today Isiah asked me if he could have a slumber party with his mom. I told him that as soon as you get out of time out, you are going to come home, and we will have a bunch of slumber parties. He said NO NANA; I want to have one right now. That just proves my point that he will never forget you and all the fun times you and he had as long as I keep you in our conversations and your pictures up and talk about the things you and he used to do. You are still very much a part of our family you know; this is a minor setback to a major comeback like Coley says!

I am having a bit of trouble sleeping at night because of these nightmares. I hate falling into a deep sleep because I can't control what happens in my dreams. Last night was intense, you showed up at the door and told me you had escaped! I was panicking and yelling at you and so mad you had done something so stupid. Then you told me you were going to run in the cornfield and asked Gracie to go with you... And she did! I said, "Gracie Jo Frisby, get your butt back in this house!" She wouldn't listen and I was a wreck and so mad at both of you thinking I was losing both my daughters. Then you told you were going to go back before they found out and asked me to drive you and help you sneak in. The feeling was awful and I was caught between helping you and you thinking it was ok if I helped you get away with it! I woke up sweating and heart pounding out of my chest until I went in and saw that Gracie was sound asleep and everyone was here. It was so real I even looked around for you to be in the house somewhere. This is why I haven't checked my email from you all week because I have to put it completely out of my mind to get some peace in my life. I get where I'm checking my email 20 times a day to see if I have an inbox and it's like a giant snowball and you are consuming my every thought until I can't even finish a sentence there is a thousand things running through my mind. I also need to focus on the other kids. It is not fair to them. They have done nothing wrong and yet all my "attention" is still on you. Cole starts college on the 17th and Gracie got her report card and has a 3.5 GPA... I should be able to allow myself to be happy for them, but when I am so consumed with your misery, I will not allow myself to be happy. I put on a great show in front of people, but it sickens my stomach if I start to enjoy something because I know you are in hell right now. I have to work this out, it is just not fair to them, they are good kids and deserve to have their mom present in their lives. I mean I am here but the blank stare and constant yawns and look of exhaustion is kind of a downer when they are excited and telling me something you know? I have so much guilt when it comes to them. I don't even remember the month of May or June; I was just going through the motions and that's not fair. Cole graduated for God's sake and after he walked out of the gym I started sobbing because you weren't there... So, did he. His grad party was nice, but he kept coming up to me saying, " I miss my sister, she should be here." You had control of our thoughts without even being here because we care about you so much we can't allow ourselves to be happy. I have to step back, and JUST BREATHE. We cannot live like this, it's like we are in our own prison. It was Cole's very last home baseball game of his entire school career on April 29th. There was 1 out in the bottom of the seventh and he was up. Mom and dad were sitting beside me and Isiah. I had not seen you in FIVE DAYS. My phone was ringing and I didn't answer because I wanted to concentrate on Cole it was his moment. I had a gut-wrenching uneasy feeling so I hit my voicemail to see your Aunt and my Aunt had left me a message, I listened to the beginning of ...

Hey, Judy, we want to know if you are ok, we just saw Mackenzie on The 6:00 news. I mumbled something to mom as I frantically hit WLIO on my phone . I walked into the restroom by the ball field, went into a stall and hit play. Jeff Fitzgerald says your name as your mugshot is largely pictured behind him as he talks about the "woman" the police have arrested in a number of burglaries in the area counties. My knees buckle, my breathe would not come out and I kept swallowing as my glands were watering like when I was a kid with the stomach flu. I braced my hands on the walls of the bathroom stall and I start to vomit, and I kept vomiting until there was nothing left to come out of my body but sobs and like a weird yell. My first thought was how am I going to hide this from my mom and dad and Gracie and Cole. I wipe off my face and look up toward God and say, " help". I walk out trying to look not traumatized and the game was over and they were shaking hands. I missed it, I missed your brother's big moment to remember and I can't forgive myself...yet I did nothing wrong. I love you so much but please know I will never forget about you, I just need a "Mackenzie break" every now and then. I can't wait to see you, I really needed you to hear that for me to have a release of some sort. I will ALWAYS stick by you and defend you until the day I die because I am your mother, but I also their mother too. I love

you more than chocolate, goodnight my sweet girl...Mom.
From: Mackenzie Basham
Date: 11/14/2014
To: Judy Frisby

Hey mom... I hope you are doing better than me, I still cry
myself to sleep at night wishing I was holding Isiah.. I miss
him so much, it hurts so bad, to hear him laughing and
carrying on in the background when we are on the phone. I
mean I'm glad he's happy but it hurts that I can't be there to
see his smile and play with him.

I know its hard to actually be happy, but you as well as
everyone else deserve to be happy and enjoy your days. I
deserve to be punished, not you, I'm doing the best I can in
here. All because of you, so relax and be happy, this will all
be over before we know it. This is what God has dealt us in
life, he obviously knows we can make it through this... I
won't give up because I love you and everyone else and I
WILL be back home ... you keep me going mom, SMILE,
you deserve it

From: Judy Frisby
Date: 11/17/2014
To: Mackenzie Basham

Hi Girl,

I just got your letter this morning. I knew when I talked to
you that you were having a tough time. Everyone that
talks to me says the holidays will be the hardest. I am just
going to stay home this year. I know I'm going to hear
about it from our family but I really don't care. I cannot go
and see everybody laughing and having a good time with
their children. I haven't had a Thanksgiving or Christmas
without my children since the day you were born, so it will

not be complete and I refuse to put on a show like it isn't killing me. Jen says I'm just at an angry stage right now... She's probably right. I love all my nieces and nephews but to see them all happy with their parents and grams and gramps makes me want to like turn up music so loud I just see their faces but don't have to hear a word they say! I do not care what others think about me right now and I'm really tired of feeling like I'm on the defensive all the time. I am always trying to "explain" your side or why or how you had a drug addiction. Today, at this moment I don't want to talk or explain anything to anyone. I get mad at people for bragging to me about their kids. I know that's insane, but I feel like it's a dig at me. I am perfectly happy with my being in my home, or at a shop, with Isiah, Cole, and Gracie and never seeing another person ever again in my life. Nobody understands how I feel so whatever. I had to start taking meds to sleep again, the nightmares are out of control. Lately, it has been coming from you last court appearance... " the sentencing". To even write about this will make me have to take an anxiety pill. The night before, the meeting the family in the parking lot, the ride to the courthouse in silence with just Cole Ryan and I in the car. Walking up I had a death grip on Coles' hand, and the second he spoke I started sobbing. He said, " Mom, you are ok, we can do this!" I don't remember if I replied all I remember was not speaking and trying to look at everyone waiting for us on the steps of the courthouse. I was saying to myself that I had to see your face then I could faint. My stomach felt like every person that spoke to me punched me as hard as they could in the stomach. By the time I got to the upstairs entrance, I felt like paralysis was setting in..... In my entire freaking body. I walked through the metal detectors and I felt like all the police officers and woman sitting at desks were all staring me down like " there she is, that's the big ALLEN COUNTY BURGLAR'S MOM." I just focused on my feet so they would walk but honestly, I wanted to punch every one of them very hard in the face. I hated them, they did this to my little girl. That is just how a mom thinks I guess. We got in and I sat in the front row, right behind where they would bring you. The last time I was on that room I was with Sharon Young and the girls and they were bringing Dick Joseph back to Lima for an appeal, and Sharon got to speak to the court. I was on the other side of the room, where the good people's side was I thought. I remember looking over and thinking how could anyone sit behind such a horrible person... A criminal. So all this is running through my head as I hold on for dear life to your brother. Then Jules says, Judy somebody is here... I look up and it's Sharon. She grabs me and is hugging and kissing me and I try to say, " the last time I was here   I couldn't finish and she knew that. Cole Ryan couldn't speak to her; he knows he was named after her boy. She was like some kind of angel that God sent me to let me know I could do this and if she was there it meant the people who truly love us were not judging one thing, they were hurting too. I took a deep breath and sat down and in walks the victims of whose houses were invaded. I started to sob, I couldn't look at them, and for a minute I felt like they were me years back glaring at those awful people sitting behind my dear friends' killer. That's when I look over at Jen and Jordy and I said: " here she comes"...I heard your chains as they walked you up from the jail. Cole jumped up and ran to the bathroom to vomit, but your Uncle followed to check on him. He came back and we were holding hands so tight as the bailiff said," All rise", I lost my breath. This was not real life, I thought I was on some secret reality show. My vision of you was blurred from crying and your attorney was saying words to me about if I was going to be speaking and asking for mercy to the judge I think, I just kept staring at you as you were sobbing and telling the entire family you were sorry and you loved them. To see my daughter in black and white stripes as the defendant in a criminal trial is an image that haunts me every night, once I can get

pushed through this I think I will be able to sleep...
Sound sleep. I know I spoke and apologized to the victims
and begged the judge, but I have no idea what I said. I do
remember feeling overwhelmed with support and hugs and
love from all who came to support you. You need to
remember that. At your lowest moment in life, when that
judge handed you that awful sentence, remember who was
in the 3 rows behind you... They will always be there. I
know Sharon writes you and I cannot ever repay her for all
the things she has done, but do you understand her hell
brought her to do this for us. She has more wisdom than us
so listen to every word she says, God knows she knows
what she is talking about and she still has faith in the man
upstairs so we have to also. I lose my faith then I can see
her face that day, tears running down her poor face, and I
think my God she has made it until now with what she went
through, we cannot lose faith it is all we have. I love you so
much and the holidays are just that, another day. We have
each other and that is bigger than any day on a calendar.
Love you more than chocolate, hugs, and kisses.....
Momma

From: Mackenzie Basham
Date: 11/20/2014
To: Judy Frisby

I know what you mean about the nightmares, they haunt me
every night... I think about court and the day I got arrested, (of
what I can remember) and I get shivers and start having an
anxiety attack... I think about when I signed my life away for 14
years because I was scared to risk it for 64... I think about the
shackles and stripes , the transfer and the car ride that passed
your road on the way to Marysville prison, the big gates that
opened an the police officer that drove me said "if your going to
run, now is the time to do it" then the gates closed behind us
and I had to vomit , but I swallowed it, then I got checked in and

they stripped me naked had me do all this bend and cough, put me in a dress , while everyone sat and stared at me. They took my picture and I sat and sat.... every minute i retold myself I was going to be ok.... all I wanted to do was be with my mom, and my son, I wanted my family and to tell them how much i love them and how sorry I am.... But now I realize sorry is just a word that is easily overused, I need to show you how sorry I am, that's why I'm staying sober and being on my best behavior, I'm taking my medications and staying busy... I'm doing anything possible to be home with you, yes God is the only one who knows what tomorrow brings... But one day tomorrow will bring me home, until that day we've got to stay strong and positive... They can't keep me forever. I love you, mom, talk to you soon!! SMILE!

From: Mackenzie Basham
Date: 11/26/2014
To: Judy Frisby

This will be the hardest year for us because it is the first year not being able to be together on the holidays but please take your mind off of me and my situation and know that I'm okay and at peace where I'm at... Enjoy your Thanksgiving with our wonderful family because you never know when it will be the last... Go and be thankful for our health and well being, give everyone hugs and kisses for me. Laugh, smile and eat until you throw up. Lol, as much as we wish I could be there, I can't... but it's going to be okay because you can be there for me and you can enjoy Thanksgiving for the both of us ..... I'm thankful for a family like mine, a support system like mine, a strong mother like mine, a perfect son like mine, and a second chance at life ..... One day things will be back to normal, but until then we've got to adjust to the situation we are in..... Go and have a great Thanksgiving. I LOVE YOU MORE THAN MY FREEDOM. STAY STRONG MOM & HAPPY

THANKSGIVING!!!!

From: Judy Frisby
Date: 11/30/2014
To: Mackenzie Basham

Hi Sis,

I got your letters on Thanksgiving and I will send out your food box this week. We had an " ok" day, but it wasn't the same without you. I went through the motions, cooked a turkey and a million other things which kept me busy so I didn't get sad. Ritchie had a tough time. It is really hitting him hard losing both his parents. I feel so bad and selfish loathing in my own misery of losing you. It has been very trying on our marriage yet made it so much stronger. We both feel like it is us against the world and at times we don't like anyone, even each other. We still very much love everyone but just don't like people. I have changed and I know that, not sure for the better or for the worse. I just looked up the meaning of traumatized:

trau·ma·tize ˈtroumə ̩tīz, ˈtrômə ̩tīz/

verb

past tense: traumatized; past participle: traumatized

subject to lasting shock as a result of an emotionally disturbing experience or physical injury.

It explains Ritchie, me, you, Coley, Gracie, baby Isiah. I guess I want answers, I want to know why this happened to us and how to fix it. I am not feeling sorry for myself; I just want to know WHY? I question why I was not a better parent to you, I question how I did not know of your drug abuse, I question why I was not a better daughter in law to Grandma Sherry, I question if I was a good enough wife to Ritchie when his mom and dads died that horrible month of June. Not like you or anyone can give me the answer I need to have peace though; I am battling this with myself in my own mind. I have done some bad things in the past but so has every human on this earth... So, my question is if this is God's plan what did I do to deserve this? There's no answer. I am at a point where I get angry if someone says anything nice to me. If they tell me I look nice, I want to say "Your lying to make me feel good, I have gained 20 pounds because I don't leave the house and chocolate chip cookies are my best friend right now and I have bags under my eyes from crying on a daily basis, and I have nervous twitches in my face and pick at myself so I look like I do crack.". If someone says that I am a good mom, I want to say, "then why did my daughter get pregnant at 16, become addicted to drugs and commit a series of crimes?" I would just rather not speak to anyone. My shop has saved my life though, it is what I love, and my customers make me happy every single day and my girls at work. It gives me a reason to get out of bed and get dressed. If I didn't have a job I am quite sure I would live in my grandma nightgown and bake and not look in a mirror and feed the rabbits and cats and squirrels in the backyard! I also looked up the meaning of panic;

pan·ic1

ˈpanik/

noun 1.

sudden uncontrollable fear or anxiety, often causing wildly unthinking behavior.

"she hit him in panic"

This is another word that describes my feelings every day. I panic when I hear an ambulance when I see a cop car when I get the mail, when I get a text message when my phone rings when I hear a noise and it's dark out. I'm sick of it. How long until I feel safe in my own body or in my

own home, I don't know but you sound like you feel safe so why don't I? The letter you wrote me before Thanksgiving made me cry. I didn't believe you for one second though I saw behind your words and knew you were lying. I cried because I know that you love me so much, you sent that and put on a happy face just so I would not worry about you and be able to have a good day for the rest of the family. Am I right, because I know you girl? I knew when you called on Thanksgiving by the shakiness of your voice and the deep breathes you kept taking that you were giving it all you had to sound ok or happy. I appreciate the effort sister! Anyway, our next obstacle is the Christmas season and I know we will survive it, but it isn't gonna be pretty, lol. Gracie is excited that we have to play "Santa" now..... Me I'm not sure. I kinda liked sleeping in on Christmas morning, hell every morning for that matter. Let me know what presents you are thinking you want me to put under the tree from you and I will get them and tell Zay that mommy sent him a present from her "school". He is so smart, as the years come his questions will get harder for me to get around to start thinking of ideas or what parts of the truth, we are going to tell him without causing him any harm. One day at a time girl, can't wait to see you for a visit. I'll get you a snicker bar from the vending machine and a Mountain Dew and we'll have Christmas dinner, haha. We gotta laugh or we'll cry, right?
Anyway, I love you, keep writing me and stay safe in there. Be strong when you have to be and don't you let anyone hurt you just because you are in there does not mean you're any less of a human being than anyone else..... Remember that. Love you more than chocolate, Momma

From: Mackenzie Basham
Date; 12/2/2014
To: Judy Frisby

So, I read your letter and first off I want you to know that the things that happened to me will never be your fault or because you didn't parent right... You have been the best mother anyone could ask for; I don't know why we have been dealt this life but I do know that God gives his hardest battles to his strongest warriors... I know that no matter where we are or what we are going through we stand together with love and support. I know that we have been through hell and back and that this trial in our life will not break us. If anything, it will make us stronger and better us... The whole situation sucks yes, but mom, we can't change it, and we can't keep asking ourselves why or what if, it's only going to make it harder on us... I'm still having a hard time coping with this, every day it runs through my head that this can be my life for the next 14 years.... I think about all the things I can miss out on in my son's life, and all the events in my brothers and sisters live I won't be present at... It hurts a lot and I become angry at myself... Then I realize that there is a reason for everything, and I realize that if I wouldn't have caught this case and been locked up for burglary, I would have been in that car with KG, even worse I would have been driving ..... I could be dead right now and Isiah wouldn't have a mom, or I could have died off of all them Xanax and alcohol... I don't even remember days upon days of my life.... Blackouts after blackouts, waking up in the car in random driveways, beside a house in the grass next to a trashcan IN my own vomit. I thank God every day and night because he saved me, mom... even though I'm not where I want to be, at least I'm not where I was, at least I have a second chance... If worst comes to worst I'll be home 4/25/2028... And yes, that seems so far away but at least I'm coming home now with the mentality I have and the motivation I'll be home sooner than you know ... miracles happen every day.... I'm taking this "time out" I was given to better myself and my thinking... I've matured a lot since I've been incarcerated, I'm more thankful and appreciative for the small things in life, I'm able to control my anger and think clearly and logically...

This will never be a walk in the park for us, but I promise it will get easier, sometimes I act like everything is okay and will be okay in the end but honestly I'm not okay with where I'm at and I'm not sure how things will end up but 'I've learned to put everything in God's hands, because he is the only one who knows what tomorrow will bring. That's why I need to tell you every day that I love you and I'm thankful for you because just in case I don't have another chance to tell you I need you to know how much I appreciate you. I pray every night, things get easier for you to deal with, I know the feelings you have of not feeling safe, truth be told I don't feel safe either... I live in the lifers' cottage so that's pretty much all child molesters and killers, having to always watch my back and sleep with one eye open gets exhausting, in the youngest one in this cottage and I have to stand my ground... But I know that all I can do is ask God to hold me in his arms and protect me, I ask him to hold my family also and keep them safe until I can come home... You've got to have more faith, mom ... We are going to be alright, I read a lot now and I don't read fictional books because life is not fictional, I read books that relate to real life situations and they teach me how to handle things And respond to situations in a positive way... Read the book "Don't Sweat The Small Stuff" also any book by Joyce Meyer... That is when you have, time,

Christmas is going to be a nightmare for me, I cry every time I think about it... But we will get through this .... when it comes to Isiah asking questions, I believe that he deserves the honest truth... He needs to know that we will never lie to him no matter the situation, when its time I will tell him that I made mistakes and did bad things and I have consequences for my actions so I am in time out, I am ashamed for where I'm at and what I've , done but I cannot change the life I live nor the situation I am in . Just because I'm in prison does not make me a bad person or any less of a person.... Everyone makes mistakes, unfortunately, I overdo everything and had to make a REALLY

BIG mistake... He needs to understand that and know that he doesn't want to travel the same path in life... He also needs to know that breaking the law is no joke and he has to abide by the law when he gets older, so he doesn't end up in prison. I want to have an open relationship with him so he never has to feel like he has to hide anything from me , he needs to know that no matter what life brings us we are a team and I'll stand by him thru anything, I want him to confide in me when making decisions so I can guide him the right way in life. He has to know that I've been there done that and mom knows best.... I'll never hide anything from him because I wouldn't want him to hide anything from me ....

But anyways mom you need to take time away from stressing over me and reconnect with Ritchie, thru all the shit I've put you guys through he stuck up with it, he works his ass off to support your f***** up 20 year old and my son, not to mention being a father like grandpa to Isiah and then dealing with you, Gracie and Cole.... LOL idk how he has done it so many years, but I love him for it, ... He's gone through a lot this last year, he deserves a 30 pack or two !!! Lol well, it's like 3am and I'm going to try to get some sleep, I love you mom and appreciate you so much... Stay strong and know that this too shall pass... Say your prayers !!!! Goodnight Sweet Dreams.

From: Judy Frisby
Date: 12/9/2014
To: Mackenzie Basham

Hey Kenz,

I did get you a food box out, I can't put more on phone until Friday which is the day you maybe should get your food. Gonna send a clothes box next and will let you know my visitation day! Love you too. Zay has bronchitis so been staying home doing breathing treatments a lot, he had a bad asthma attack Saturday night, so I took him to St Rita's emergency. I called them on my way and told them I thought it was an asthma attack so when I pulled up they had a nurse waiting and a respiratory nurse all set up and gave him oxygen and back to back breathing treatments and he was instantly breathing better and not coughing. I am getting him in with a specialist so we can have an inhaler at home too. He was so sweet and good for the nurses you would have been proud of him! Anyway, he is better and going to school half a day today. Talk to you soon.... Mom

From: Mackenzie Basham
Date:12/9/2014
To: Judy Frisby

okay, thank you so much mom I love you ... you have to have the boxes ordered by the 15th .... I'll talk to you Friday, something happened and I'm going thru a lot right now I wasn't going to tell you because I don't want you to worry but my head is really fucked up because of it .... I need my mom... Courtney went to the hole for me and got out today because of the situation... I can't thank her enough... I'm worried about zay please keep me updated. let him know i love him so very much ...love you mom and miss you.

From: Judy Frisby
Date: 12/21/2014
To: Mackenzie Basham

Hi Sis,

It's been awhile since I have heard your voice and I'm missing you so bad. Christmas is coming, I have been trying to put it off but just like life, it is going to happen. Not sure how I can "celebrate" with this empty space in my heart, but I'm going to try. You were always the one most excited on Christmas morning and the one that always got all the other kids up and ready for presents. I guess Isiah will take your place. He is just like you. Not a day goes by that Ritchie or I say, " you are just like your mommy"... Then we laugh! I just figured out that the reason I am having such a hard time with you being gone is that I am such a good mom. Since June 17th, 1994 my entire life has revolved around my children. If it didn't then this wouldn't be so tough. My mom was a mother just like I am, she could not function without seeing or talking to or checking up on her children so it's a good thing I'm like her in that sense. Lately, I have been working a lot staying busy, so I don't get sad. I don't get sad when everyone's home, or at work around people... It's the alone time. Driving in the car by myself, at night when everyone is asleep, at the store by myself I see something, anything that reminds me of you and then I start to cry and have to leave the store. I thought I saw you at Walmart and it was the back of some girl. It was like the nightmare was gone and I got this warming feeling throughout my body and I smiled really big then she turned around and I looked like a complete idiot standing close to her as I knew her. My smile fell and once again the coldness was back in my body. I have not tried to Christmas shop since.

I am so excited to get to visit you on Christmas Eve. I want to make sure we have a happy, positive visit for Gracie and Isiah. I am either bringing Cole or Grandpa Shepherd with Mom and me. I am nervous and scared and happy. I hate going there. They treat us like we are beneath them. I understand they have to be strict on the woman on the inside to do their job, but the visitors didn't do anything. I am nervous about how dad will handle the experience. He is tough, he's a marine, he had been in awful places, but he had not ever been in this situation. He is trained to protect and save the things he loves, but he is going to feel helpless in there. I feel that every time I go. I hate when the clock ticks I just want to be able to be with my own child as long as I want, I mean I gave birth to you and I have to be watched and monitored to see if I hug you too long or kiss you or hold your hand or lean over the table to close. I want to rewind the past year. Sometimes in my head I do and it's fun and it makes me smile but the truth is you were on drugs then too. I just want the daughter you are now without the bars. I don't think I'm asking a lot. Isiah has been asking about you a lot lately. This week he has 3 days in a row. It crushes my heart. I can tell when he is thinking about you and I get ready for a meltdown. I'm not telling you this to torture you, but who else am I going to tell? Nobody else really wants to hear that it's too sad or it makes them angry at you for doing this to him. I know you love him more than anything in this world just like I do, I also know you never meant to hurt anybody especially Isiah. I don't care what other people think about you I know what's in your heart and I know all the good in you underneath the hard-tough shell you would put on. It's your defense mechanism. Isiah will be fine; we have to look at the big picture. You will be fine too. I'm sorry what happened to you in there, it makes me throw up in my mouth and eats me alive. I want to pay a visit to that nasty woman and tell her what's on my mind and let her know if she ever tries to hurt or touch my little girl again, she will regret it... But I can't. That was my worst fear of you in there, and once again I have to deal with my worst fear. You fight back, scratch, bite, scream, whatever you have to do to survive. It kind of puts things into perspective for me out here though. My survival and yours are two totally different things. If people knew what they take for granted this world would be so much better. We can't change horrible people; we can change ourselves and you are trying to so keep it up! I love you just as much as when I first saw your sweet face at 2:01 in the morning on June 17th, 1994. That Mackenzie, will never change no what you

see in there, or go through, or have done. My Christmas
will not be complete just like the giant empty space in my
heart, but we still have each other in our mind and we are
still sleeping underneath the same big moon and that
comforts me the devil puts awful things in my head. I
choose to think Your guardian angel is protecting you and
no matter how bad it gets for you in there, you are going to
survive however you have to come home to me. I love you
more than chocolate. Isiah just told me he wants to buy
Santa a present, a T-Rex.... But a nice T-Rex. See you in
three days, chin up baby girl, Love Momma

Year Two

The Move

From: Mackenzie Basham
Date: 1/6/2015
To: Judy Frisby

so I called you and you were acting angry, I just called to ask you about the green dot card because you said you were going to get it... then I told you ill just call you back later and you said I know you will ... like you didn't want me to ... so I feel like you're getting sick of me ..which would be understandable if I was home but I'm not and I know it's nobody's fault but my own but I'm feeling like in time you are going to forget about me... and it hurts. I just want you to know I love you and miss you and hope everything is okay on your end... and I'm sorry... I'll call you in a couple days ... give you some space... be safe . kiss bubby for me. I'll figure something out here.

From: Mackenzie Basham
Date: 1/11/2015
To: Judy Frisby

hey mom, you've been on my mind a lot today, hope you are having a relaxing day, I know you don't have to work and zay was excited about you two staying home! I haven't done much today, went to church but it was too packed so I had to leave. it's okay though, someone else must have needed the service more than me. I love you with all my heart and want you to know I appreciate you so much, I couldn't ask for a better mother, because I've got the world's greatest... I hope everything is going well at the shop, I miss going there so much. We were talking about the things we want to do when we go home and all I want is to lay in my mom's bed with Isiah and my mom lol. I don't care how old I am, I just want to barricade myself in your house.. get all my family to come over and just talk about all the good times we've shared. I can't wait until we can look back on this trial in our lives, ... hope your keeping your faith, because I'm keeping mine, somethings going to happen and I'll be home sooner than expected... well I'm going to go, I'm calling you after 9:00 count so I'll talk to you in about an hour....... LOVE AND MISS YOU MORE THAN MY FREEDOM!!! SMILE BEAUTIFUL.

p.s, one day we will actually be on the beach like in this picture, can't wait until I can sit in the sand again :)

From: Judy Frisby
Date: 1/16/2015
To: Mackenzie Basham

Hi Kenz,

I needed to write you today. I'm having some deep depression and I don't know why I can't shake it. Maybe it's because it just really hit me what really happened, maybe it's because I miss you so much, maybe it's just me today. I am in a constant darkness every day. I try to put on a smile lately, but I don't think my face muscles go that way anymore. You are doing so much better than me! I am very proud of you staying focused on getting home early. Isiah just completed his second day at preschool wearing big boy underwear all day with no accidents. He is so smart Mackenzie. I refuse for him to be a "statistic" like other children of single parents or children that's parents have been incarcerated. He is going to be an all-star at whatever he does if it kills me!

I don't know why you are worrying that we will forget about you. That will never happen by the people who love you I promise. People are going to communicate with you less the longer you are there, but not me. I have already noticed who

my real friends are and who in the family is sticking by. It is
sad but it is just a hard fact of life. I have been listening to a lot
of music and that helps me when nothing else makes any
sense. I know you can listen to music so here are a couple
songs I want you to buy. Anna Nalick sings " Breathe (2am)", it
is why Kendra and I got the tattoo on our wrist. One line that I
relate to so well is...And I feel like I'm naked in front of the
crowd

Cause these words are my diary, screaming out

loud And I know that you'll use them, however you

want to.

Another song is "Ghost" by Ella Henderson...I keep
going to the river to pray

'Cause I need something that can wash all the

pain And at most I'm sleeping all these demons

away But your ghost, the ghost of you

It keeps me awake......It doesn't mean you the ghost, it's
the whole damn situation that has happened to our family. I
have these awful nightmares and I'm always in prison or
I'm trying to get out of prison, and nobody hears me. I just
can't believe you are there. My sweet little girl who cried
every time Cole got hurt in a game or even cried when
Gracie Jo had a high fever you are so softhearted... Not a
"criminal". It's like they don't know you, but that girl I saw
on the 6:00 news I did not know either. I am glad I have
you back even if it is behind those walls. I hate drugs and I
hate money. I have had a little and I've had to worry about
how we were going to pay the electric bill and it does not
make you any happier it just makes life a bit easier. All the

money in this world could not put my broken heart back together or bring you home or take away your addiction. I went to church on Christmas Eve. I had not stepped foot in our church in 9 months since you went away. You know I never miss a Christmas Eve service at night. I was worried I would cry or be sad. The music, the memories of you and Coley in Sunday school and preschool, the people who are going to look at me as " that mother". It is my own battle in my mind. I cried all the way there and most of Christmas Eve and Christmas Day and New Year's too. I'm glad you called me on New Year's Day I needed to hear your voice. I have to make some pretty big decisions about my shop. I am failing to try to have this career and now be a full-time mom to a 3-year- old. He is, of course, my number 1 priority plus I think I need to heal my mind because my thoughts are not healthy. I feel like I brought a stick to a gun fight and I have never felt so NOT in control of my life ever, I hate it. It's because no matter what I do, no matter how hard I try or yell or bitch or research... I cannot fix you. Only you can, and you're working so hard which is awesome. I'm glad your dad wrote you; I know how you desperately wanted to hear from him. I didn't mean to make you cry on the phone when I told you I just gave in to him and her, I just wanted you to know I'm done fighting, 16 years in and out of court over money and "power" is a waste. Maybe if they think they won by suing me for money he can have a relationship with you. One thing no one can ever take from me and Ritchie is Isiah or the memories of you and Cole growing up, that means more to us than any amount of money. We were just talking about when we took our kids to Kings Island. The 3d movie you kept jumping and moving out of the way like something was coming at you, haha. Then remember when you started spinning that water tube and Cole was so pissed because he was terrified of that ride! You were never scared of anything, except mice haha just like me, I guess. Well, I have to get ready to start my day. Every day I wake up is a day closer to you being home girl. I love you so much, take care of yourself in there and keep dreaming of us on the beach! Love you more, Mom

From: Mackenzie Basham
Date: 2/16/2015
To: Judy Frisby

Hey mom, sorry it's taken so long to write back... It's really hard to sit down and write you because I just want to be able to be home with you. I lay on my mat and close my eyes and picture laying in your bed with you and Isiah and Gracie and Cole... Laughing and smiling .... then I open my eyes and see where I'm actually at, where I will remain for idk how much longer... I think about my baby sister growing up so fast and seems like she isn't able to enjoy her teen days with all the things going on around her, then my little brother that needs someone to just listen and guide him through the bullshit he is facing of turning into an adult fending for himself...... My grandparents getting older each and every day, begging God not to bring them home before I can return home to make up for lost time.... a sweet baby boy that is growing up without his mom to be there with his making unforgettable memories, wanting to beg him to forgive me for the pain I've caused on his little fragile heart... And my mom that now has the world on, her shoulders because of me, when you should be able to be living a stress-free life doing the things you've always wanted... I'm so sorry... I know all I can do is stay strong and focused on the finish line ... Music is also my escape from reality, I listen to it all day. I sometimes act like I just live out of state and this is a town but then I snap back to reality... I haven't talked to you in a couple days and I'm worried about you guys ... I really miss your voice and zay always making me laugh on the phone ... I swear after this is all said and done, we will look back and talk about how strong we have become, I get my strength from your mom... No doubt about that. I couldn't ask God for a better mom or family period .... Well I have been accepted into 4 more groups !!!!! After I complete them I will file my clemency so please start getting letters sent to me, I need as many support letters as possible and with my good behavior and completion of groups, something positive should come out of this !!!! All I can do is put it all in God's hands though ... He knows what's best... I can't wait until I can walk out of these gates and never look back... Well, mom, its late 3 am, I'm going to get to sleep... I love you and miss you more than my freedom. Give my little angel kisses for me and always remind Him how much Mommy loves him !!!! Tell everyone hi and I miss them, love them all.... thank you, mom, for everything, for always standing by me, for being my crutch.... stay strong and smile beautiful, we got this !!! LOVEEEEE YOUUU!!!

From: Mackenzie Basham
Date: 2/19/2015
To: Judy Frisby

love you momma !! thank you for taking care of my baby while he is sick ... I love and miss you... talk to you soon. tell chunky butt I love him...

From: Judy Frisby
Date: 3/20/2015
To: Mackenzie Basham

Hey sis, how are you doing? Sorry, it has been so long since I've written, just way too many words in my head to write down. I am glad we get our 15-minute phone calls but I like for you to get to hear Isiah's voice as much as you can, so I don't get to tell you things. This morning at 5:00am Ritchie brought Isiah into my bed and said he wanted his Nana. He had been up with him for a few hours. He just sat up in the dark, so I asked him what was wrong. He chokes out the words...." Nana, I miss my mommy." I said, " baby I miss your mommy too" and he curled up next to me and just cried his little heart out. Why am I telling you this? You need to know. I carry this heartbreak every day and I just don't think you get it. My day will suck, Isiah will be a grouch at school for being up way too early and this happens on an average once a week! You got a sentence, but so did we. This will not stop until you are home and done with that kind of lifestyle. You were young when you were sent away... I am not. Slap your 14-year sentence on my age and I may not be able to enjoy a single day or night until I'm 55. That is crap because I did nothing wrong. I guess I am mad, at you.... at the world. You have a chance if you want to start over making a change... Start fresh, but me, on the other hand, will be aged and broken and tired and I'm a little pissed off at you about that. I love you so much you already know; I have your back forever and always but you need to hear this. I forgive you for every single shred of heartache your old " habits" have caused me but there are a few things we just swept under the rug and why should I keep them in now... our business was on the 6 o'clock news? If I cannot ask you then we will never really heal from this. When Ritchie found the drugs in your room and you flipped out to another level because I called the police and told them I did not want drugs or anyone using them in my house... Why in the hell did you say to the police that they were not yours they were probably mine? Who says that about their mother? Then when I walked outside to try to breathe you came out and told me if I gave you back the drugs, you would leave Isiah with me.... Otherwise, you were taking that baby in that car with trashy drug addicts. You tried to make a deal with your son for drugs. That is sick and makes my blood boil that something you smoke, or swallow was more important than your beautiful sweet child who was just up crying in the night because he wants you to be able to hold him. If that isn't motivation to change then nothing will save you. You told me one time in a drug-induced craze that if I wouldn't give you money you needed you wished my house would burn down with me in it. Do you remember that? See I do from time to time and it really pisses me off. You wanted to get high or pay off some lowlife drug dealer so because I wouldn't help you-you didn't care if I died. I know you were in a completely different mind frame then, but I just know that I would never speak to my mother like that... Ever. I don't think your sentence was fair, and I don't think you deserved to go down alone or to be put in the media like you were, but you put yourself in that situation and for that, you sure are paying the price. God is teaching you a lesson perhaps one you didn't learn from me. You are responsible for your actions not responsible for your addiction. Does that make sense to you? You are not responsible for being bipolar, but you are responsible for not taking your medication to treat it. Cole lashes out at me because he is heartbroken. He told me that the reason you are in prison is that I didn't get you the medication you needed so you medicated yourself. I will not take the blame for that. You could drive to a party or get drugs, but you couldn't drive to your counselor and the pharmacy? You were 19 and wanted to be a big girl out on your own yet it was my fault you hit rock bottom and made a deal with the devil? No. It was not my fault. I need to heal also and these things I needed to say to you. I will be forever sucked into this black hole of a situation that surrounds us now. I have to work on climbing up every hour of every day. We are coming onto a year since you have been gone and it took this long for me to write what I just did. I love you so much. We can get through this, but I get mad too and I have to able to tell you why and move on. I put money on your media so buy the song "Gravity" by Sara Bareilles.

Something always brings me back to you. It never takes too long.

No matter what I say, or do I'll still feel you here 'til the moment

I'm gone.

*You hold me without touch. You keep
me without chains.*

*I never wanted anything so much than to drown in your
love and not feel your reign.*

*Set me free, leave me be. I don't want to fall another
moment into your gravity.*

*Here I am and I stand so tall, just the way I'm supposed to
be.*

But you're on to me and all over me.

It just explains how just when I think I could see the
sunshine in the day, it's there.... the sadness of it all. The
situation, my missing my little girl and Isiah's broken little
heart missing his mommy. Then I'm brought right back
down to be sad and depressed. It is not your fault that I
cannot shake this, but those choices you made are your
fault and you are not the only one that is in prison
suffering a sentence. I am serving a 14-year sentence too.

I love and miss you so much and so does bubby and
Gracie and Coley. We have to, as a unit, repair our
brokenness along with you so we can all find happiness
and look forward to you coming home to us. Hopefully, I
can see you soon and I will bring Isiah, that should help
him a lot. Talk to you soon, love you more than chocolate,
Momma

From: Mackenzie Basham
Date: 4/25/2015
To: Judy Frisby

Mom, so its Friday night at 1:38 in the morning and I can't sleep... I'm really deep in my thoughts and I'm missing Zay like crazy. Everything is just a mess right now and damn I'm trying so hard to be positive and stay strong but I'm tired, I'm tired of living this lifestyle, I'm tired of being everyone's laughs and disappointments, I'm tired of hurting the ones I love and I'm really tired of acting like nothing can phase me, like Wonder woman and I can take on anything... I'm really working on my relationship with God because he is the only way I'm going to make it out of this... I get so mad and irritated with these dumb broads in here I just want to lose control and do what the old me would do and fight. But I just think about zay and how he doesn't deserve this, let alone me not trying with everything I got to get home... Then when it's all said and done, and I've relaxed I'm proud of myself because of how much I've changed... But I'm scared, I'm scared my anger that burns deep inside of me will not go away, I'm trying so hard, to find out the source of it and heal myself but what if I can't? What if I stay this angry my whole life because every time I think about zay and what he is going through I HATE myself for it and want to just knock myself out ... I never wanted to hurt him, I never wanted to not be able to hold him or watch him grow up. Mom, I'm so scared I won't be able to be there for him until he, is 17... I have this empty spot inside me and it won't go away ... And it won't until I can be home with him... I know that everything will be okay, I know God will bring me through this and I KNOW GOD WORKS MIRACLES, this is one big lesson that saved my life, and I know it's going to be hard not only for me but for us, all of us ... I'm sorry you all have to suffer for my mistakes. and I don't think you understand how thankful I am to have the family and support that I have, some people don't have that, some people don't have

anyone or anything... I cannot change the fact that my father doesn't want me in his life, I never could... I need to realize that, why do I keep punishing myself for his mistakes? Why is it I'm the one hurting so bad? Why am I the ONLY one who cares? He makes me feel worthless. Like I don't deserve to be loved. . .. He is hurting me still by saying nothing... I just don't understand ... I'd never leave my child's side no matter if they blew up the white house... If we go down, we go together because we are a unit, we are one... I'd never push my child away, and I really need to keep assuring Isiah that I love and miss him and just because we cannot be together physically right now, I'm with him always in heart. I'll always be there, for him, n I'm sorry for the hand we've been dealt, just don't give up on mommy yet, I'm still trying to get it together. And I won't stop until I've did what I've got to do to be home to be mom again... I like to remind him of the times we've had and share memories with him because I don't want him to forget, I don't want him to forget me or the memories we've had , .. Ugh, i just hope and pray God has something up his sleeve for me, because I'm ready to come home to my baby boy and my family .... Well, I'm going to try to get some sleep. I'll call you tomorrow, I love and miss you mom, more than the biggest juiciest steak... We've got this, and WE ARE ALL WE GOT, so stay strong and know that people want to know about us because they couldn't deal, with the hand we were dealt...
GOD GIVES HIS HARDEST BATTLES, TO HIS STRONGEST WARRIORS.... smile beautiful, we are soldiers.

From; Mackenzie Basham
Date: 5/10/2015
To: Judy Frisby

hey mom, just wanted to say I LOVE YOU AND HAPPY MOTHERS DAY!!!!!!!!!! I'll call you after 4:00 count

From: Judy Frisby
Date: 6/14/2015
To: Mackenzie Basham

Hi Sis,

I have started this letter about six times but I either have to stop because Isiah got too quiet or I got all choked up and don't want to get upset! You have been on my mind so much the past few weeks I think because of your birthday on Wednesday. The BIG 21....did you ever imagine "celebrating" it in that hell hole? I know you didn't, neither did I. You always got so excited about your birthday, and you would remind me every day for 3 weeks before (haha). I love you so much, you still make me laugh just from memories of you growing up. I guess one of my biggest fear is those memories going away or me forgetting them when too much time passes. As people get older, they forget things and those are all I have of you and my God I cherish the times I remember of you and Cole and Gracie like nothing else on this earth. I am so excited for our visit on Wednesday and we will "celebrate" your 21st with Mountain Dew and coffee and vending machine chips and candy bars! Party on, right? It doesn't matter I can't wait to hug you and kiss your cheeks and hold your hand and stare at you for 3 hours because those are fresh memories I can use on my dark days. I miss you. This is killing me. I thank God every night for your life, for the gift you left me although at times he is pure rotten. I thank him for Cole and Gracie and for bringing Ritchie into my life when he did. On days when my attitude is horrible and I'm ready to throw the middle finger up to life and this screwed up world, I can always count on him. I tell him some days that I hate everyone I just want to live the rest of my life in my house with him and Zay and Gracie and

Cole. I don't want to look at or see or even hear one more person breathe outside of my home. He tells me I'm just having a bad day I will be ok. I tried antidepressants, anxiety pills, uppers, downers, alcohol, but the support from Mr. Frisby you can't put in a bottle and that's the only thing that works. Hopefully, I can be that drug for you, lay it on me sister! It's hard to dream with a broken heart but when we are stripped of everything on the outside and we get down to our bare, raw inner thoughts and dreams it's the people in our lives at this moment right now that gives us the strength to get through the days and nights.

As I am writing you this with tears running down my face, Isiah comes running in and jumps on my bed and he's stark naked with only his camouflage slippers on and says," I love you, Nana". I am cracking up; he is hilarious just like you were. He hates to wear clothes so the other day he came into the kitchen wanting breakfast with a t-shirt on and his cowboy holster with a gun in one side, a sword in the other and nothing else. A bare butt and bare pickle. He saw nothing wrong with that, so we just ate breakfast with a semi-naked cowboy/ninja. He tried to be so good after my surgery, but he is nonstop dawn till dusk little chubby ball of destruction and noise! I wouldn't trade him for all the money in the world. He brings a smile to our face on a daily basis and makes me say cuss words that I never said when you kids were young. He kinda teaches me to slow down and appreciate little things even if just a tiny bug or a spider web I would usually just hurry and not even notice before. Sometimes I feel like all people should see things through a 3-year-old's eyes, life would sure be simple. Grammy Shepherd and Josie and Jordan and Jenny were a big help this week too. Of all the people who offer help and were there at the beginning of this nightmare, it's your Aunt and Jenny that have consistently followed through with the support of Isiah so far. I know I can count on them when I need help. You know they do that out of love for you. Not a lot of people have that kind of support from an Aunt or Uncle, so you are lucky to have them. I am proud of you for mentoring those women to get their GED, that is awesome sis. I am proud to tell people about your accomplishments like that. I hear and see parents constantly putting their kid's victories and then some parents don't say a word. I say celebrate any kind of victory you can, in the big giant scheme of things it's really what matters to us anyway in our hearts and minds. A mother whose child gets voted in as president of the United States is no more proud then I am because at your drug addiction group you were the only one who hadn't tried heroin. I am proud as hell you didn't try that. Well I have to go wipe Isiah's butt haha, he is yelling "nana, there's a big something coming out of my butt" aaaaaand my lavish life continues! I will get to see your face in 72 hours, and we will celebrate your birthday because we will be together and that is OUR kind of victory to celebrate.

Grammy Shepherd will be coming too she's missing you badly and she will make us crack up anyway. Maybe she will ask if you are getting a Starbucks on campus haha. Campus you are not on, brown flavored water with maggots is your Starbucks huh? I often think that you never knew the price you would pay for what you did, did you? I mean I don't know maybe you did know, maybe in the frame of mind you were in you thought you were invincible? Nobody is invincible. We have all learned that. Well, I have to tame the wild animal now, and not the dog. Sweet dreams my angel, I love you more than ever don't forget that. When your sad at night, look at the moon and think about me and Zay because we are not that far away and under that same moon. No matter where we are, we'll always be together, always. Next time I see you, you will be another year older and that much closer to being free and back home where you belong... With your family. I love you more than chocolate, Momma.

From: Judy Frisby
Date: 6/15/2015
To: Mackenzie Basham

Are you ok?? I'm worried I haven't heard from you in a few days! Please let me know if you are ok. I have an uneasy feeling something is not right! Please call or message!

From: Judy Frisby
Date: 6/17/2015
To: Mackenzie Basham

Happy Birthday to you, happy birthday to you, happy birthday MACKENZIE... Happy birthday to you!

We are getting ready to come to our visit, hopefully, everything is ok. I haven't heard from you since June 6th and I have an uneasy feeling, hopefully, I am wrong. There has to be something we can do about them over-medicating you like that. I will keep calling until they get sick of my voice. I love you birthday girl, see you soon... Momma

From: Judy Frisby
Date: 7/27/2015
To: Mackenzie Basham

Hi Sis,

I'm sorry yesterday's call ended in me yelling and you crying before they shut it off. I don't understand and I'm frustrated. You don't see my point and I don't understand yours. That's going to happen. I have a visit Thursday and we can talk, I did, however, I put some money on your media to buy you some songs and when I woke up this morning and turned on Pandora this song was on... It's called "Brave" by Sara Bareilles. Please buy it and listen to the words.

Everybody's been there,

Everybody's been stared down by the enemy

Fallen for the fear

And done some disappearing,

Bow down to the mighty

Don't run, just stop holding your tongue

Maybe there's a way out of the cage where you live

Maybe one of these days you can let the light in

Show me how big your brave is

Say what you wanna say

And let the words fall out

Honestly, I wanna see you be brave

I don't want to argue the seconds we have to speak; I'm still struggling with all this and still not knowing a lot of things are making me crazy. I love you more... Momma

From: Judy Frisby
Date; 9/2/2015
To: Mackenzie Basham

My sweet girl,

Haven't written to you in a while, just our short MONITORED

phone calls. I cannot really talk around Isiah and if he's not at school he is with me. We are having a rough time with him as far as going to school (leaving Nana), acting out at home usually against me and Gracie Jo, and asking some pretty intense questions that I continue to lie to him about. Every month when it's the days around the visit with you is hell for me. I will not ever quit bringing him to see his mommy, but I don't think you know what he and I go through. He will wake up in the middle of the night telling me he is ready to see his mommy and asking over and over again if we can go "right now". He will not sleep for hours and then when I finally do get him back settled down, it's time for me to get up for the day.

He has meltdowns where he hits me, says a lot " I hate you", and then we got the throwing things and crying tantrums. I know you tell me to discipline him more, but here's the thing....I raised my kids, I don't want to yell and punish all over again. We do make him mind but Mackenzie he does not have the life of any other 4-year old that I know. We don't know what is going through his little mind. After our last visit, he was in the back seat with Ritchie and Gracie and I was driving talking to Gram and I was discussing your case not even thinking and all the sudden he says out loud..."Oh my God, is my mom in jail?" Ritchie said that's enough talk about (that). I told him, of course, his mommy is not in jail, we were talking about someone Aunt Carolann knew? Someday he will read these prison diaries and hopefully forgive me for lying to him all these years. I feel terrible about it but the look of terror in that baby's eyes when he asked that question was gut- wrenching. He thinks you away at school and I refuse to break his heart, I can't do it....he does not deserve this. You say you want to always be truthful to him, well tough shit sister. I am making the call and after that happened last week, I know for a fact he is not ready for the truth, not now. I am dedicating my entire life right now to surrounding him with love and trying to teach him the rights and wrongs just like I taught you and I don't feel like it's your option to choose what we tell him. I just love him so much and I know how having both my parents shaped and formed me into the person I am today, I want to try to give him that same foundation except in his situation. I get mad and I cry because he does not have either parent to raise him. His beautiful innocent little baby heart should only have warm fuzzy loving positive energy, not the giant ball of thunder we are living with right now. His birthday is coming up. Last year I had a party at the house, and I knew a meltdown was coming, I just didn't know when. I couldn't sleep the entire night before, so at 4:00 am I went to Walmart to buy party decorations and candy and anything a 3-year-old would want at the most exciting day of his little year. I cried in Walmart. I smoked cigarettes all the way home with a nervous stomach he would be awake, and I had to put on this big fake happy face and say" Happy Birthday" when all that was going through my head was I want his mommy here. Until the last 2 years had you ever had a birthday without your Mom? No, and the last two years were absolute hell for you, and me. He is going to be 4 and only had one parent with him on his birthday 2 years. I am 42 and on the day of my birthday I look forward to hearing my parent's beautiful voices sing to me like I'm still their baby, it makes me feel safe and loved and like everything at least for that ONE day, is going to be alright.

This girl is what goes through my mind when he is having a screaming, kicking meltdown. Sometimes I grab him and just hold my arms around him as tight as I can, I usually take a few punches, but I am one tough Nana. I just want him to know that no matter what he does to me, or says, or throws, I am never leaving him, ever. I will be at every birthday, every ballgame, every school event so helps me, God. He needs to have that from me and Ritchie so he can live the life he deserves. That takes me to the next thing....taking care of myself. I am doing that now. I have to be healthy and be able to keep these strong shoulders for Gracie Jo, and Cole and Isiah....and you. at my last Dr visit, this specialist for my stomach says, "its plain and simple Judy, you HAVE to start taking care of yourself." I have had 2 major surgeries in the last 6 months, I'm on more medicine than a floor at a nursing home, and I was not ever in the hospital until 41. It's stress they say and I'm drowning in it. From this point on I am ridding anything that gives me negative vibes. My business has suffered the most. It's too much for me now in our situation, I love people, but they are what I fear the very most. I don't want to talk about you. It still hurts very bad and I still want to kiss your cheeks and hold you as I used to my little Kiki Lee when you were little. I cannot handle the emotions that I feel every day unless I am in my home where I feel safe from the world. I'm getting weird but I am in survival mode right now. I am done talking about it, I want my daughter back home now. Enough is enough. They don't give killers or rapists as much time as you. I want to walk into that police dept and freak the hell out. I want them to sit there while I scream and cry and ask them if their kids have ever made a mistake or did anything illegal. I know, it wouldn't help, and I'll probably get arrested anyway. I'm helpless and I hate that feeling more than any other. Well, I have to try to move forward even if it's just baby tiny steps, getting out of my granny nightgowns means it's gonna be a good day. I have to go, for now, I feel better telling you some of this. I love you so much, stay strong baby girl. I talk to you every night in my prayers, I love you more than chocolate, Momma

From: Mackenzie Basham
Date: 9/4/2015
To: Judy Frisby

hey mom, I'm going to call my dad today after I move and get my stuff situated.......... I hope you have a good day at work and zay is good for Ritchie, I think karate would be a good discipline and venting sport for him. plus he loves ninjas so it would be enjoying to him also. look into it and the cost of it... I'm going to write later, got to go to lunch and see what is over there and if it has a side of maggots or not. lol, I love and miss you.

From: Mackenzie Basham
Date: 9/4/2015
To: Judy Frisby

Thank you so much for giving Zay a great birthday. love you

From: Judy Frisby
Date: 10/17/2015
To: Mackenzie Basham

Hi Sis,

I haven't written in a while. When I write you, it helps and at the same time brings up a lot of pain. After you called me Saturday, I had a huge meltdown after everyone went to sleep. I hate when we have to end a phone call and your crying because it's all I can think about. I closed the beauty shop thinking it would be easier, my life, but I think I may have made it worse. I no longer have an identity other than "Nana". That is great don't get me wrong, but I've slipped into a funk. I live for your phone calls and look at the website of where you are every day as if it makes me be close to you someway. I have been making videos for you to watch when you get home because I don't want you to miss out on Isiah, Cole, or Gracie's life. I had a Brittany Spears moment yesterday (haha). The past 3 weeks I have avoided phone calls and basically humans to live in my giant Hawaiian nightgown, combing my hair every few days and with my only joy being the hour-long Tom and Jerry cartoon on before nap time with Isiah. I have baked more cookies in the past 3 weeks and ate them, then a bakery. My body actually hurt from not doing anything, oh and I'm totally addicted to smoking cigarettes.

I always liked to have a cigarette but now, well they are my best friend. I'm a sad excuse right now. Yesterday I decided I had to make the best of the day, so I took a shower, got out my scissors and cut the hell out of my hair. I put on makeup and put on a dress and went to the dentist haha. That was it, but it's a start I suppose. This just sucks, I miss you so bad.

I was telling a good friend yesterday that the nightmares now are coming from me worrying about what's next. I try to stay in the moment and not hurry life but here's the problem... I don't want Gracie and Zay to get older, but I want time to fly because that will mean I will get to be your mom again and take care of you too. I feel like however; I think it's unfair to my kids. I also was thinking about how to help Gracie feel safe and protected like the counselor told us to and that leads to thinking about what made me safe when I was a kid. My dad made me feel safe in my home and like I was protected no matter what. I think that's why the respect I have for that man is out of this world. The one thing that scared the hell out of me as a child was a robber breaking in my home. The other thing was when, as Elva put it, the "nuts got loose from the nuthouse". That meant that a prisoner had escaped from the prison. I would sleep on the floor in my mom and dad's room and I knew no matter what I was safe, I remember crying when a prisoner was loose, and dad went to the store or something. He said I would be fine it was daylight out, but I had the fear of God in me that one of those monsters would come to my house and kill us. Fast forward to now. Don't take this literally but the very thing I want to make them feel safe from, the monster, is exactly you and your situation. I would never be scared of you nor would anyone who really loves you, yet you're a prisoner and in there for people going into people's home. How can my little girl be the very thing I feared as a child? How can I make them feel safe when I freaking take them to prison to visit and expect them to be ok with it? I will never quit coming to see you and I will always bring them but what if Gracie or Zay one day say they don't want to come? What do I do, which kid to I pick? I'm worried about you mentally surviving that life and I'm also worried about them mentally seeing you like that every month. I guess we will cross that bridge when we get there. People will say you choose to do what you did so I should not worry about what you think. You are my baby girl who I love with the deepest parts of my soul and every single ounce of my heart, I will always worry about you and try to do what I can to ease your pain. I feel the same way about Cole, Gracie, and Isiah so what does a struggling mother do? I'm just rambling but just want you to know the crazy things going through my damaged mind. I've been listening to a lot of Eminem lately before it was just music but when you use music to heal, I think Eminem may be a genius. I love his loyalty and rage and he makes me want to use the big "F" word fluently haha. I'll put some funds on your media so you can buy the song " monster" by Eminem it came out after you got locked up. References the show intervention which we used to watch and ironically, I called them when you were spinning out of control with your use of drugs.

------*think it went wandering off down yonder*

And stumbled on 'ta Jeff VanVonderen 'Cause I need

an interventionist

To intervene between me and this monster

And save me from myself and all this conflict

'Cause the very thing that I love's killing me, and I can't conquer it

My OCD's conking me in the head

Keep knocking, nobody's home, I'm sleepwalking I'm just

relaying what the voice in my head's saying

Don't shoot the messenger, I'm just friends with the

I'm friends with the monster that's under my bed

Get along with the voices inside of my head

You're trying to save me, stop holding your breath

And you think I'm crazy, yeah, you think I'm crazy

I love you, sis, I can't wait to see you and if you get to go to the library lookup Centurian ministries. I am writing them a letter and want you to also I will tell you about a few other groups too that may be able to get you a new sentencing hearing also. I will not give up; you do not give up either. Clear thinking and positive attitude every day in there so you can hold your little boy again. Love you forever, Mom

From: Mackenzie Basham
Date: 10/22/2015
To: Judy Frisby

hey so I didn't mean to come at you crazy mom, I don't know what it's like to be on the outside looking in, but I do know what it's like to be on the inside looking out. I know you're not going to stop worrying about me if I tell you to, or even if I simply say everything is okay. but I will never tell you the shit that happens or the shit I've seen, the animal I get made to feel like. I simply try to tell you minor things... and the only thing I look forward to is seeing you and Isiah . I don't like fighting ... I'm tired of it, I'm tired of having a fucked up attitude but I have to in here, or I'll be made someone's bitch. sometimes when I call home I forget who I'm speaking to , I forget that you all are feeling pain as well... but I have nobody to talk to , nobody to cry to... especially not now... so when I'm already pissed off and stressed out because I don't know if I'll have pads to stop me from bleeding all in my pants I tend to get irritated. then the last thing I want to hear is I have to wait to see zay, so I am sorry, and I know that you are also enduring pain, ... I know that the situation I'm in is only because of my selfish acts and nobody else's. and I'm thankful for every visit and every penny you still provide me with... I love you and I miss you, and this will pass us, we've got to remain strong, and my grandma didn't say anything negative about you or any situation. I'm just fucked up right now, with my surroundings and situation. it has its positives with its negatives...

From: Mackenzie Basham
Date: 11/4/2015
To: Judy Frisby

Hi mom, yeah I've been a wreck myself lately.... my friend Brayden that you cut his hair... well his dad shot himself in the head.... so, I've cried and I've had to be strong on the phone.... yet have not spoken to Brayden and I'm nervous too, but I know that he needs to know that my prayers are with him and I love him and his family. I cried because I think about past times at Brayden's watching the walking dead with his dad, or when he would come over to the house on Murphy and Elizabeth to fix things and we'd smoke a limb together.... then I go to call my grandma to tell her I've been down lately and she tells me about Bob, Becky's husband,. so, Becky gets on the phone sobbing singing the "big mac" theme song.... and I can't do nothing but start crying with her... then I'm locked in my room with nothing but thoughts...... and I wonder how many people aren't going to be here when I come home, and I pray that God doesn't take anyone from me that I won't be able to handle. When I'm in a closed room with nothing but toilet paper and a mat, (the hole) I know that on the outside I still have my family.... that when I get out Isiah, you, my grandparents, brother and sister, aunts and uncles are still here for me and waiting to hear from me.... I know Thursday is going to be a new thing for you but it's going to be alright,... no matter the situation I wouldn't let nothing happen to you, grandma or Zay ... nor would I want you to endure something that you can't handle. I've done enough to you guys and I'm sorry... we'll get through this, I can't wait to see you ... I've got to go, for now, is count time. I love you and miss you. see you soon... "God gives his hardest battles to his strongest warriors"

From: Mackenzie Basham
Date: 12/4/2015
To: Judy Frisby

mom, I love you ... and I hope things look brighter for you soon. tell Isiah I love and miss him. god don't give us battles we can't win. stay strong, and positive. is everyone okay? I've been worried about you guys. just keep me posted please whenever you can.

From: Mackenzie Basham
Date:12/18/2015
To: Judy Frisby

Awww, he looks so grown. I miss him so much mom, and I worry about him all day. I just hope he keeps his nose clean because I couldn't take the thought of him in prison or dead... I couldn't live without my brother.... damn, I miss you guys so much. I can't wait to see you. I love you all and we are going to get through these hard times, together... *

we eat with who we starve with* .... be safe, and Merry
Christmas, it is almost 2016, another year down.... love you

Year Three

The Petition

From: Judy Frisby
Date: 1/10/2016
To: MACKENZIE BASHAM

Hello Sunshine,

I haven't wrote since before the holidays. How are you holding up? I know I am glad the holidays are over just like you.

People say time heals wounds, but I think this year was just as hard as the first day you went away. I'm sure a lot of people have " moved on" but not me.... Or Isiah, or Gracie Jo, or Coley, or my mom, or Ritchie. I feel bitchy saying that, it makes me feel angry seeing those closest to you having holiday parties smiling having fun saying they love their life.... Blah blah. I can't help how I feel. I loved seeing you on Christmas Eve and so did Gracie and Zay, but I think it traumatized the Greezer. She had a panic attack as soon as we got into Dayton and I yelled at her. I don't know what to do in those situations and I HATE seeing my children upset.

Bless her heart she wants to see you so bad but it upsets her just as much. She has got to be one of the bravest 14 year old's I know. Isiah is a freaking pro now, except when we have to leave the visitation hall, then he has a meltdown. I still believe I am doing what's best for him by not letting his bond with you be broken. The good out ways the bad and when your stuck between a rock and a hard place you go with your heart and stick with it. You make those decisions all the time and I'll stand by you even if the world doesn't understand.

You've become a different person now, I hate that but I get it. It's like when you have been on the floor in the depths of hell, beat down, stripped of all integrity (literally), you have no choice but to become a different person. That was one of my biggest fears of you being in there. I know who you really are and so do those closest to you. Some say you deserve this life for the crimes you were involved in... I am telling you that you do not. Not just because I'm your mother either. There are fifty five female inmates from Allen County in prison. Four are in Dayton maximum security. You were used to make an "example" out of just like the detectives from Allen County said and they needed to "somehow put the community at ease".

Apparently a bunch of grown men who cannot get the job done needed a 19 year old girl to make them look good. I think about it all the time, so many unanswered questions still. Why didn't the judge, or prosecutors office even bring up the question of how in the hell did ONE 19 year old girl break into 8 homes carrying out a big television and 7000 dollars worth of stuff, load it in your little Chrysler Sebring, take it into a pawn shop, all in 3 days. All by yourself, with a 2 year old?

Nobody questioned the obvious of the others one time in court, and I am pissed as hell that they all stood in that court room knowing your involvement and the others involvement as you just plead guilty to every single thing. I wonder how they slept at night the next week when you were in a jumpsuit and that string of burglaries happened in Bath Township? They freaking knew and sat back as you sit in a prison cell. I have a new outlook on our law enforcement because of this, just like you. I had the utmost respect right up until this. DePalma is in a minimum security prison and is a thief but a much better one then all of your colleagues lol. He was stealing AND he was getting paid to do it, and got to carry a gun.... Take that. What a piece of crap. I think I'll write him a letter and tell him he owes me restitution for helping pay his salary while he put my daughter away! Ugh, this is so frustrating to have our hands tied right now girl. It will come out, hopefully before the damage to our lives is permanent. Lesson learned now. Your paying the ultimate price for doing wrong times a million. I am sending you pictures of Isiah's first basketball game, he had a huge cheering section and he loved it. He is number #13 if you can't pick him out ha ha. The only thing going through my mind was, how much I hate that you were not there. Those moments we can never get back and it's soul crushing. I love you more today then ever and I always will. I dream of the day you and Isiah are hugging each other and your free.... Free from judgments, free from your own mind, free from the tortures you will take with you after being in the hell your living in right now. We will survive, it's what we do. Stay positive and stay strong because someday hopefully before you expect it, the nightmare will be finally over. I love you more then chocolate, Momma

From: Judy Frisby
Date: 1/12/2016
To: MACKENZIE BASHAM

What is going on? I haven't heard from you in five days, are you OK?? Please contact me soon! Love you mom

From: Judy Frisby
Date: 1/27/2016
To: MACKENZIE BASHAM

Hey Sis, You have been on my mind since last Thursday after our visit. Wasn't that a great visit though? I feel like we did a lot of "good talking" and it made me feel not so miserable.

You have reached a new level of maturity and it's refreshing. I read about an exercise where you write down small phrases or words of whatever is on your mind at that particular moment. It's supposed to help you let go or release bad vibes or bad energy so I tried it. I think I sound a tad bit insane but it was a breath of fresh air getting it out.

Where did you go

Who are you now, I'm afraid to know anyways

This level has made me feel like a child and taught me how to hide

Think I'm an inventor, because I invented some new emotions no human has ever known

I miss your presence here, voice is not enough for me

If I had known, would I have done anything, or put that in the closet and shut the door?

Everyone has an image to uphold

Mine is different than yours

How did they get so far apart

It's always been all or nothing with you, mental illness is not found in a yearly physical

People just assume normalcy

Perfect family in photos

I think I have some of the same thoughts as you, am I the real criminal?

Bold letters, fear, regret, guessing of self, failed...panic I was not strong enough to hold you down

Tired of making excuses

Perception through actions

Disappointment of the real father you cannot erase that's how we are the same

Our bond is a steel rod but so are your
chains Oh those chains, they cause my
blood loss

So many questions, will it be a vicious circle? Do I have the
strength to be the stopper?

I am not completely innocent, you are my addiction and
now he is

Trying to make up for you not
here Am I really helping or just
hurting?

Is he the reason I can't let it go for one
second I'll cover him with my hard shell

Take words, stares, talk..... like a beating a slave would
take The sun never fully shines and I hate people who
always think like that

I have experienced a new kindness and a new
hate Should I keep my circle so small, or are they
for real? I keep searching for a reason

Nobody really gets it

New appreciation for my own parents, they shouldn't have set
the bar so high

Fully understand words like nothing, anxious, sadness, hurt,
empty, love, happiness, killing, heartbroken, confident, trust,
and need.

Disappointment of family and people I thought were true New
findings, research, does it solve the problem or fuel the fire?
I should have.....

Will your demons go away or will the demons beside you stay until the end?

Cages are for animals
Human life is precious

Your body is a sacred temple that you should not allow just anyone in

Mad red rage when people intrude the temple, their human flesh should burn

Even in darkness your allowed to smile, it's like a cold drink of water, water is refreshing to your mind

I love you more then you know girl. I can't wait to hug you and kiss your sweet cheeks. you'll always be my little girl, I love you more then chocolate milk.....Mom

From: Mackenzie Basham
Date: 2/8/2016
To: Judy Frisby

Do you pray at night, or thank god for your food? how about for

just being able to look at the moon... I pray for one night, to count

stars with my son...

Lord, please bring me home, while he is still young... my tears

don't come out normal anymore,

I've become numb all the way to my core. they've tested pain in

my blood, hate in my eyes, to say that I'm healing would be a lie.

will I ever get better, or maybe just feel, love, faith or hope... Lord show me its real... I try and try to please everyone else,

how about just trying to please myself...

have you ever jumped right out of your sleep? yes, you're 21 but for your mom, you scream.... you have a son, he just turned 4, flashbacks of playing with toys on the floor...been through enough, get ready for more...

few people know my battles behind my cell door,

suicide doesn't cross my mind, homicide is more than a reoccurring thought,

I'm afraid of myself when I'm angry....

in don't have a routine, don't want one either... that's when you know your use to this shit...

don't blame yourself, we all have our own lives we have to live,

you are stronger than you know, just believe in yourself...I believe in you

the past is the past, everyone says.... but

I'm addicted to thoughts of (what if?)

I have faith, but in also have doubt, not of god but of myself...

why am I so violent???

that's a million-dollar question ...

why am I so angry?

will I ever know??

you say money is evil, but even without it, I'm still evil... I've always thought I was invincible; I'd never get tired......

reality check...

I've got pride issues... is it because I use to get

bullied?? all my problems big resort to fighting, that's

not normal...

my body is tired, my mind is exhausted why do I get thrilled
from the actions of evil

what is peace? I don't know....

nor do I care anymore, I'm tired of looking for the great
world of joy love and peace everyone talks about...
NEWS FLASH IT'S NOT REAL !!!!!!!!!

I don't fear hell, because I'm here...

I don't plan on coming home before the world ends, so I'll
see you in heaven ...no hope I make it. if not it's just me
being a failure... no surprise right,

black sheep in the family.... or just simply the fuck up.

do you think I wanted my life to be like this ??

Because I didn't, but I don't know how to fix it !!!!

I won't give up though I promise ... please don't give up
on me...

You say you want to know what runs through my head....
don't judge me...

they say I'm crazy, that I have no heart...

they say I'm more than one person, but I can't tell them apart

I'm trying to find the root of my pain, yet I don't know
where to start...

things I've done makes me sick, ashamed to admit,

the shit I've seen haunts me every day when I close my eyes

my life replays.

I feel like a cement block, no love no hope no fear, only hate... I

hate people for no reason, I may not even know them... maybe it

is just because of my situation... maybe it's really me, hate turns

to rage, the rage I can't control,...

I want to do good, get right with God

but my desires are of sin and he doesn't like fake

he knows what I'm thinking, I know he doesn't approve

but why did he create me, was I set up to lose?

I don't care what others think of me, but I'm constantly trying to
impress my family... when can I just be me

Mackenzie, Mac, kenz, kiki or zee, do I even know the real
me?

I wish I could go all the way back before I was born, maybe I
could pick my dad...

they say to get better you've got to open healed wounds, re-
feel the pain. just to create a small amount of relief and more
shame

I have days I feel unwanted, unloved ...... a failure

anger boils toward myself, the embarrassment for abandoning my son...

I didn't want to...

I'm scared to get to close, scared to open to wide... who will strike next!???

I'm paranoid... on edge, this cannot be

right. I'm the product equal to fucked

up....

do you know me as much as you think you do,...

I don't think I know anyone anymore, not even myself... why am I not normal ??? why am I so different??

From: Judy Frisby
Date: 2/8/2016
To: MACKENZIE BASHAM

Wow your writings are great, does it make you feel better? It does me. I will put on some media money tomorrow or Wednesday. Did you get the pics I sent you? Here's more.

From: MACKENZIE BASHAM
Date:
2/9/2016 To:
Judy Frisby

Yeah it helps a little, how is Gracie . I've been trying to call you. I love the pics, I need a better one of Cole, Gracie, and Zay together for the background of my player

From: MACKENZIE BASHAM
Date: 2/13/2016
To: Judy Frisby

love to see ya but hate to tell you bye...
I wanna kill the world for seeing my little brother cry. i
gotta stay strong, hold in the pain...
show my siblings strength, that I'm here to carry our team.
we'll get thru this one day at a time.
when the visits done I'm ready to break the machine,
how dare they take you away from me..
,ice cycles on the ceiling, the only thing with me is my mind
and my memories....
I'd give my arms and legs to be on your couch,
seeing the house made me flashback to the things others
would think of as small,...
everybody's gotten older , grandpas aging ... lord let me get
home to make a couple more memories,,
I'm so mad , I'm so angry ...... this shit isn't rehabilitating me
!!!!!!

From: MACKENZIE BASHAM
Date: 2/18/2016
To: Judy Frisby

I lay in bed at night and can't help but think about things I'd
change.......
if I had my life to live over , in would have talked less and
listened more. I would have invited friends over instead of going
out.. I would have taken the time to listen to my grandparents
talk about their youth. I would have spent more time focused on
the image God wants from me rather than the image of the
world . I would have taken more time on the softball field then at
Robb park. I would have kissed my siblings every time we went
our separate ways. I would have held the hugs tighter and
longer with my dad . or feel The scratch of my grandpas beard

against my face... I would have tickled Isiah more just to hear his laugh, . I would of been more respectful to my step dad , more understanding to my mother . wiser with my choices and more patient financially ... I would have cried and laughed less while watching TV and more while watching life... there would be more I love you's more I'm sorry's ...... but mostly given another shot , I would stop every moment, look at it and really see it, cherish it, live it, and never give it back. .... what would you do???

From: MACKENZIE BASHAM
Date: 2/25/2016
To: Judy Frisby

had to go to Dr today for back im in so much pain. . they charged me of course . i shop next Friday and have to pay for that. will get in touch when phone pin comes in mail. love you

From: MACKENZIE BASHAM
Date: 3/14/2016
To: Judy Frisby

let me tell you that I'm
sorry for causing so
much strife tell you that
I'll succeed
in leading a better life
I know that its not
over yet its a long
road up ahead
but I appreciate the little
things because I could be
dead
I've learned to live each passing
day as if it were my last
in look forward to the future and I'm learning from

my past........

......haven't been able to sleep the last couple nights, just been in my head a lot about everything..... I miss you. love you and will call tonight or tomorrow.
give say kisses for me tell him I love him more than oatmeal cream pies , I wish I had one of them right now
. :-) smile

From: MACKENZIE BASHAM
Date: 3/14/2016
To: Judy Frisby

I know I'll survive this .... I know we'll get through this .....
I'm a strong person, I know my glass if half full.. I hate people that tell me its full, I've sipped a few and spilled more than enough.
I will fight and will not be beat, but I am allowed to say I'm tired. even people who win get tired.... I've got a lot to do, and plan to do as much as I can, but first if I need to cry I'm going to ..... if I need to yell I will.....
God has seen me through a lot of stuff and I know he'll give me the strength to pull this off.... this is tough one for me , but I'll handle it in my own way. some issues are bigger than others.... mine seem to be huge, but my issues are what defines me, creates me.... imperfectly...
I am going to fight, and I'm going to win... I will work at being stronger ,even though I may not like it...
life is for living , and we each have our own life to live, complaints should be kept to a minimum... we've all got something, and at least I've got people who care.... I see this sentence as a punch
in my stomach, it takes my breath away, it will leave me sore, but I'll end up walking away with my chin up....
I will cherish life more, I will pray for strength, I will not be bitter, I will be strong, I will laugh, I will cry, but most importantly I WILL WIN!!!!! ... if your not first your last ;) "shake n bake" ... hahaha ..

From: MACKENZIE BASHAM
Date: 3/25/2016
To: Judy Frisby

if Cole isn't here today don't bother coming tomorrow cuz i wont be able to get visits... and make sure you tell him i said fuck him and don't ever speak to me again. period. happy birthday by the way, hope you have a better day,. love you give zay kisses for me

From: Judy Frisby
Date: 3/25/2016
To: MACKENZIE BASHAM

OK we won't come. All I have to say is if you didn't commit crimes, none of us would have to go through the pure hell of getting 2 hours away to see you, be treated like shit for your crimes, searched, spend money and have our paperwork.
Apparently you still have not matured enough to realize that while you are in a horrible situation, you, not any of us put you there. How you feel right now being let down by your brother is how your 4 year old feels everyday because of you. Ritchie and I and Gracie Jo live with his heartaches everyday because you wanted to steal stuff instead of work a job like we have to do. Sleep on that little miss and welcome to my hell of being let down by someone you love more then anything.
BTW I just worked a 10 hour day so we could afford to bring your son to see you for Easter, but throw a damn fit because of Cole's stupid crap... That's fair!

From: Mackenzie Basham
Date: 04/21/2016
To: Judy Frisby

Isiah,

today after our visit. I couldn't get you out of my mind...
not that I wanted to, but I have to put my mask back on,
and one day you'll understand what I am talking about...

you are growing, and getting so big, I'm not used to it yet
and try not to think about the time that has passed since
I've been gone... it eats at me every night that I'm not
laying next to you and the pain that. keeps me awake is
the worst pain I've ever felt in my life...

I wonder what you're doing a lot, or what you're thinking if you're
having a dream or a nightmare and what's the last thing you
thought of before you fell asleep or the first when you wake up. I
know mine is you, ...

every day I learn something about you, and it eats at me that I'm
not the first to know... I'm so sorry that I'm not there and I
haven't been these last couple of years but I promise you when I
come home I'm home to stay, nothing or anyone will ever keep
us apart .... thank you for being so strong and patient for
mommy, thank you for loving me unconditionally no matter what.
I can't wait until we get another "play date" but honestly, I can't
wait until we get to have a playdate without a time limit and a
goodbye... I'll see you when you get back from Memphis, have
fun "big boy", take a lot of pictures, be safe and listen to your
nana, papa, and Gracie... hugs and kisses from mommy . I love
and miss you sooooooooooooooo much, more than slushies and
hot Cheetos !!! :-) :-) :-). :-). :-). :-).

To: Mackenzie Basham
Date: 5/21/2016 10:05:00 PM
From: Judy Frisby

Hi Sis,

Going to try to write to you but I'm having a pretty tough day here. When we hung up the last phone call, I was heartbroken. I put on a fake smile and took bubby to team pictures like I'm supposed to do, but I was choking back tears. It breaks my heart when he gets sad talking to you. This is not "getting easier " and I want to throat punch people who say that. I feel like every day I get to look forward to pouring salt in a wound... Sometimes 2 or 3 times a day. Poor baby doesn't know why he feels sad. It's taking a toll on me as you seen from the last visit. I try to keep pushing, climbing to the light at the end of the tunnel (or 12 more years) but I'm failing. The darkness pulls my feet and my hands are greased with oil on the ladder out of my hell. I want you home. I don't want to celebrate another birthday of my child's surrounded by bars and restraints or using up my 2 hugs in 3 hours. Who do they think they are? I BROUGHT YOU INTO THIS WORLD... A mother should not be told when she can hug or kiss her own baby. I just hate you being in there. You still consume my every thought, but my worries and fears are not as intense as 2 years ago. Well, kind of like you say you get so depressed missing Isiah that you can't look at his photos or get out of bed, the same scenario. Will we ever heal from this damage? Will we be able to function as a "normal family" when you return? I am different and each and every person in our family is by going through their own way to cope with where you are. I got Isiah signed up for counseling and in play therapy this past week. Do you know when they asked me where "Mom" is I still freeze? My mouth at that moment, in that room, with the physiologist, would not move. It felt like forever then I said, "Dayton Correctional Institution ". I cannot verbally say the sentence.... My daughter is in prison. I'm typing through tears just writing it. Not my daughter, my sweet little Kiki Lee with the cute rosy little chubby cheeks I love to hug and kiss. The salt just went in the wounds again. When will this be all over? I will never stop missing you or loving you so taking it day by day sucks. It's very dark knowing that tomorrow when the sun comes out and the Good Lord has kept me another day, that I know I will be sad. At some point every day.... I'm sad. As I type this I'm sitting in my dark room, only the light of the phone. My sadness has taken hold of me today. I have fewer days like this I will admit. They are cruel and consuming, and they make me feel sorry for myself, and for Zay, and Grace, and Cole. We are a pack and our souls are connected by a strong bond that is being put to the test right now. I am thankful for these days for the reason of being forced to appreciate my own self-worth. I am pretty freaking bad-ass if I can be at this low of a point, then Monday be a T-ball mom and cheer him on like I'm a pro.... with a giant smile on my face.

Mother's Day made me ill. I still hate birthdays, holidays, the day you were arrested, the day you were sentenced, hell most Sunday's just because. Sunday makes me think of a family day, I just cannot handle the concept of doing anything family without my entire unit there. I gotta shake it, but I revert back to a 10-year-old child--I don't want to!!! Anything that makes me the slightest bit emotional I avoid at all costs. I get strength through Gracie Jo and Coley, you, and even Zay. Nobody else in this universe can connect to the same frequency we are riding through all this. People try, but they don't understand our specific situation. I probably sound selfish, and inconsiderate to all the hurt and tragedy in the world but today, I am going to put myself first.

Well, sis, I feel a little better writing to you, it's as therapeutic as it is brutal. I am scheduling a visit for next week(or try to) and then one on your BIRTHDAY, 22 years old already! Oh, how I miss your sweet face. I love you more today than ever before... Stay strong stay smart baby girl. You are in my heart forever and always. Love you more then chocolate ice cream, Momma

Prison Diaries: The Petition May/2016

It is Memorial Day weekend and I'm home alone. It is times like these that I think of my Mackenzie. What is she doing on this holiday weekend? I still cannot partake in any cookouts, hotdogs and hamburgers, corn hole games, drinking ice cold beer which I used to love oh, so much. I am overcome with a sense of emptiness inside and I'm sad. Being alone in my own home is something I used to live for back in the day. The day when we had all four kids at home and it was always chaos, I would say repeatedly. "I would just like a day to myself, ONE DAY is all I ask". Now all kids are grown except baby girl and we are starting on the next generation with the brown bear. I sit down to my computer to relieve some stress and pour out my pain and suffering into words and I get an idea. A petition. What if I take around a petition for people to sign to get Mackenzie a shorter or new sentence? I start searching sights for ideas and I come across a site that will let you compose your own petition and start from there. I become obsessed with the thought of sharing my daughter's story so that the public will know more than just what they have seen in the evening liar and on the nightly news. People are going to think I'm crazy and that is fine, it's a risk I'm willing to take. I have not ever known anyone in my real life that there has been a petition about. The only petition I have ever signed in my forty- three years was a petition to keep a man on death row after he murdered my friend when we were in high school. Of course, I signed that he deserved to rot in hell. How will people respond to signing and supporting a cause that is FOR a criminal in prison? I fill out the questions and I write a brief story of why I think people should sign my petition. I attach a photo of Mackenzie and Isiah with beautiful smiles and their arms around each other at a prison visit. Oh wow, am I really going to put this out to the public? This is scary putting it "out there" what Mackenzie has admitted to and the injustices I believe she has endured from our local law enforcement and the justice system. What if I get a negative backlash? What if people blow it up with reasons why she should "rot in hell" just like I thought of the man that murdered my friend? My daughter did not hurt anyone physically, surely people will embrace her story and support her through this petition. I am nervous and my gut is telling me to do it. My gut feeling has got me into a lot of trouble in the past, but this, this is different. I click on the button that says, "create petition now" and it asks me for my title that I want people to see first thing. Voices for Mackenzie Basham....oh my god I am putting her picture in a prison uniform AND putting her full name on the petition. I fill out for the names and comments to be emailed directly to the Ohio Governor, the Ohio Attorney General, and the Ohio Parole Board. I click the button "SHARE" and that's it....it is public. My daughter's story of crime and drugs and is now available for all to read and judge all over the world wide web. I share it on social media then I get off the computer and decide to not look for the rest of the day. I going to write Mackenzie a letter telling her how much I miss her like all the other letters I write to her. I wonder if she will be mad about what I just did? Oh well, I can't pick up the phone and ask her permission so it will have to be a decision I stand by.

It has been three days since I started the petition for Mackenzie to receive a shorter sentence. The last paragraph of my letter is to beg people to sign this petition, I state that Mackenzie will be released in 2028. She will be thirty-four years old and her baby will be seventeen. I have never written that down on paper or even been able to comprehend a time so far away, I just knew it was way too long. When I wrote that date, I started to think to myself how old I would be, and my parents, sisters, etc. I try to dream at night of the day or days leading up to Mackenzie's release, who will go with me to pick her up? Where is the first place we will go? Who will be the very first person she wants to see(other than her baby boy)?

Then an overwhelming sadness hits me in the chest. My parents. If my parents are seventy-five and seventy-seven now that would make them eighty-seven and eighty-nine on her release date. What if the Lord takes my sweet parents' home before they can be with Mackenzie again in the free world? Oh my God, what if one of them dies while she's in there? Will she be able to go to their funeral? How in the living hell will I be able to deliver her the news of one of her grandparent's death? Why am I thinking this?

I am beginning to get panicked because the realization of my parents dying while Mackenzie is in prison is now in my head. I have never before this thought about that, it was nicely tucked away somewhere in my brain where I could not find it. My children are as close to my parents as I am to Isiah. They helped me raise Mackenzie and Cole when I was a single mom. I am confident in saying that I could not have survived without my mom and dad back them, maybe even now. I will never forget the time my mom was watching the kids and I was a twenty-five-year-old single mother. I had just worked a long Friday and had anxiously waiting for the night to come so I could go out and enjoy my new single nightlife while feeling warm and fuzzy inside with my babies at Grammy's. I went out for drinks with some friends from work. I walked in and to my surprise there sat the devil himself at the bar. The man who had not seen our children in months because he needed to "sew his wild oats". I would have liked to sew his "oats" for him.... with a very sharp needle and thread, literally. I was crushed that he had chosen that place over spending time with his children. I was getting one night away, and I had to see him. As he tossed shots back and got in his wallet to splurge on rounds of drinks for people who he thought were his new friends, my blood began to boil. This was not going to end well. My coworkers did not have children at the time, so they did not get it. How am I supposed to sit here and enjoy people and conversations and alcohol when all I can think about was my two precious babies at home whose own blood couldn't give two shits about them I thought? He is supposed to love them as I do, he is supposed to worry and care and have his world revolve around them as I do. Fueled by hurt and alcohol, I explode. I approach him and probably started to make a scene. I wanted everyone sitting along that bar to know that while he was so freaking awesome buying their drinks, he had only provided his two and four-year-old with a package of bologna, a gallon of fruit juice, and one pack of diapers in the past three months. Well everyone knew now as I followed him out the door making sure he didn't escape without being humiliated. He was trying to get his key in the door and he just was not quick enough. I hit him right upside the head. It felt good. I was now screaming and crying and hitting him as hard as I could. I wanted him to feel pain because I feel pain. He just stood there as I unleashed my anger of our divorce on him with his hands in his pockets. As I look back now, I appreciate that he didn't hit me back. It was not my anger; it was for my children. He just didn't get it; it was about my babies. I realized that night that I was alone in this adventure of raising children, so I needed to get it together. I can't be beating his ass every time I think he craps on the kids. I stormed off back into the bar to tell my friends I was leaving. They had just seen me unleash the "crazy" and I think they were a bit scared of me now. Oh well, I can worry about that later. I had business to take care of. I got back to my apartment I now rented after losing the house in the divorce. I jumped in my car and drove to my parents. My dad was in the garage as usual and was surprised to see me. I was visibly upset, and he knew it. I started in the house on a mission. My dad asks me what I'm doing back, he thought the kids were having a sleepover. I said, "I'm getting one of your guns, I'm going to kill that son of a bitch for what he is doing to my kids." I start to march by my father in a mad, crazy, rage. He firmly grabs me. I was instantly defensive and began to yell at my own father. "You have no idea how I feel Dad, you and Mom have been married forever and you do not know what I'm going through. Leave me alone, I just want to hurt him, not kill him. He shit on my kids, how can someone do that to their own flesh and blood?" My screams were now turning into a sobbing kind of yelling. I had just lost my cool for the very first time right in the driveway of perfect mid-American suburbia. These things did not happen in my world or my family's, I thought. My dad grabbed both my arms and yelled at me. His face was red and I could see the bluish veins emerging through his neck. To be totally honest it kind of scared me. I had never really been yelled at by my dad, I was a good kid, most of the time following the rules. That's when my dad said something I will never forget to this day, he was serious and visibly upset I could tell by the tears in his hardened eyes.......He said, " Do you think I don't know what you're going through? Don't you understand that your mom and I are going through this too? I watched my mom and dad fight all the time and get divorced. I hate it that my grandkids have to see the things I saw as a kid...I still remember. My dad was an alcoholic, he wasn't a good dad, but you know what....I still loved him. You cannot do this; these kids need you both. "

I had made my dad yell at me and get teary eyed. I no longer felt sorry for myself on this journey. That night really opened my eyes to a lot of things. The bond between my parents and my children was as strong as steel, just like the steel doors separating them now. They cannot die until Mackenzie is free, that just cannot happen.

From: Judy Frisby
Date: 7/18/2016
To: Mackenzie Basham

Hey Sis,

I'm feeling very anxious about this Saturday. If you look at it from an outsider's point of view it's a little scary. I am going into a maximum-security prison with my little 4-year-old grandson to spend the day. Ritchie tells me that I will be fine and that he is confident "Mack" would never let anything happen to her baby or her mom. I know that's right. You make me feel safe in there....but what if your hand is tied so to speak? I am very thankful for these 6 hours for Isiah, he is beyond excited! He misses you still as much as when you first left. Your bond with him has never been broken.

I have had quite a few sleepless nights and oh so many butterflies in the stomach because of this extended visit. Last night about 3:00 am, I think I figured it out. I am going to see with my own eyes where my little girl lives. The inside. In my mind, I try to make it crappy glorious, so

I am not eaten alive by my own worst worries and fears. At our normal visits, your sitting at a table....so that's how I leave with that image in my mind. I am afraid of the image that I will have after I see where you really are living. That is my own demon to deal with. A mother cannot stomach seeing her child in that kind of environment and not have feelings of terror, especially when there is not one thing I can do about it. The feeling of helplessness is incapacitating. I'm sure like all the "firsts" before in this nightmare, I will recover. Be able to function after a while, but every time we fall down a few notches it takes a lot out of us physically and mentally. I'm tired but not tired enough to stop fighting the world for you sis. Human life is precious, you don't just give up. Some of your family members have or let their support for you and bubby fade...... but I will NEVER. You are not replaceable to me or Ritchie or Gracie Jo or Coley. I sure do miss the girl you once were. That is no more, you're a young adult now. My worry is you becoming an adult incarcerated will have an irreversible effect when you finally do get home. I read an article of a man who was in prison 32 years then went to Harvard and got his master's degree:

"Some literature suggests that people in prison experience mental deterioration and apathy, endure personality changes, and become uncertain about their identities. Several re-searchers found that people in prison may be diagnosed with post-traumatic stress disorders, as well as other psychiatric disorders, such as panic attacks, depression, and paranoia; 15 subsequently, these prisoners find a social adjustment and social integration difficult upon release".

Well, we will cross that bridge when we get there. Focus on today, right now, this weekend. I will be there with Isiah and we will have the best day ever. I have done a whole lot of things I never would have imagined I would do because of you, child. This being a big one, haha.

Here are some song lyrics to read, it makes me think of mothers watching their children grow or enduring troubled times. When I get extra, I will put on your media account to buy the song.

"She Used to Be Mine" (Sara Bareilles) It's

not simple to say

That most days I don't recognize me

That these shoes and this apron That

place and its patrons

Have taken more than I gave them It's

not easy to know

I'm not anything like I used to be

Although it's true

I was never attention's sweet center I

still remember that girl

She's imperfect but she tries She is

good but she lies She is hard on

herself

She is broken and won't ask for help She is

messy but she's kind

She is lonely most of the time She is

all of this mixed up And baked in a

beautiful pie

She is gone but she used to be mine

It's not what I asked for

Sometimes life just slips in through a back door And

carves out a person

And makes you believe it's all true And

now I've got you

And you're not what I asked for

If I'm honest I know I would give it all back For a

chance to start over

And rewrite an ending or two For

the girl that I knew

Who'll be reckless just enough

Who'll get hurt but

Who learns how to toughen up when she's bruised And

gets used by a man who can't love

And then she'll get stuck and be scared Of

the life that's inside her

Growing stronger each day 'Til

it finally reminds her

To fight just a little

To bring back the fire in her eyes That's

been gone but it used to be mine

By the way, I finally listened to "Dear Mama' from Tupac you sent me long ago, was afraid it would make me cry...but it's a rap song ??, anyhow I was good until close to the end... remember me, you and Cole...the struggles of being a single momma...You kids longing for your dad's attention......us against the world, and I started sobbing. In the car, at the grocery store. I'm sorry I lost my composure at the visit on your birthday. I felt crippled sitting there. I wanted to sing "Happy Birthday" to my baby girl and I wasn't allowed. Dear God, this is not how I imagined spending your 22 birthday. I hate when I lose it in front of my mother, or Isiah. The entire freaking day I cried. Maybe there's something wrong with me, or maybe I just love and protect my kids too much.

You are my sunshine, my only sunshine...you make momma happy when skies are gray. You'll never know dear, how much I love you....please don't take my sunshine away......I'll love you forever, Mom

From: Mackenzie Basham

Date: 7/19/2016
To: Judy Frisby

Hey mom, I've got to make this quick because I have school but everything will be okay, it's not as bad as its made up to be.. and my hands would never be tied when it comes to protecting my family most importantly my son and my mom. you should know that. 1000 years in the hole wouldn't stop me from that, better yet the death penalty ... everything will be great we will have a nice time and get to act like we aren't in the situation we are in for a short period of time. I am so excited to be able to play with him and have more time to spend with him... this week is a big week for me, I get my green shirt on Thursday and I'm trying to get into a better dorm also... where Zaria lives (my Muslim) lol.

you know people do change in prison some for the worse and some for the good... I can honestly say I've changed a little of both, more so good though... I have fought a lot of battles mentally within myself and built up confidence and courage to fight my demons... I used to not want you or the family to know a lot of things about me but honestly, I don't care anymore because I am who I am... I don't know, there is good and bad with this, but let's see the positive outweigh the negative, it will help us mentally.

it's okay to lose your composure, it's like letting out the bundle of pain and getting yourself refreshed for another load...

one day we'll look back at this and you will understand and be able to support someone else who is in the situation you once overcame.

smile and I'll see you Saturday. I love you. thank god for the blessings, good or bad...

kiss bubby for me tells him I can't wait to see him !!!!!!!!! and look nice for our pictures.

Mommy/Child Day 2016
Prison Diaries: July 23, 2016--- Part 1

Observations of spending the day at the prison
with Mackenzie and Isiah.

These are MY observations and experiences only.

This entry will not be going to Mackenzie.

Isiah woke me up at 4:00 am in total excitement. My
nerves started about 8:00pm the night before which led to
me finally falling asleep around 1:30 am. After showering
and getting dressed for the day we made a live video to
show our emotions/mood before we visited. Isiah was
very happy and extremely excited to spend the day with
his mommy. We left the house at 5:20.

We arrived at Dayton Correctional Institution at 6:52 am.
We made another live video to show emotions/mood right
before we entered the prison. Isiah was good until he
actually got out of the car, he just became a little quiet is
all maybe having some butterfly's in the tummy himself, I
really don't know. I felt the need to vomit or empty
otherwise at about the "Dayton 12 miles" sign on I-75.
When I got out of the car, I gagged a few times, hands
were shaky and I was finding it hard to finish a sentence
or collect my thoughts...just focused on the task ahead.

We entered the prison check-in area at 7:00 am. The employees
were very nice and stern. Doing their job as expected. I had
brought several changes of clothes just in case Isiah and I's
clothes were not "policy". Nothing was going to stop us from
getting in....covering all alleys so I did not have a broken-hearted
4-year-old or a broken-hearted 22 years old. We just sat and

observed the workers checking in for work, the conversations in the lobby about the child/mommy day going on. As we were waiting, I witnessed an older black woman walking with a cane approx 60ish in age being escorted by 2 corrections officers to the opposite side of the desk. They checked through her 2 Ziploc bags of prescription medicine as the woman was very antsy and anxious. Just then the male officer says out loud to the woman, "Inmate
******, you are no longer welcome here".

The woman says very loud, "That is fine, praise Jesus!!"

She has just served her debt to society and was being released. No one else in the lobby said a word. I was overcome with joy for this lady and just wanted to hug her or something. I just smiled at her, but she hugged her husband, he grabbed her box of belongings and they were quickly out of there! I have no idea what she did, nor did I care I just felt compassion for the woman. Then I started thinking of the day they walk my girl to that other side of the desk and say that to her. I can just tell you it wouldn't be quiet on that lobby because I can name about 25 people who will be there with me anticipating Mackenzie's release. Thirty-six woman was granted this special day out of the population of eight hundred some inmates. They took us back in groups of about 15. Isiah and I were the very first ones called back (I think my petition has a part in that, maybe not...). We entered through our normal visitation set of security to where regular visits are. Then the caseworkers told us to follow this officer to the family day festivities.

He told us we were going to be taken through back hallways and around buildings to keep us away from the "general population"...I felt a sigh of relief, to be honest. Isiah as well as all the other children just stared and took it all in. It was very hot in and outside, but everyone kept up with the same anticipation. We walked out into a large

The Real Prison Diaries

fenced in area which was locked after we entered. We were told to not go past the caution tapes as the fences directly behind were electric and would alert a security alarm. There was some blacktop and 2 old basketball hoops out there. We were then taken into a gym looking area filled with tables and chairs. An inmate or two were sitting at each one of the tables.

It was about 105 degrees in the gym, just then Isiah spots a beautiful girl with 2 huge dimples and the prettiest smile across her face. He literally ran shouting "Mommy"...some of my emotional overloads was relieved. They hugged and kissed and hugged more...it was overwhelming with emotions. That's when this girl got her hands on Mackenzie ha ha. Oh, I'm smiling just typing this. I hugged the crap out of her and kissed her warm red (still chubby) cheeks like nobody's business. It was a beautiful release of love between us three.... all at the same time we couldn't get enough of each other. At that time a man gets on a microphone and announces for us visitors to sign in and turns on some music!! It was the rap song "Teach me how to Dougie".... you could feel the entire room relax and people started walking around and it was awesome. The love exchanges between the mommy's and their children were one of the most honest things I have ever seen. Nothing else mattered in those moments, nobody cared who did what, how long since that much contact with each other.... just tight hugs and a massive amount of love. It reminded me of the saying "you don't know what you've got until it's gone" kind of moment.

Recap of activities: Corn-hole playing, jump roping, basketball playing, face painting, coloring, dancing, eating popcorn, sidewalk chalking on the blacktop, and throwing frisbees.

Recap of food/snacks: Popcorn, bottled water, Capri Sun juice drinks for the kids. Lunch was a hot dog with bun, a small bag of chips or Cheetos. Dessert was snow cones with 3 flavors.

Mackenzie got our lunch for us, her and Zay got snow cones together, they held hands most of the time and were inseparable. I walked around a bit, but the heat was almost unbearable for this ole' gal.

Mackenzie and Zay were both sweating but that didn't stop them. I really enjoyed watching the interactions, the different cultures, and the prison way of life was interesting to me. I did feel like I was on the Netflix series " Orange is the New Black". I only could watch one episode, but those directors are spot on minus the dirtiness and inmate glamor.

To be continued...

Prison Diaries: Part 2 of Mommy/child day.

The things I observed from being an outsider with no experiences of crime, prison, or ever being separated from a family member are as follows.......

The inside of a woman's prison is another world in itself. It answered a lot of my questions and confirmed some of my worst fears. I'm not sure how to phrase this other than being brutally honest. The so-called "class" of people in there visiting was not as diverse as I thought. My opinion only is that about 25% of woman in there was from the background/income Mackenzie has come from. The other 75% were noticeably lower income. I would say that about 50% of inmates I observed were so-called comfortable with being there, maybe have been to prison before I don't know. About 75% of the woman just in that gym were white leaving the black inmates a minority only among the 36 approved for the visit day.

Mackenzie definitely looked "out of place" not by race just by her young age and how she presents herself acting

timid or apprehensive being there. My question now is, "
Does money really rule the world?" In my own case, if I
had been able to hire a top dollar defense attorney instead
of Mack getting a court-appointed attorney, you bet your
sweet ass she would not be sitting in there right now. That
is water under the bridge now we play the cards that we
were dealt.

I observed the cliques of inmates, just as it was a high
school lunchroom...........

You had the inmates who were scared as hell to even be in
prison, shedding tears on and off with their family members
(Mack fit in this group). You had the badass chicks I would
not want mess with inmates that did not shed a tear and
treated their children as one of their "homies". You had the
men/woman inmates who were trying to keep up their
persona inside the prison but still connect with their family.
You had the older more motherly grandma looking inmates
who it was obvious had been there a long long time with no
hope in their eyes so to speak. You had the girly girls that
wore makeup, hair done and strutted provocatively around
flirting with other inmates trying to, I'll just say it.... hookup.

Something happened when we ate lunch that made me almost
lose my composure. We got in line for our lunch of a hot dog on
a bun and a snack size bag of chips. The hot dogs were kind of
lime green-ish, buns were soft. Going through the line it seemed
as if Mackenzie was so proud of 1. us...2.the gourmet lunch she
very much appreciated. I felt as if I commented on the "probably
wouldn't feed my dog" lunch it would hurt her feelings. She was
so proud of what they were serving us obviously it was a better
meal then she is served daily. I told her that I didn't really eat hot
dogs because of a diet I'm on.

That was a bullshit line I just wanted to let her get more food.
She said, 'Oh mom are you sure?" as she looked down at the
floor. At that moment my heart was completely broke. I'm crying

typing this. I watched as my shamed little girl savaged down those two lime green hotdogs as they were steak. She looked down the entire time as if embarrassed to be eating like that. Oh, how I cannot stand to see her like that. She asked me if I wanted another bottle of water. I said sure, do you? She said she was going to drink as many as she could because they do not get "water in bottles" normally.... Broken.

My child was not wanting Buckle jeans, or Nike shoes....she was damn near beg-full of water in a bottle. Take that in or maybe read this to your own children. I am well aware my daughter committed a crime, but is this humane? She does get water. Lukewarm, possibly infected with hepatitis C water out of the bathroom faucets. Dear God, bless her heart, I love her so much this is killing me to watch. Her and Isiah ate their lunch and smiled and she finished every scrap of every bite not wasting a crumb or drop of juice or water. Same with the snow cones we had after.

I really take for granted just running to the grocery or through a drive-thru to grab whatever the heck I want, whenever the heck I want it. If I'm done, eh toss it in the trash no big deal.

My daughter would eat that trash. She's becomes not just physically incarcerated but mentally. She is poisoned.... kind of animalish like a predator protecting its prey or latest kill.

We walked outside to shoot hoops and jump rope and it was "yard time" for the general population. There was a track woman were walking, there were picnic tables they were gathered around, there was a softball game going on a homemade ball diamond, and inmates sitting in the grass every here and there around the yard. When some of the families stepped out to play in our special area it was like the old medieval times of spectators all around in bleachers looking down on the fight or event about to take place. We were being watched by 95% of them. The guards were positioned here and there for our safety. Mackenzie looked a few times over to our "audience", but I noticed she tried to stay between Isiah and them fence so he was being seen as less as possible.

I think I'm a pretty tough gal, and I think my daughter is a badass and I probably wouldn't mess with her, but at that moment I felt small, tiny, weak, wimpy, unprotected, vulnerable, violated and scared as hell. My usual smile and talk to everybody were not going to work with the inmates staring at me through the fence. I was being watched. I wanted to grab Isiah and Mackenzie and run as we've never run before.

To be continued....

Prison Diaries: Part 3 The final entry of our Mommy/child day at the prison.

When you're a parent, well most parents, you can't always give your child what they want with material items. You can, however, give them love and comfort and security and as much as they can take until they are content. This leads you to, as a parent feeling accomplished, or valued maybe, even let's say completed in your internal goals of parenthood. It doesn't matter if you have a newborn baby or a 70-year-old child you will only ever be as happy as your most troubled child. I am so proud of and in love with my other two children, but I am still empty. Am I just supposed to forget that I have a child suffering even though she got herself into this mess?

How do people just turn their back?

I am here to tell you that if I only got to see my mom for three hours a month, I would be sad. If the only time I could talk to my mom was occasionally for 15 minutes I would be sad. I cannot imagine how little Isiah feels at 4 years old. Maybe like those whose mommy's have died and went to heaven, or maybe not.... I'm just an observer. He is so emotional the weeks leading up to our visits and after and when he looks through his baby pictures. I am 43 years old and I am having trouble functioning......he is 4. Oh, how I feel for these children with incarcerated mothers. They did nothing wrong, not one damn thing! They are messed up socially, mentally, they have behavioral issues and separation anxiety overload. Some do not believe me and that's cool. I would like to invite them to stay in our home the nights leading up to a visit. You will not sleep. You will hear yelling, profanity, crying, and that is coming from little Isiah. He doesn't even know how to feel.

Yesterday I tried to do live video as soon as we got into the car which was about 15 minutes after he said goodbye to his mommy. The mood had gone from excited in the first video to quiet in the second video, and the third video was a tiny minute piece of the full-on meltdown that lasted about oh, the rest of the night. Saying goodbye to Mackenzie after spending 5 hours together was awesome....then it was time to go. The officers announced on the microphone to wrap things up and the entire mood of the room changed. People were hugging and crying, and some were acting as if they didn't hear the announcement. That was me.

I freaking hate leaving that place without my child. I'm not protecting her, I'm not making her feel safe, I'm just not doing my job as a parent dammit. I am not the only one like me, there are many, many others. As we said our goodbyes, I kept going back for seconds. " One more kiss sissy, I would say" we would laugh and hug again as we...

Ok, just had to take a break, meltdown. I imagine why writing is therapeutic is because I don't have to physically say it with my mouth. Sometimes even typing what's in my head makes me go into a sobbing episode but like Mackenzie told me in her last letter..." It's OK to lose your composure, it's like letting go of all the pain and getting ready for another load." I'm ready for another load now.

We followed our instructions and exited the prison. Isiah was happy about making new friends who were all in there seeing their mommy's just like him. After we went through the final doors we were sweating, tired, emotionally just freaking over it. Isiah likes to race me when we leave there. I walk the steps and he runs up the ramp. Yesterday I got to the top of the steps and turned around...no Isiah. I yelled for him to get up to the top because I was hot. He said no. He was sitting down on the cement ramp. This started the meltdown. He was not going; he wanted his mommy. He wanted his mommy again, and another 10 times. I walked back down the ramp and told him I would take him to his favorite store and buy him a toy and I lied and said that mommy had to go back to class, and we were coming back later. He got up and after about 3 more stops on our way to the car, I had him in his car seat. I do not care who judges me for bribing the little guy or telling him false things to get him to go. Let them live in my life for a day.

At that moment I felt like Mount Saint Helen's on the verge of eruption. I wanted to start sobbing and yelling and I wanted to fight someone, you know... punch someone very hard in the face. I was in pain and so was this little boy and nobody gets it. Only me and Isiah get it, why do I feel like that?

I promised him a fishing pole from Walmart. I tried to take a live video of the emotional change after we pulled away and had driven to probably the Troy, Ohio exit. I got off 75 and pulled into a gas station. I was a nervous wreck and had to just regroup thought maybe some caffeine was needed. He was crying and gagging and just a mess. It was a mix of no sleep, being sad, and being mad I suppose. I turned off the video and got him calmed down by stories of fishing poles and Walmart. All the sudden it was quiet, and he was asleep.

Sweet Jesus he was asleep. I wanted to smoke a cigarette, it would be the very best cigarette in the entire world, but I was not getting outside of the car in fear of the door shutting and waking him up. I just got back on 75. No caffeine, no cigarette, just get home to our comfort zone.

Didn't happen. At the Wapakoneta exit Isiah woke up crying and yelling he wanted his fishing pole, he wanted his mom, I was a liar, he hated me....Bless his little heart. I got off at that exit and we went to the nearest Walmart and I put on a smile and "Nana" tried to make everything better. I bought him a fishing pole, some bait, and a spider-man net, with money I do not have on my credit card. It's the same thing I do when Mackenzie asks for money on her books to buy a "food special". I picture things like, OK, her eating the green hot dog and I will put that bill off...We are getting this girl any food she wants. I am not saying it's right, but Do I care at that point, nope. Please be happy for a minute so I can feel happy for a minute. Just please don't be sad Isiah.

I was told in a private message that I am being over-dramatic with the petition I will not stop pushing and the prison diaries I write to help get through this, and that's OK. My thoughts are this......

It is not being dramatic if it is real. I am simply sharing my daughter's story. Her story is not the worst there is, and she could be dead, and she could be in for life, and she could have terminal cancer, and it would still be HER story and my feelings would still be real. At least I have these feelings for my child, and I have her back no matter what. Judge away I say.

I am being talked about, sued by my ex-husband, putting

off bills, closed the business I dreamed of having my entire life, looked down upon, changed the places I go to in public, back to toddler years, getting thrown up on, peed on, lost friends, gained friends, lost family, owe my ass to people, lost self dignity, could have lost my marriage, been publicly embarrassed, humiliated, done things I could not picture myself doing, ate my feelings, took (prescription) drugs to self- medicate, and apologized to a lot of people, but I am real and I will never stop loving Mackenzie until the day I am no longer on this earth. She could have murdered someone in cold blood and guess what, I would still be at every visit longing for every hug and kiss and so would Isiah because LOVE is blind, it's no matter what. I've told her that before. Our last three years have been dramatic!

I have sat at every arraignment, at her court hearings, at her sentencing, at Marysville every month since the day I was allowed, and I sit in Dayton as much as I'm allowed, I've heard her tell me stories that are haunting, stories of her past I didn't want to hear, things she has done, stories of what has happened to her in prison that violate my every thought sometimes.... why?

I only hope we get to go again to a mommy/child day.

Prison Diaries: August 2016

Cell Bock 6

It was Monday morning and I was enjoying my coffee in my favorite thrift store giant purple Hawaiian nightgown when I hear a knock at the door. I look out the window and I see a county sheriff's car in my driveway. The blood starts to leave my body because I knew this was it, they were coming to inform me that Mackenzie had taken her own life in prison. It was just Isiah and myself home that morning. I started to panic as to how I was going to keep this little 4-year old from hearing the most devastating thing he will ever hear in his life. I go to the door and open it seeing a police officer standing holding a paper in his hand. I close the door behind me with the screen door open to shut out as much sound of what he is about to say as I can from my poor little brown bear. Oh my God in heaven this is horrible. The officer says that he was looking for Judy Frisby and I say that was me without breathing. I could not breathe; my ears were ringing I think from the lack of oxygen. The officer then says that he had a warrant for my arrest. Wait, what? I let out a long exhale....and start to laugh. I was actually laughing and asked him what he had just said.

He was being serious though, he was not smiling and trying to come off stern. He repeated himself that he had a warrant for my arrest. I asked (still smiling) if this was a joke...I actually asked if I was being punked! He was not humored as he said: "Ma'am, I am here to arrest you". I said that I did not understand as I try to think very quickly if I had committed a crime in my past that I couldn't remember.... still laughing this off. I told the deputy that this had to be a mistake because I have only ever had a speeding ticket, I have not ever committed any kind of crime. I could not possibly be the right person, I explained.

The officer told me that I was being arrested for "failure to comply" and that he had to take me right now. This was really happening...I felt the sharp pain in my chest. It was a complete confusion that quickly became a reality and I was scared to death. I asked if this was about the petition, I started for my daughter calling out the local Sheriff or my ex-husband's work but there was no answer. I told the officer that he could not do this in front of my little grandson because he had already been traumatized by his Mommy and the "police" ...... I was all he had. He cut me short by saying, "Ma'am, I know who your daughter is, and I know about your grandson. If you do not have anyone for the little boy, I will call child services to come to get the child".

I hear a little shaky voice say, "Nana...are you going to jail because I'm scared", to even write this makes me sick to my stomach and shakes me to the core. I have not ever been so scared in my life. The thoughts going through my head was that I should have not started that petition because I had pissed off the wrong people, I was so stupid and now my beautiful baby Isiah was going to pay for it. Frantically I call Ritchie and tell him to get home, I was started sobbing hearing his voice. Ritchie is my safe haven, my solid foundation that I lean on every day to survive this nightmare, but he could not make this go away or fix it. I had hurt Ritchie; he was scared I could tell by his voice. My husband always fixes everything, but this was out of his control. I ask if I could change my clothes as the officer stood attention directly inside my front door. He was inside my home, my fortress of safeness, I was invaded. Isiah must have found his way into the police officers' heart because he said he was not going to handcuff me until I got into the police cruiser.

This is the hardest entry to write in my prison diary. I have stopped three times.

All I remember was the long drive in the back of the police car. I was rethinking ever saying one word about how my child was treated by the police in our town. I remember getting myself into a situation in middle school with a teacher when I was younger and having the same feelings in my stomach...except it meant getting grounded by my parents for my grades, not anything remotely close to this. I have never been in a situation like this in my entire life. I could not stop the tears from running down my face. I thought of my sweet baby Zay back at home and the additional "damage" this could be doing to him. I thought about poor Gracie Jo and Cole and how if anyone found out how embarrassed they would be. Then I thought about my Mackenzie.......

I arrived at the station and the officer said he was going to un-cuff me because there was no need to keep me like that. He must have seen the crybaby in the back seat on the long drive, or that I was no security threat. They walked me into the back of the police station and put me in a room to sit in a chair. An officer came in to get my name and information and as he was entering stuff into the computer, he looks up at me and asks, "what were you brought in for?". My answer was one that I would end up giving to about five or six officers that day that looked at the papers attached to me, and it was "failure to comply". The officer looked puzzled but did his job to check me into the computer then send me to the next room. I was placed in a room that had a shower in it and a bathroom maybe, and racks of these jumpsuits that were black and white striped. Oh, my dear God I remember those when I saw Mackenzie in one, I was not putting one of those awful things on my body. I also was not removing my clothes in that wretched place, it looked filthy. Two officers came in and told me to stand on a mark on the floor because they were going to take my picture. A mugshot, a freaking mugshot? Is this real-life right now? I felt like trash; it was embarrassing. I am not like these people. The officer taking my very attractive photo of me sobbing said something to the officer of my "charge". The officer said it was a bench warrant brought on by my ex-husband for a medical bill from 2011. They knew of my ex-husband because he used to work for that Sheriff's department. The two officers were discussing they could not believe that they actually went and arrested a 40 something- year-old Grandma in her nightgown on a Monday morning in front of her grand baby for a medical bill. If this was the work of the ex, why would he do this to his own actual grand baby? It was the work of the devil.... whichever man had wanted this. That is inhumane, to say the least. I still didn't know. I was escorted to a holding cell. It was a disgusting cement hole of a room that was locked by a steel door. It smelled of urine and was filthy. People had written all over the walls and floor. There was a toilet in there...a metal toilet. I would hold my pee and piss myself before I sat my skin on that thing. I was in a holding cell for hours, but it seemed like years. As I sat in a corner on the cement floor I thought of my Mackenzie, and I started sobbing. My baby lives in a place like this. This is not fit for my bulldog. I wondered if

Mackenzie was in that same holding cell. I studied the writings on the walls to try to see her name. I tried to put myself in her shoes at 19, sitting in that hell hole missing me like I was missing her. I couldn't even think about Cole or Gracie or Ritchie, or my sweet little brown bear or I would become hysterical. This was the worst place I had ever been in my entire life. It made you feel more alone then a person could ever feel in the outside world. I was in here for about 8 hours. My child has lived this for years.... she will never recover from this. I think I will need therapy for the 8 hours I spent and that is no lie. After probably hour 2 they knocked on my steel door and offered me a cup of water and a tray of lunch. I declined. I would not eat in that place. I would rather starve to death and hopefully die...it would be better than there. I had so many thoughts racing through my head.

Was it the petition, or the medical bill that landed me in there? I began to get strength from the thoughts of Mackenzie. Wait a minute if she can survive this, so can this girl!! I stand up after about hour 6 and knock on the window. An officer came over to me and asked what I needed through the tiny slit in the door. I told him that I never got a phone call and I knew I was allowed to have one. I'm sure they didn't know that I was practically a lawyer from all of my "Law and Order" marathons I had watched since the show started. He said he did not know that I never got a phone call...yea right Barney Fife, I bet you didn't. They unlocked my cell door and escorted me to this big desk. They handed me a phone. I called Ritchie. I told them that this was my "one" phone call and I wanted to know what he found out from our attorney. Ritchie told me that to get me out he had to have bond money in cash. He asked me how much we had in the bank accounts......not that! Oh my God, I was going to have to stay overnight in there? I would die. I could not survive that horrible place for another minute. Where the hell was my family at? Where were my friends? I do everything for everybody....so this is how it is? Boy, this sure makes my priority list of people drastically different now. I was so scared. I say to Ritchie as I started to cry hysterically again..." Ritchie...you gotta get me out of here...I can't stay here". I felt so bad putting this pressure on him. He was all I had to save me. I understood so much more now about the calls and letters I had received from Mackenzie while incarcerated. While most all of Mackenzie's family withered off from keeping in contact with her, only a few remain. She cherishes those who write her or help out her son and she has absolutely no use for anyone else. I get it. Ritchie replied to me that he was doing everything he could to come up with the money by 5:00. If not, I would be having a sleepover in cell block 6.

A lady correction officer came and retrieved me out of the holding cell. She was very nice and said she knew who I was. This woman told me that she had helped out Mackenzie when she was in there also. She said she felt so sorry for Mackenzie back then. I told her how I appreciated her watching out for my girl and expressed that I had to get out of there as soon as possible to get home to Mackenzie's son. The female officer spoke in a lower voice so not all could hear. She told me she had to make me get in stripes and shower shoes. I must have had a terrified look on my face because she said: "Honey, I'm not making you get naked and get in that shower in front of me". I was instructed to just go around the corner and get changed behind this wall and put my clothes in a bag I was given. For the first (and last) time in my life, I was in the dreaded black and white stripes. They were no doubt man's clothing as I looked like one with the high-water pants bunched up around my stomach. They smelled of a certain fabric detergent that smelled familiar to me. I will never forget that smell. Maybe that is the smell of Mackenzie every time I get that one big hug before and after every visit? I'll never forget that clean smell. I was given a giant pair of white cotton underwear and a white sports type bra that made me look as if I had just had some sort of surgical procedure done. Very institutional to say the least. I was then given white socks and orange slip-on sandals that were me, I think. I cannot explain how I felt standing there. Even on my worst day, in my comfy clothes, at Walmart, early in the morning...I have not ever looked like this. I wanted to die. The thing was in all seriousness, I had not committed a crime! I go to my thoughts of all the people out there that this judicial system has complete control of, and I began to feel sick. If a cop, or a public official, or an ex-former sheriff you had children with, want you in jail....you are just shit out of luck. Is this a free country after all? I was arrested and taken to jail, and I did not commit a crime. Not one single crime. I did what I felt was right, and for that, I was standing in a jail uniform getting ready to be locked down for the night. I asked the female officer if I was going to have to be taken to a cell, and she told me yes. I started to tear up again while she assured me that she was putting me in "the best one" where they would not mess with me. Oh Jesus, Mary and Joseph what the heck does that mean? She told me that she heard a rumor that someone was there trying to bond me out so I may get out after all and not have to stay. Ritchie.... Mr. Frisby...the only person I can count on in this life of mine....it had to be him. The officer takes me upstairs I think...I was panicking and opens a steel door. This was going to be my living quarters until someone got me out of there. There were what felt like a hundred set of eyes staring me down the second I stepped inside. It was a much larger cement room than my last one, yet still one room. The bathroom had a curtain separating it from the steel slats that were bolted to the walls to make bunk beds. All the female inmates sat on their beds as if protecting their "spot" from me. I got the point that I was not to sit on any of them and that I was going to sit down on the floor and live because that is where I belonged. Before the nice female officer left me in the lion's den, she told the girls to teach me the ropes and that I wouldn't be in there long. One tall very very skinny girl jumps off her bed and grabs the bag they gave me with a blanket and a mat and shampoo, toothbrush, soap, cup maybe...I really don't know, I blacked out in fear, I think. She made my bed and told me to sit on it because room checks or counts, or something was coming and I was not to move off that mat. I followed orders. It got very quiet and as I lay on my side on a mat on that cold cement floor I started to cry. I had my arm under my head as my pillow. I was missing my family. I was so sad, and it had only been less than 8 hours. Poor Mackenzie. I thought about her knowing it was going to be an eternity before she could be with her child, and mom, and family as she lay I'm sure on the same floor overcome with sadness and fear the days that led up to that horrible deal she agreed to. I felt connected to Mackenzie right then. She was no longer the only one she loved that knew where she was coming from, I knew just a taste. One of the girls who was very big, and very scary looking asked another girl why I was crying. She did not look like the kind of person to scare easy, to say the least. I stopped breathing for a second, holy shit I made the toughest bitch in that cell block not like me already for crying. My tall skinny hero came to my defense as she says back to the chic that looked like she could make me into a human pretzel.

Another girl asks" hey what are you in for" as now there were conversations started within the room. I answered that it was "failure to comply". I believe there were 8 or 9 girls in there not counting me, and they all said the word..." WHAT". They asked what I failed to comply with, and I told them it was either an unpaid medical bill for my son's car accident to my ex- husband from 2011, OR I had started a petition and called out the head Sheriff for corruption. One girl, who looked mean as a junkyard dog sat up in her bed and said, "what is your daughter's name?" I was scared as hell to answer. What if Mackenzie had had a beef with this girl, oh my God what if she decided to get even by hurting me? I answered reluctantly hoping to get on her good side.

Once I said Mackenzie's name about 3 or 4 more girls came over to near my mat. They all said they knew about the petition I had started for Mackenzie. Most of them talked how bad of a deal Mackenzie got and none could understand the 14-year plea deal she was given. Thank you, Jesus, I felt like Mackenzie had saved my life right then...who knew? One girl said she had heard something else about Mackenzie Basham's son, some kind of program. Ok, now Isiah is gonna save my butt, I said: "Was it The Isiah's Hope Project?" The girl got up and sat at the end of her bed closest to me and remarked: "YES that's what I was thinking off!" I told her that it was a project I had started that transported children from whose Mommy's were incarcerated to have a visit every month and get a photo to keep. Now all the prisoners were engaged in my conversation. They all were talking about how that is such an awesome thing to do and some asking me if I could bring their children up to the county jail to see them. I asked about some of their situations and they were all horrible ones. My skinny friend who had big sores all over her said that she would love to see her children but lost all custody because of being arrested so many times with heroin. Ahh now I understand her looking like a human skeleton with track marks up and down her poor skin, it was such a sad sight to see. I honestly have never been within touching distance of a heroin addict and knew it. The one girl starts to cry and says loudly that this is such bullshit that they have done this to this poor grandma (meaning me). She said that I reminded her of her own Mother, and it broke her heart for me to be sitting in there for something stupid and not criminal. She was in for drugs and overdue fines. She told me how she had missed her little boys second birthday and by this time she was sobbing. She reminded me of my Mackenzie. The oldest person in the entire cell block was probably 26, and then there was me. I quickly became the "Queen of the dipshits" so to speak. I had become one of them, like the pack of wolves had brought me into their pack. They asked me if I would start a petition to get better living conditions in there because some had up to a year to spend. I suddenly became Dr. Phil of cell block 6. I was listening to problems and things about their cases and their baby daddy's keeping the kids from them. I felt for them all, but honestly, I was glad I was still alive. Supper came and I gave all my food to my new roommates. One told me I had to eat something, or I was going to get sick. I assured her I could live a long time and not starve to death, and that I was too upset to eat. They all scarfed down those trays like a feeding at the zoo. They spoke of this one correction officer that was apparently the scariest thing on earth in there. Every single one was scared of her. They said she will call you fat, or ugly, or stupid, or make you clean the grossest of things, and that you do not ever want to mess with her. They had a nickname for her. The girls finished supper as I sat on my mat staring at a brick wall. They all had chores to do and informed me that if I stayed the night, I would be given a chore to do also. They cleaned like no joke and returned back to their beds to sit for count time. The door buzzes and in walks another female officer I had not seen before. It was like Mufasa from the Lion King was walking through the other animals because not a single sound was made while this lady walked in and out of each bed. This had to be the one they just told me about. She looked stern, I did not make eye contact and just kept staring at the wall. I was scared to death of her and I didn't know why. She yelled at a few girls and they answered quickly both very respectful answers. She walked out the door and locked it. I was trapped in there and I didn't know for how long. I had no idea of the time, the weather, the world....it was so scary to feel that confined. I did not move for what seemed like hours and the buzzer went off and the jingle of the keys began to open the lock. All the girls sat at attention as "Mufasa" herself yelled..." FRISBY". I became paralyzed. What did I do? Oh God please save me...I was terrified of where she was going to take me or what she was going to do. The other inmates were all staring at me scared for me I think as I answered her. The officer said, "Get your things, you're getting out of here"

......the room began to cheer. I mean that literally the girls were clapping and telling me they were so happy for me! A few told me not to forget them or their kids to see if I could get them to a visit. I gave them all my "stuff" and it was like I was passing out bars of gold, except it was bars of soap. I walked out into the hall and waited for my instructions. The officer completely changed her face and told me that I don't belong there, and it was bullcrap I was brought in any way. Oh, thank you, God, she was nice to me. She told me she knew my father in law that had worked there and how good of a guy he was. She nodded her head still in disbelief of me being put in jail. She was a very nice woman, and she did her job well as her reputation preceded her. I was taken back downstairs to change into my street clothes and sign all of my discharge papers. They gave me my paper and told me to exit through a certain door. When I opened that door, I saw Ritchie standing there with one of our best friends Steve. They had not ever looked so beautiful to me in my life. They put their arms around me as we walked outside the courthouse doors and I was crying. That was the most disturbing and scariest day of my life. Ritchie offered me a cigarette and I took him up on his offer. He said he was kind of turned on because he had to pick his badass wife up from the clink...we all laughed but mine was half laugh/half cry. We got in the car and my cousin called Ritchie to see if he had come up with the money yet, and to ask if he had heard from my attorney. He told her he just sprung me out (I will never hear the end of it) because our buddy Steve and his brother Jonboy had given him enough cash to get me out. He asked me how I felt to tell Kendra and all I remember saying is..."I feel like Kid Rock". That meant kinda badass, kinda dirty and trashy. I will never in my life forget what those three men did to get me out of there that day. I now know that I am not tough, or strong in a place like jail, or prison. I could not have stayed overnight or days in that place. I am still traumatized by that day. My respect for my daughter is at an all-time high because she did it....it still does. Ritchie told me that our old neighbor from the town we raised the kids in saw him in the waiting room of the jail. Our old neighbor was a sheriff. He was a good, honest guy. He had been working there for years, and he knew us and that we were good people too. He asked why Ritchie was in there and Ritchie told him he had been waiting for over an hour to pay my bond money to get me out. Our neighbor replied "Judy is in here" as if he was shocked about it also. He told them to come back into his office and got on his computer and brought up my mugshot. He got on the phone and told whoever he called to get "Judy Frisby" down here right now. He was pretty high up in rank as far as offices held at the Sheriff's Department I believe. That's when they got me released. He knew I shouldn't have been in there, and he was a good cop...an actual good guy. After the corrupt Sherriff and crime scene investigator were arrested, he actually became head Sheriff. I had a new hope for our town in him. He served one week.... then passed away.

From: Judy Frisby
Date: 09/06/2016
To: Mackenzie Basham

Hi Sis,

Very emotional day today, Isiah went to school for the first time by himself. He is such an awesome little kid, he missed you... I miss you. I had a crying spell yesterday because I just want my daughter home. Motivates me to keep trying harder to get you back home where you belong. Lately, the nights are my favorite times because I dream of you being home playing with Isiah and laughing with Gracie just like old times.... It's the daytime that is my actual nightmare because of reality sets in. The petition I started just hit the 1000 signatures goal yesterday. You are not alone, always remember that! If you think about that, there are

1000 people on this earth who want to see you home with your little boy and not in the hell you are in....you do not deserve to still be there that long. You have paid your debt to society, this is no longer your time. It is time being served at the actions of someone else's mistakes. I love you, we have to try harder and not stop until you have your say in court. Stay strong my sweet girl... I'll love you forever, Momma

From: Judy Frisby
Date: 09/14/2016
To: Mackenzie Basham

I don't have any money, I might in 2 weeks. I want to come to visit next week a lot to tell you. The county Sheriff was served with a search warrant and the FBI and Attorney General's office are in Lima investigating him for corruption. Some say stealing money out of evidence room....this is huge. Our 1000 signatures were emailed out Tuesday morning to attorney general's office and Wednesday they were in Lima investigating him. He hasn't been to work since then and now has hired an attorney. Love you I will put money on your phone this weekend though. Call Friday after 4:00, love you!

Prison Diaries December 26, 2016

It's been a while since I have written in this diary. I didn't even know where to start. Mackenzie's situation is once again consuming my every thought and is mentally wearing me thin. The holidays are over which is like a giant breath of fresh air to my little family. The things I wonder about are, why is there so much pressure to be happy and joyful during Christmas? It is really a celebration of the birth of Jesus, so all the other red and green and trees and Santa Claus and presents and family acting like they all love each other for 2 days is just plain nonsense. I am the most real I have ever been in 43 years and I am unable to "put on a show" for other people. I am no longer happy or joyful. I am on a mission. I am motivated. I am determined, those are the words that describe my personality now. I used to be happy and joyful because I remember.

I can no longer write Mackenzie letters due to the fear of them being brought up in a courtroom. I know they are read before given to her just like our phone calls are recorded, I have learned. We just had a visit on Christmas Eve. That has become our new tradition. I hate it. I would never tell Mackenzie that because it has nothing to do with her, it's that I cringe saying out loud that I spend my Christmas Eve in a visitation hall at a maximum-security prison. When I was growing up, I can remember the "magic" of Christmas Eve. It was the anticipation of family coming over, presents, the smell of dad's wood burner downstairs, and the aroma of mom's cooking from upstairs. As a child, you do not know any behind the scenes stress of the holidays. You do not notice any "empty chairs" of loved ones that have passed away, or out of town family members missing when you are a kid......it's all just gingerbread houses and giant candy canes. Fast forward to mid-life and I become the definition of the phrase, "Debbie Downer".

This Christmas Eve I have never felt so angry and betrayed. My family went on about their business and had food and merriment and alcohol (lots of alcohol), without me or my family. How can they be so happy? Don't they know the deep hole in my heart without my Mackenzie? It makes me feel betrayed and hateful. Nobody understands, not even those who share the same blood as me. Why did this happen to MY child and not one of theirs? I try to put myself in one of my sibling's shoes with the situation, I try to imagine if one of my niece's or nephews were serving a fourteen-year prison sentence. Would I have a party and be able to go about my merry Christmas? I just have no connection anymore with my family that once was such a tight bond. I feel like everyone has forgotten about my child because she made a mistake.

She is embarrassing to the family may be, she is a square peg that does not fit in the round mold of normal. Mackenzie is fitting in more and more now in the prison system and that kills me. She is like an empty shell of a girl that's life revolves around the "prison life". Did I want her to fit in there? Hell no, it's disgusting and filthy and full of criminals......not my child.

She is not a criminal to me or her baby. I've always wanted Mackenzie to fit in somewhere, but here? She never quite fit in with her peers in school. She was bullied. Why didn't I do something? I just desperately wanted her to fit in with the normal kids.... the girls on her teams. She was different. She had an intensity that made her a superstar at sports but it's that same intensity that made her an adrenaline junkie which once she tried drugs, that was it. Hooked, line and sinker. Out of the name calling came a toughness, the defense mechanism was created. Kids would call her fat, a lesbian, a man, a tomboy, crazy.... now all those things seem to make her fit right in where she is. How ironic that the very hurtful things she would self-medicate about, now makes her hold her head high. It makes me want to punch society in the face. It makes me hate the school she went to; it makes me hate myself. It eats me alive that I should have done more, or something different right when Mackenzie was about 15 and everything went to hell. I have always fit in. I am accepted by everyone, people like me. How can my own child be the complete opposite of me? I still yell at her when I go to visit, and she says something I don't want to hear. It is becoming more like two adults sitting there talking and less like a parent and a child talking. When she left, she was a scared 19-year- old girl, very immature, very self-indulged. Now Mackenzie is almost a 23-year-old adult woman who has been through more troubled times than me at 43. She has had to fight for her life physically, she has been violated and raped mentally and physically, she has hustled to survive, seen a human take their own life, been treated like an animal, learned what the true meaning of love is, battled her own thoughts to survive, compromised all morals to survive, been beaten, broken, and stripped mentally not to mention the body cavity searches she endures on a regular basis. All of this before you turn 23 years old? Where the hell do you go from here? Dear God, how will my girl ever be able to live a normal life? It seems to me the prison system in our country creates criminals. It creates demons, animals, psychopathic humans without a conscience. If you were not before you enter the system, you will become a menace to society before you leave. Some leave in a body bag, some are let go into my normal world. One of these people that will stand out like a sore thumb and be "labeled" will be my child. My beautiful little brown bear's mommy. I worry about his future; I worry about their relationship when she gets released. I am still mad at her. I love her more so then when she left if that is possible.

It is now the 7th of January at 4:02 am and I have not heard from Mackenzie since December 24th at our visit. I worry her depression may have a hold of her. At our visit, she was able to rock Isiah like when he was a baby. She sang "you are my sunshine" and hugged and kissed her little boy as much as she could so it would last her until she was able to have contact with him again.

Isiah has his first basketball game today. Today we have yet another life milestone of Isiah's that his mom will miss. He will do great and Ritchie and I will be there like we have been for this baby since the moment he entered this world. At least she has an excuse for missing everything in his life, right? What is his other parent's excuse? Same as Mackenzie's other parent I suppose......and the cycle continues. I will not be at ease until I hear her voice. Isiah has been asking that question again, the one that can make the room silent. It is not like any other kid I know that misses their mommy because they will eventually at the end of the day see them. This is the, "When are we gonna see mommy" question that you can feel for hours. It breaks my heart; I always try to make up some lie followed by a promise of a toy or candy or some kind of bribe. This child should not have to endure this at 5 years old. Why him? He did nothing wrong. I want to slap both of his parents; they don't deserve such a beautiful child. I try to tell myself that this child is a gift from God....to me. How lucky am I? I am very thankful to be in Isiah's life, and this is how I will choose to look at the situation. I am also thankful for my three children, thankful to be in their life no matter what path they are on. Why am I worried about Mackenzie more than Cole or Gracie? I guess it's because I can see them by walking in the next room or dialing up facetime. I cannot explain my worry for her, it is an instant panic. A worry that takes over your mind and your body. I'm on edge. I can't sleep. It is not a worry that your kid is being made fun of at school, or yelled at by a co- worker, it is a worry that your child is being tortured by their own thoughts. It could even be tortured by someone else for not "behaving" as she should. It is a sickening feeling, an acid coming up from your stomach kind of worry. I need to see her soon for my own health. When I get to visit her, it is how I get my mind right, it is like a prescribed medicine I cannot live without. I can't explain it, only her and I know. I just wonder do other parents feel as I do if they have a child in prison? I guess I'm not so "Normal" after all.

Year Four

The Mental Breakdown

January 9th. 2017... Sixteen days since I have heard
from Mackenzie.

I am beginning to think there is a reason we have not heard
from her. At our visit on Christmas Eve as Isiah was playing
in the playroom assigned for children of prisoners, Gracie
said something to her sister that changed the mood of the
visit. Out of nowhere, Gracie blurted out something to the
effect of...."why don't you quit acting like a spoiled brat, you
don't need anything, you're in prison." Oh no she didn't! I
have to admit I was a bit nervous about the shit that was
about to hit the fan. I had warned Gracie on our drive down
there that the last time we had seen her it was like visiting
someone in an insane asylum. She had started a new
medicine so it may have been the meds, but I was a little
afraid. She used words fluently like murder, cut, enialate,
make certain people pay....what in the holy hell? She was
just referring to what she would do to people if they hurt her
family while she was gone. It's an obsession now and if she
hears of anything big or small, she writes it down in a
notebook with the month, day, and year. Maybe it makes
her feel comforted in there acting as a "protector" of things
since all control is lost when you're incarcerated, even if it
sounds insane. Mackenzie had got word that some thug
had robbed Cole when he passed out at a party, she found
out his name and the date. She said he needs to apologize
to her brother when she is free. I believe her. Mackenzie
became visibly upset. Gracie argued her point back.
Mackenzie became enraged and then we were in a full-
blown argument right there smack dab in the middle of the
visitation room. Gracie never raised her voice, but it did get
shaky at one point. Mackenzie started to become so
irritated and upset that I was keeping eye on the officers
who had noticed the disturbance. I looked at them with a
look of almost begging....my girls needed to have this

discussion. It is about two years overdue. Baby girl is becoming a woman, a very smart woman at that. She has questions and they need answers. I commend baby girl for speaking up to her sister as difficult as it may have been. It has stayed with her since as I catch tears in her eyes often. It is not fair to her; she has had to sacrifice just as much as Ritchie and I have. Gracie is mad at her sister and I really don't think she likes her these days. Mackenzie had an equal argument. I love them both and had to excuse myself to the prison restroom area to sob in a stall until I could get my composure. The arguments were as follows; Gracie's words at Mackenzie......You think you are living in some kind of fancy hotel. You act like a princess. You hound mom all the time for money and she gives it to you and last week mom and dad sent you money for steak! You are eating better than us at home. I'm sick of mom being stressed out over money and you calling all the time. You're the one who put yourself in here. We do everything for you, ask your dad's family for something.... they do nothing.

Mackenzie's words to Gracie Jo.........You think I like asking Mom for everything? You have no idea how it makes me feel asking Mom and Ritchie for money to buy tampons, and soap to wash my body and laundry soap to wash my clothes. All mom has to do is tell me "NO" and I won't ask again. (Mackenzie's voice became louder and the tears were turning into a sob coming out at this point.) Let me ask you this Gracie....Have you ever ate maggots because you were so hungry, and they were in the only food you were going to get? Have you ever been jumped by four girls with a razor blade and sliced your arms while they stole your shoes off your feet? Has anyone ever stole all your clothes and the only blanket you owned while you were fucking sleeping? I have to depend on people for everything and I hate it. I hate asking for money. You are really lucky to be born to two parents that love you and care about you. I have never had that. My Dad doesn't give a shit if I starve, or care if I have no blanket when I'm cold or a fan when it's smothering hot in this hell hole. He doesn't care if I have money on my phone to call and hear my son's voice or talk to my family on the holidays. Mom and my other Grandma are my only lifelines outside of this place. They had a Christmas special and you could buy a Bob Evans dinner prepacked and warm it up in the microwave that was real eggs, real hash browns, and real meat that was a piece of ham and a piece of steak. That's what I asked mom about. It's not like I have a fancy steak dinner or even meat that is not green or doesn't have a layer of green mold on the top of it daily. You have no idea what it's like little girl to ration things for months until the next time you might get real food. I don't get pop or coffee or milk or fruit or meat like you can just get hungry and run to the store or drive through to get! You don't think I live with my mistakes every single fucking day of my life? I wish I could take it back, but I can't! Your life has been easy because your parents love each other, you just don't know. I will never ask mom for anything again.

Gracie's rebuttal......Chill out psychopath, it's good for us to get this stuff out. It's healthy to get it off our chests. (Mack would not look directly at us and continued to sob.) I'm fifteen and I don't do drugs or get pregnant for someone else to raise my child. I have to help mom raise your kid and I'm still a kid.

I had heard enough. I was angry at both of them, but I yelled at Gracie. This was not the place to bring it up. I told her that. Gracie replied, then where is the place?

The rest of the visit was awkward. When I came back from my meltdown both of my girls were sitting there in silence. It really sucks when you have to sit across from someone, and you don't want to talk to them. The ONE thing we are allowed to do when we visit Mackenzie is talking, no phones, no walking around, no purse to look through, just your body facing her body (with no contact). I was my usual self and tried to break the silence with a joke. They were both stewing inside of the things they wanted to scream at each other. Mackenzie was instantly a prisoner. She had put on the mask, the very mask that she hates. In kicked her defense. I was getting pissed, I refuse to be intimidated by my own child. That's when I said something I regret. I feel like a real piece of crap even writing this. I said, "Don't act like a bad-ass to me little miss, I will leave and not come back!" Oh my God, I just threatened her with her own freedom. I needed to get through to her, she needed to feel the sting of her actions but what I said was ridiculous. When you have a child at home you can make those threats, the ones that will really hit em' where it hurts. You take their phone, or their car keys, put up the video game, the computer is off limits, or ground them over a weekend. First of all, Mackenzie is not a child, second, she lives in hell on earth. There is one thing she lives for....visits. Mostly seeing Isiah, but she loves when a family member comes too, and I just threatened her with that. She immediately puffed out her chest..." Do you want to leave?" She was hurt and angry and I was seeing a very disturbed person sitting there that honestly, I was a little scared off. I said, "No, but I didn't drive an hour with these kids for you two dumb-asses to get into a fight." ......

Well just give me the "Mother of the Year Award", why the hell did I go there? I made it sound as if it were an inconvenience to go visit her. I would be so hurt if my mom had made it sound like a job to drive to see me. I am not a good person, God forgive me.

Silence....we all just sat in silence for what seemed like hours. We were all thinking about the things we had said to each other. Then up walks the sunshine in all our lives with a game of Uno. It was dirty and the cards were old and torn. Isiah says, "Hey guys, will you play cards with me?" and just like that the silence was broken. We all fixed our attitudes, and our faces, and smiled and said yes. Children have magical powers. I asked

who needed another pop, and what snacks do we want for our
card game. We played some dirty old tattered Uno and got
along and laughed and enjoyed our Christmas Eve as if we were
sitting around Grammy's big table at home with the entire family.
It was a silent agreement amongst myself and my daughters, an
agreement that this little boy would not see or hear anything but
love. He deserves unicorns and rainbows for God's sake, and
we were all going to give it to him. The rest of the visit was
actually very nice and loving. Mackenzie held Isiah until he fell
asleep in her arms as she cried with remorse and regret. I cried
because I could feel her pain in my chest. I look over at baby
girl...she was crying. She loves her sister and her nephew to the
moon and stars and back again, she just hates our situation.
She hates the pain we all feel. She needs someone to take it out
on and today she snapped. I admire her honesty and she has
more balls than me to just spill it out there to Mackenzie's face to
face. We said our goodbyes with hugs and kisses and
tears...lots of tears and sadness. The guards told me that we
had a package at the front security station. When we got
through the other steel doors and as I was returning my badge I
asked for the package, the officer gave us one, and then
another, and then another. They were clear plastic bags with
inmate number 090219 wrote on a piece of paper stapled to
them. I signed a form and the articles were released to me. As
soon as we got in the car Isiah started to rip into the bags.
Two bags were labeled "Isiah" on the inside, and one bag
was labeled "Gracie Jo". Inside were homemade Christmas
gifts.

Isiah had a headband ear warmer that was crocheted in a
beautiful bright blue. There was a pair of homemade sewn
boxer shorts for the brown bear that had hand painted the
Michigan logo on them with blue and yellow fabric paint.
The other thing in the bag was a pillow. It was hand sewn
by his mommy. It has her handprints dipped in paint in
bright blue on a white fabric on the one side of the pillow
and on the other side read the saying "Hand in Hand

Mommy's Always With You... wrote in the paint. The note in the bag said to lay his head on the pillow and put his hands on hers every time he got sad and missed her, this would mean they were together. The bag for Gracie included a handmade jewelry box that was painted green with black music notes and a great big "G" on the front. It was made from poster board of some sort and has a button glued on the front as the handle. Inside was a headband that Mackenzie had crocheted for Gracie to wear. It is a very pretty tan with shiny gold pieces running through it.

This was to keep in her new jewelry box.

The money she had asked for before Christmas was to buy the materials to make Isiah and Gracie Christmas presents. Gracie's eyes were opened a little more to her sister's intentions while being incarcerated. I wish she didn't have to experience adult lessons at the age of fifteen, but this is the hand we have been dealt. God, please bless both my little girl's hearts.

The long ride home was quiet, the kids slept. Both were emotionally drained, I think. I thought about my sweet Mackenzie all alone on this Christmas Eve in that cell. I wonder if she is laying in her bed crying, or if she is cold, or restless. Will she be excited to wake up the next morning just because it's Christmas? She will be alone still, in her cage still, with no family still, no holiday drinks or home-cooked favorites. Mackenzie's memories of Christmas pasts are her gift and that is all she has. I think I'll just stay home again this year functioning is not an option. I'm not gonna lie, some nights I get out that pillow and place my hands on hers because it makes me feel close to her knowing her hands touched it.
Year three, not any easier.

Prison Diaries: January 22, 2017

I just got back from a visit with Mackenzie. I took my mom and Isiah with me. Tonight, Ativan was not enough to level me out, so a side of writing it is. The patience I need to have with my mom I am far away from. She loves Mackenzie as I love Isiah. I should understand that. My mother should not have to at 75 have to go through security and metal detectors to hug and kiss her granddaughter....that's just how it is. I got my fix of Mackenzie like a drug addict just scored a small hit. I am unsettled and not at peace with the events in this past month. When I started calling, I was feeling brave and determined to get to the bottom of where the hell my daughter was. Today I feel like a kid that just got bullied in the schoolyard. What is her path? Why is Jesus making the road Mackenzie is on such a difficult one? I am just a spectator, a spectator whose hands are tied tightly behind her back. If I don't write about how I feel when I saw Mackenzie today, I may be in the same living quarters as her. Now I'm in prison in my own mind and I feel connected to my girl. This, I'm pretty sure is not normal.

When I had not heard from Mackenzie, I had the "feeling" I have had about 3 or 4 other times since we have been on this journey. Something was wrong with my child and I felt it. I swear to God and the Holy Spirit that I feel it when she is in pain. I just went to the bathroom and vomited up my morning coffee. The image of Mackenzie yesterday is burned in my head and is coming out my mouth. My hope that when Mackenzie is in the free world someday, she will not "appear" any different to the public is now shot to hell. She is marked, branded almost literally, and her physical body will show it for the rest of her life. When I finally got a hold of the head caseworker after a week of calling, she told me that I hadn't heard from Mack because she was in segregation. Ok....why? At first, the caseworker told me it was probably a rule violation. Good enough, I have accepted her "violating rules" before. We talk about it and move on. The next part of our conversation is what is disturbing, the caseworker told me to hold on the phone and she needed to look up something. Oh, the things running through my mind. When she got back on the phone, she told me that Mackenzie had not broken any rules but that she was admitted to solitary confinement by mental health.

Gosh dang it this breaks my heart. The caseworker goes on to tell me that my child has been on suicide watch for three weeks. I asked if I could visit her, I was told to make a reservation but to call the day of to see if she was stable enough for a visitor. I thanked her very much for the information and told her I would be calling back every day to check on my child and make sure she was alive. Definitely not what a mother likes having to do on a daily basis. I sat in my sunroom in the quiet as so many things ran through my head. I was upset but I was calm. How could I remain calm?

Something was wrong, but my child was not going to commit suicide. I am at a battle, I am on the front freaking lines of this war and Mackenzie is right there beside of me, she's not going to quit! I am working way too hard for her to coward out. If she does this to her baby boy, I will never forgive her. Mackenzie is tough, she is a warrior....warriors do not take their own lives. The holidays are hard, but suicide? My worst fear has shown it's messed up little face. My day of that phone call consisted of a hoodie sweatshirt with the hood up, comfy pants, a call to my doctor for another bottle of Ativan, the curtains pulled, and sleeping. I would sleep, then stare at the wall, then sleep again, then stare. I could not function that day, it was a Tuesday. I was worried and angry and nauseated and a whole lot of other emotions, I just went back to sleep. Maybe it would go away. I asked my close circle to pray for Mackenzie and pray hard. It was the only thing us spectators could do out here watching the game with our hands tied behind our backs. I prepared myself for the news of her death. I prepared myself for the discussion I would have to have with her brother and sister, but nothing was going to prepare me for the discussion I would have to have with my little baby brown bear. Now I'm pissed at her again. I am now paranoid when I hear or even see a car coming down the road. I googled: "How are you notified of inmate's death in prison in Ohio?" This was the answer: Police personnel will make death notifications in person whenever possible. Deliver the notification with tact and sensitivity. Before arrival, learn as much as possible about the next of kin. Extra precautions in the notification may be necessary if the next of kin is elderly or of fragile physical or mental health. Wow. Please don't let a police car pull in my driveway, this is going to be a long night.

The next day I didn't work again. Human contact was not going to be possible once again. I was nervous picking....at my face, at my head, on my dog for God's sake! I now had these beautiful fever blisters all over my mouth from stress. The bags under my eyes were not able to be camouflaged by even the best makeup. Wednesday could just go away. That night at about 8:00 my phone rang. It was on the kitchen counter and I was rolled like a burrito on the couch. It kept ringing. Ritchie told me my phone was ringing...I know, I don't want to speak to anyone. He got up and answered it. I was irritated and I closed my eyes so that it would not be a lie when he had to tell the person on the other end of the phone I was sleeping. He said, "Jude, it's Mack!" Sweet Jesus thank you. I took the phone and said, "Hi sis, how are you?" Mackenzie said that she had just got out of solitary and it felt so good to be out. I'm thinking that was odd because if she was in this horrible state, in or out of there she would still have the depression. I then told her I had been calling to check on her and that made her feel happy I could tell by the tone of her voice. I told her I knew in my soul that something was wrong. Mackenzie told me that they had just called for checks, so she had to go but very quickly she needed to tell me something. Mackenzie said, "Mom they probably told you I was on suicide watch, but I really wasn't. I would never take my own life. I wouldn't do that to Isiah, or my family." She then was whispering quickly and said, "a few weeks ago I was walking alone to get meds and I was in the yard at a spot out of camera view. I was jumped by FOUR inmates and beat pretty bad then left there. I made it back up to my room to clean myself up but when I went to school the next day the teacher questioned my appearance. I told her I fell out of bed, but she didn't buy it. I was put in solitary because I would not tell who had done this to me and so my wounds would heal. I do not want Isiah to see me until the bruising goes away and the black and blue around my eyes heals up. I lost weight, I am now dehydrated and my private is sore. I was held in a small room completely naked, no clothing articles allowed. I started my period, I was given a pad but with no underwear, it is very hard to use while you bleed for a week. They told me that running water is a privilege and I'm in prison....nobody cares."

My emotions and feelings were now completely different. I wanted to put my fist directly through a brick wall. Nobody does this to my child. I listened to her and had just one question...What are their names? That's all I want, their names. Mackenzie would not say it, and she just kept saying she was fine now and for me to just, 'LET IT GO!" Oh, little girl, I cannot let it go, I will never let it go. This Mother bear is ready to battle. A physical battle. Let me at them, just tell me their names. She said to wait a few days to schedule a visit and that she loved us so much. She told me she was sorry I had to think she was suicidal but if you don't rat on who did it, they put you in solitary. She told me she is not a snitch.

Obviously not or she wouldn't be serving a 14-year prison sentence. I just wonder what kind of trophy you get on the street for "not being a snitch"? Must be some big thing because she is going to take that crap to the grave. Her grave almost presented itself at 23. I want to report it, but she says ABSOLUTELY not. They will get her again. It's the prison way, the prison life, you gotta play the part. She's a badass, hardcore, tough as nails, just survived a horrible beating, blah blah blah......She has her mask on and as sick as this is, she is fitting in pretty well in there. Two black eyes, two busted eye sockets, a broken nose, cut with a razor blade, multiple abrasions and dark bruising and Mackenzie was so happy to tell me that it was fine, they left her teeth. Mom, she says, I didn't even get one tooth knocked out!

Is this real life right now? Does she honestly expect me to "let it go"? Will they really retaliate or kill her this time? Dammit, why are my hands still tied behind my back? I will do nothing to keep her safe. That is sick as hell. I got a visit for the following Sunday night.

This is how I feel seeing her tonight, Ativan. That's all, nerve pills and I think I'll put another hoodie on. Isiah was so sweet waiting on his mom walk through the door. He is so smart and knows the drill. He pointed out that as soon as you hear a loud buzzer and big door opening a girl walks out from around the corner. He sat perfectly still in his seat with his head turned completely around watching that corner. We heard the buzzer, we heard the loud steel door unlock and open....in walked his mommy! They were so cute, they hugged and kissed each other and he just hung on her for quite a while. He missed her; 4 weeks is too long with no contact. I really think Isiah knew something was up because he had a lot of sleepless nights until we got that phone call. I let my mom at her next. Grammy hugged and kissed and pinched just like grandmas do. Then it was my turn. I cannot explain the power of that first hug. I squeezed her and just held on to her body as long as she would let me. I kissed her cheek, then I kissed the other cheek...I was feeling brave and did not care if I was breaking the visitation rules of contact. Arrest me I thought. Mackenzie whispered in my ear that she was not feeling well. She was just trembling and her hands and face were very clammy and she was very pale. I asked her if she had been drinking fluids or had eaten anything. She mumbled, "running water is a privilege, I'm in prison nobody cares". I bought her some fruit punch out of the vending machine and a yogurt and some cheese crackers. She did not have an appetite which is odd for Mack. My mom asked her if they had a Drug Store there where she could buy some medicine? Oh, Gram, we both laughed hard. I explained to my mom that most of the inmates are drug addicts of some sort, and most are thieves. If they had a Drug Store it would be robbed by drug addicts every day probably! My mom laughed, then whispered to me, "Well do they at least have an ATM in this awful place?" Bless her heart....I could not say anything about Mom's crazy questions because I had gone to the bathroom and when I came back Mackenzie asked me if I had my pants on backward. Uh, no? She said there was a softball logo on the bag leg of the sweatpants I had on and they looked backward. Oh, my Lord, I am my mother. I did have my pants on backward and I had gone out to eat with the kids, went to the grocery store, and went to the dollar store before heading to Dayton. My life is in shambles.

At one point Isiah had to pee so I asked my mom to go with him so I could talk to Mackenzie alone. The second they walked away, I said let me see your arms. She gave me a dirty look and said for me to stop staring at her and just drop it. I am not exaggerating when I write that her right arm on the front and back looked as if she had been carved up like a Thanksgiving turkey. It was sickening. The razor blade marks were long and short and going all different directions. Dear God, why would someone do this to my little girl? Her other arm had a large lump on it that was a healing black and blue mark and her eyes were healed up to a yellowish color all around both eye sockets. I was ready to whip somebody's ass. I told her I was going to buy a photo and to make sure her right side arm was showing so I had evidence in case there was no documentation. She got mad at me. I bought a photo of Mackenzie, Isiah, and my mom and guess what, she completely hid her arms. This is so frustrating. I wanted to march right up to the officers in that visitation room and make a scene. I wanted to ask how come they have officers there to monitor how many hugs I give my child when she walks in, but not a damn person was around when she got beat and sliced and diced by four woman inmates and left to bleed to death in the yard! I could tell Mackenzie was very uncomfortable with the looks on my face and me staring at her. She begged, "please mom, just don't say a word" and she meant it. I won't right now, that is all I can promise.

The positive things about today's visit are that she has all her paperwork ready and mailing out Monday morning. "The Appeal" ...this will be a long chapter but I anxiously await for us to go through this process. I believe the justice system cannot possibly fail her again. Hope is my word of the day. I'm mentally stronger now that I've had a visit with her but leaving her there was very hard knowing she would have to walk at night, back through that same yard, unprotected, just because we came to visit. I feel selfish in feeling better after having a visit. I have to drive a hour....she has to get 2 strip searches and walk through the "war zone" to get back to her cell, if I could trade her places I would in a second. I hate this. I hate her being in there.

January 25. 2017

I am home today in my nightgown. It feels so comfortable when I am needed at home. Isiah woke up in the middle of the night saying he couldn't breathe.... that damn asthma. Gracie and I know the drill. It was 2:30 am and the bathroom lights come on and Gracie props him up as I plug in the breathing machine. After a few minutes of big breathes, he is falling back to sleep. The loud sound of the aerosol treatments does not even wake anyone in the house anymore, even the dog.
Of all the things Isiah's dad could have given him, asthma

had to be it. I rearranged our morning plans and am staying home to take care of my little brown bear. I wait on him hand and foot. Pancakes, sausage, apple juice, were some of his morning requests. I love making him happy. In a way I know it's because I feel like in some way, I am helping his mommy. If I can't comfort her or make her feel safe or take care of her when she's sick, at least I can her baby boy. I do not think I overdo it, or Ritchie, we both get it. My husband and I have been through this nightmare from even before Mackenzie was arrested. The nights she would call obviously out of her mind on drugs and asking us to come to get her because someone was outside with a gun. She had owed some lowlife drug dealer yet again and needed us to rescue her. Some nights we went, towards the end we did not. I can't help but think that if I had just gone to save her with the money she would not be in prison now. It needed to stop, but I could not help Mackenzie. This was a lesson she had to learn for herself. Oh, how she is paying that price today. Enabling, we did it for a long time. All the while her baby was safe and warm and comfortable in our home. Every night after Isiah falls asleep, I pray. My prayers always include to keep my family safe, and I never miss a night of saying "thank you god for Isiah". Before her arrest, my prayers were always focused on Mackenzie and her safety. I would ask God to watch over her wherever she was, or whatever state of mind she was in. I was prepared for the call. The call I was prepared for was from the police.

They were either going to tell me Mackenzie was dead, or she had been arrested. I had prepared myself for her death back then, so why do I still fear it now? I guess I thought if she escaped death from the drugs or the dealer we were in the "safe" zone. My family doctor told me that everything happens for a reason and that we were going to be just fine....as she hands me scripts for anti-depressants and nerve pills. Our doctor was very honest in saying that if Mackenzie had not been arrested she would have been filling out her death certificate. Mackenzie had gone to our same family doctor since kindergarten as well as my other kids. Our doctor knew her, had been through sports injuries, the teen pregnancy, she had even called me when she was admitting Mackenzie to the hospital psychiatric floor after an entire bottle aka the "Zanny" overdose. I could sleep at night I thought if she was safe in jail. It's years later and I have to worry about her being killed in prison. There is always a battle with Mackenzie, and as soon as I feel we are settled.... on comes another. My daughter committed a crime. The crime was fueled by an addiction. The crime deserved to be punished, I will never argue that. The crime was not a fourteen-year maximum security prison sentence crime. Am I enabling again thinking this? I question myself often about my fight for justice for Mackenzie. I am not excusing what she did, I am very confident in my beliefs that she was over-sentenced. They didn't even know her, and they didn't want to. I think if anyone in that police department would have known just one second into her past things might have gone another way, a better way. They arrested a nineteen- year-old cocky, drug addicted, stoned out of her mind, mean, smart-mouthed, Billy badass on April 29, 2014. They did not arrest the Mackenzie I know. The loving, softhearted, makes everybody crack up, worry wart, a little shy, protector of her family and friends, child loving, caring Mackenzie Lee. The only thing that can make a human being be these two different people is drugs. Mind-altering, body destroying, eats your soul for dinner, drugs. My sweet Mackenzie was not born a criminal. She was not a criminal in elementary school, or middle school, or even her first year of high school. It is those damn drugs. Something needs to be done in our country to not clump together the words addict and criminal. They are in the same class and that pisses me off. If someone has cancer and smokes weed for the pain they are not in the category of criminal, yet still illegal. Addiction runs in my family, and it runs with a vengeance. I know some of my genes are in my child and it scares me. I have the powerful "shut off" switch...Mackenzie does not. Being bi-polar may contribute to her addiction as well, I do not know how that feels. I feel sorry for Mackenzie and I am judged for thinking that way....simply because she is labeled a "criminal".

From: Judy Frisby
Date: 1/29/2017 11:42:40 pm
Sent To: Mackenzie Basham

Hi Mackenzie Lee,

How are you doing? Bubby just got home from a birthday party and he is sound asleep. He is such a good boy, and so sweet. He did so well at his basketball on Saturday, you would be so proud. I want to start sending you material like Aunt Jenny did so you can make blankets to trade for food and your hygiene products. Having those to tie and put together will keep you busy and pass the time, I hope. I just can't get you off my mind since the last visit. I know I can't talk about it but it's consuming me. I am fighting a battle for my own peace of mind every day. What happened to you is unacceptable. It breaks my heart and it makes me cry when I think about how you looked last Sunday. How would you feel if Isiah looked as you did? Wouldn't you be upset or mad, or sick to your stomach? You get upset just thinking about if kids at school make fun of him because of the color of his skin. Please don't take any chances in there, protect yourself for Isiah. It is very important to him and me that you come home alive and in one piece!! We talk a lot about what we are going to do when "mommy comes home", that makes him happy when he is missing you. I love you so much and I like to talk about when you come home too! I'm really missing you tonight, so much going on lately guess it's just hitting me tonight. Amazing Grace just came on the TV on a show and it's making the tears pour out girl. Have you bought that song yet? If not, I am going to put some money on your media account this week when I get some and I want you to buy it. Your Grandma said she was able to send you some new headphones. That is great, music is so therapeutic. I have another song that Gracie Jo listens to a lot and it's by R.E.M., you probably have no idea who they are because I used to rock out to them in the '90s. It's called "Everybody Hurts" and you know what, it might sound sad at first but it's not! It makes me think of when you do get to come home how much you will have survived.

Literally. You can be an inspiration to a lot of people you know, especially teenagers. You need to look forward to your life when your home, your NEW LIFE. It's gonna be awesome, and positive, and we will be able to sit in our pj's all cozy on the couch, eating homemade food, laughing at stinky butt Zay, talking about...."remember when we would write each other letters"......and you'll never have to be away from us again.

Picture a ladder, and the very bottom rung of it, you have been there. The rest of your life is only looking up sis, right now you probably feel like you're moving slowly or not at all, but you are. I am very proud of you for the person you are today, and I want to just tell you that and make sure you know. You are important to me. Please try not to get consumed in the world you are living in or the "prison life". That's not your home, it is just temporary, ok? Your place in life is with Isiah Lee and your family and being my daughter. Ok, I am feeling better now, ready to take on another week, another day closer to your release. I'm already planning your "FREEDOM PARTY"...it will be off the hook, and every single person that has supported you on your road to being free, and sober, and following the good Lord, and awesome is invited! No drugs allowed, we'll get high on your favorite cheesecake and steak....lots of steak and A-1 sauce for you!

Well, I love you more than chocolate turtle cheesecake, look up at the moon because I am looking up at that same moon, we're not that far apart. Hold on sister I'll love you forever and ever, Momma

When your day is long

And the night, the night is yours alone

When you're sure you've had enough Of

this life, well hang on

Don't let yourself go

'Cause everybody cries

And everybody hurts sometimes

Sometimes everything is wrong Now it's

time to sing along

When your day is night alone (Hold on, hold on) If you

feel like letting go (Hold on)

If you think you've had too much Of this

life, well hang on

Everybody hurts

Take comfort in your friends

Everybody hurts

Don't throw your hand, oh no

Don't throw your hand

If you feel like you're alone No, no,

no, you are not alone

If you're on your own in this life

The days and nights are long

When you think you've had too much of this life to hang on

(R.E.M. "Everybody Hurts")

From: Mackenzie Basham
To: Judy Frisby
February 6, 2017

hey, I'm writing you back from the last letter you sent me ...
I don't like to even think about the situation because my
blood starts boiling, I am okay, and trust me when I say the
situation is taken care of... I just got a new tat that says
"your karma's my revenge" I think tattoos are beautiful and
therapeutic, I know all mine have a meaning behind them
and each holds separate memories, good or bad... I've got
something out of the situation. . . nobody can hurt me
worse than the pain I feel being away from my family and
watching zay grow from a distance. my scars only show
the battles I've fought and overcame. I know telling you not
to worry is like telling a dog not to bark but trust in me
mom, I've got this I'm okay and I will be until I come
home.... I don't want to worry about you worrying and
losing hair because of the stress. Right now mentally &
emotionally we've got to stand ten toes down and take care
of ourselves and trust God to be with each of us since we
can't be ... sometimes you just got to look in the mirror and

say "I'm unstoppable" I tell myself I'm invincible a lot just to put more confidence in me for the day and it prepares me for the battles the devil brings me each day...... well I'm going to end this I'll write again. love & miss you

April 19, 2017

We are approaching the three-year date of when Mackenzie entered into the prison system. I just read back to my very first prison diaries from May of 2014. I am trying to find the positives of how Mackenzie or I have moved forward by going back and reading our letters. She has come so far; her letters have matured so much. Mine, however, are still describing the pain of missing my child being with me in the free world. I do not think a mother can ever stop feeling when a piece of her heart is missing. Maybe some parents handle it just fine, I wish I understood how they do it. My relationship with my daughter is made up of a closeness and bond that I cannot describe. It is not like when you are in love with another person, or even how you feel about your so-called soul mate. That is being IN love. My love for my children is different, it's the kind of intense love that is part of the makeup of the human body functioning. My body can function if my heart beats normal, my lungs perform normal, my kidneys, liver, brain, blood flow, all do the job they are supposed to do. The part that stops the performance of my human body is my piece of mind. I think this is the part of my human body a doctor cannot see, nor treat. The piece of mind is what allows all those other body parts to keep running smoothly. I have not had a 100% piece of mind since April 2014. I do not feel content or feel as if I am performing at my fullest. My heart is damaged, it is not whole. I have to have my daughter back home. I have to see her holding her baby boy, playing ball with him, getting him ready for school, being the kind of mother that I am. It feels like I have a cut on my body......a cut that will not heal. On occasion, you forget about that cut but it's still there. The cut hurts so bad at times and at times it is just a small thumping where the wound is. You can take medicine for that cut, or put a bandage on it, but it is always underneath when you take off the bandage.

We just had Easter 2017. Isiah started his second year of t-ball. It hurts me when we go to ball practice and I see the little guy noticing all the "mommy's and daddy's" there. Ritchie and I are always there, but it's not the same. He knows, he is old enough to know now and notice he is different. Kids say things that are no big deal to most, just simple questions like "is that your mom?". It happens when I am a room parent for his class too, or when Ritchie and I go and eat lunch with our brown bear. When a child innocently asks Isiah if I am his Mommy it causes a paralysis over my entire body. I do not want to answer for him. If he wants to say I am his Mom, then I want him to feel comfortable saying that. If he wants to tell his friends that I am his Nana, I want him to feel comfortable with that also. The breath holder is when he tells them I am his Nana and they ask that horrible question, ..." Where's your mommy and daddy? Oh, dear God, why does this five-year- old have to deal with this? I do not know any other five-year old's in his grade that has to worry about such a simple question like this. I am sure there are other five years old's out there that have the same situation as Isiah, in fact I know there are some. I help them through The Isiah's Hope Project. It still does not hit home like when Isiah is confronted with the question. It's not fair. Isiah didn't do anything to deserve heartache. I wish I could put a hard shell around his little tiny heart to protect it until he is strong enough to handle our situation. He has been having nightmares lately. They actually scare him so bad that he cries for several minutes. He runs into my bed and says, "Nana will you hold me?' as he trembles and cries with both hands covering both ears. I ask what the nightmare was about he usually says he doesn't want to say it out loud. Two nights ago, he was up an entire hour after the nightmare. He wouldn't tell me until the next morning before school. While most kids have bad dreams about scary animals or monsters or zombies, my precious Isiah has much more complex nightmares. He told me, as he teared up again, that he dreamed that he came home from school and his Papa had blood coming out of his mouth and wouldn't wake up. He said he kept yelling and shaking him, but he was just dead. Then he asked me if I would pray with him. Isiah folded his hands and began to pray...."Dear Jesus, will you please take the nightmares away". I assured him that it was just a dream and his Papa was alive and well and just at work. When I picked him up from school that day, as soon as he got in the backseat at pick up, Isiah told me he cannot get his dreams out of his head. He is afraid if Ritchie or myself go to sleep at night. He asked me how old Ritchie was, then how old I was. He asked me if I could live until 1000. I told him some people live until 90 or 100. Isiah said he was scared because after 40's come 50,60,70,80,90 then we will die. He said that's only 5 days. I assured him those are years and we won't be in our 90's for a long long time! The very fact that a five-year-old is worrying about all this breaks my heart. He has separation anxiety so bad. He was two and a half when his mommy dropped him off at our house for the last time. He does not remember that exact night, but he does remember living with his mommy. Sometimes the very thought of sending him to school makes me have a mental breakdown. It's sending him into the world unprotected, I feel like he needs my protection more than when my own children went off to school.

Mackenzie feels so bad about what her mistakes have done to her little boy, and I think she will spend the rest of her life trying to make up for it. I'm not sure if that's healthy, but I am at peace finally with the fact that I have no control over what happens when Mackenzie returns home to her child. It is going to be very difficult for both. Mackenzie seems to have stopped time in prison. She is on the mentality of everyone being the same age as when she left, she does not want anyone to age or grow because it hurts her too bad to know she has missed it. She still treats Gracie Jo as if she is 12, she refers to her brother as a teenager that needs her protection, and Isiah will always be that 2-year-old baby from when she saw him last on the outside. The reality is that Gracie is a 16- year-old young lady now who is very independent and speaks up for herself kind of girl. She is more mature than some adults I know, and she can handle just about anything now that is thrown at her. Cole is an adult, a 21-year-old man that doesn't need his sister or Momma to defend him or come to his rescue. He has changed so much since his sister has been gone, just in the short time, the one that will bother Mackenzie the most is her baby. Isiah has lost that sense of innocence that kids do when they start their school career. I have slipped into the role of his mother even if he calls me "Nana".

Mackenzie gets visibly upset when we are at a visit and Isiah comes to me instead of her for permission for something, or when his actions towards her are that of just any other family member.... not his mother. She knows, and she always tears up. I know what she is feeling but neither of us says a word. It is a subject that is not to be brought up yet, Mackenzie cannot handle the thought of Isiah thinking of anyone else as his Mommy....even if it's me. I try to say things like, "tell your mom about your game", or "tell mommy about what you learned in school last week" so that she can feel that sense of being a parent. Isiah loves his mommy just like any other child loves their mommy, I just see that little by little his bond with her is slipping away. That very thing terrifies me, that day in the future when Isiah says to me. "I'm tired of going there to see my mom, I don't want to go". Who do I feel for? The little boy who only gets to talk to his mom for 3 hours every month, sitting across the table in a chair being monitored by correction officers, or the child who spends her days inside barbed wire fences and nights locked in a cage? She lives for those 3 hours; her entire existence right now is teetering on 180 minutes every 30 days when I bring him to visit. I feel like I'm holding my breath that he keeps wanting to go, because if he ever says "NO" ....I have no idea how to handle that. I understand why and I don't blame him. If Mackenzie would ever hear him say that, she would give up. She would spiral into a place that no human will be able to pull themselves out of, I know her. I pray to God that day never comes.

Prison Diaries: Behind the glass.

August 1st, 2017

The last time I have seen my child was June 15, 2017. I have spoken with her via Jpay email or through another inmate relaying a message from her. I have had no contact with her even that way since July 25th. My mind and worries are getting the best of me. We will leave today to travel to where she is, spending the night in a hotel to take some of the "pressure" off of the day for Isiah. The traveling, the visit, and more traveling is a lot to handle for a 5-year-old. I was notified yesterday that our much-anticipated visit will be allowed but behind the glass. No physical contact. No hug, no kiss, no sitting on his Mommy's lap for Isiah. Our conversation will now be recorded and monitored. I now have to relay what is going on to my child, without saying it. I have to see her face. I worry about her safety and her mental state. The last time I saw my own child she was becoming someone I did not know. Her looks are hard, and her attitude is harder. Prison has done this. I question the entire "Rehabilitation" system for those who have committed a crime.

Everyone's crime is different, yet everyone's prison is still the same. You cannot tell anymore if my child's crime was selling stolen property for money, or committed a 1st-degree murder. She looks the same as them, and nothing can prepare you to lose your own child while they are still alive. My big concern now is how she will ever fit back into society being raised behind bars. At 19, she still needed my guidance and love and she was isolated and caged for committing a crime. She brought this on herself and will suffer and pay for what she did until the day she dies, and so will I. I hope she can feel my love behind the glass. I hope I can comfort her so for that short amount of time she won't be scared, or alone. Maybe she can come back to being my little girl full of smiles and laughter and love for her baby....behind the glass. My heart goes out to any parent who God forbid has to live through my same circumstances. Only those who have to watch your child grow behind bars understand. Only those who are looked down upon for that child's upbringing will understand. I do not feel sorry for myself, I raised 3 GREAT children.... all the same teachings, all the same rules, just not all the same children. I love them all the same, but all 3 will never be the same again. I am not strong I am scared. I do not want to see her behind glass. I hope I fall apart before or after I see her. I have God's protection and that I am confident about. The place doesn't scare me, seeing the woman my child has become does. There have been many "1st's" in this journey with Mackenzie. All of them I have survived, but all of them break me little by little. This 1st I will survive too, but I hate it. I hate my child needing her mom and I can't help her. I hate seeing my child be scared and I have to leave her behind. I hate seeing her baby cry leaving his Mommy. I hate watching my daughter's cry talking to each other. I hate that my child looks like the real monsters who sleep right below her in her cage. I hate it, but I will do it because I love my child even behind glass.

Prison Diaries: Orange and white stripes August 6, 2017

It has been 96 hours since I saw Mackenzie for our visit. I am traumatized. The image of my daughter is burned in my brain and I am going to struggle to function until I can see her at my next visit. This was like no other visit I have had

with Mackenzie since the day of her incarceration. To type
what I saw makes my hands tremble and the vomit starts
to come up in my throat. I do not know of anyone who has
experienced what I saw, I was not prepared. If I don't write
it down and forget it my head is going to explode.

We entered into the prison like any other normal visit with our
inmate. I was prepared for her to be behind glass which made
me anticipate just being sad. I would kill for that to be the worst
of my fears. Isiah was missing his Mommy to the point of him
repeating, "I want to see Mommy" over, and over, and over
again. I think it may have even irritated the correction officer
working the check-in desk. Gracie was anxiously waiting to go
through the metal detectors as Isiah wanted to go first like it was
a ride at the county fair or something! We went through and
went to our normal sets of steel doors shutting behind us after
we entered a room until we came into the visitation hall. The
desk officer is a nice man. He always makes it a point to speak
to Isiah or ask me how I am doing. He does his job but doesn't
use his billy club as a license to treat others without respect. He
went through the same motions as far as taking my license,
checking my visitor badge and telling us we could be seated. I
was thinking, "Oh man, we are going to get to have a contact
visit...I got all upset for nothing." I said to Gracie that maybe they
forgot we were supposed to be behind the glass. Gracie told me
to "not be THAT KID. The kid in class that raises his hand and
reminds the teacher that they had a homework assignment due
today". Fair enough. After most of the visitors' inmates had
entered the hall a correction officer came walking up to us. My
heart started pounding like I was in trouble. "BASHAM," she
said. I nodded as she motioned for us to come with her. We
were escorted to a section with a large window divided into
sections. The phone is on each side of the windows. I was
thinking, Ok....I am going to be fine. Isiah and Gracie can handle
this we just cannot touch Mackenzie. I suggested that Isiah go
find a puzzle or book in the playroom as I was afraid of my own
emotions when I finally got to see my child. He went and

grabbed some free popcorn and made himself at home in the play area. He was talking and playing with the play area workers and I appreciated them being kind to Isiah. I imagine they know how stressful these visits can be because they themselves are inmates probably longing to see their children/family. As Gracie and I wait in silence, I nervously talk about nothing. We were seated beside a large window overlooking the entire prison. We watched the daily routines of the prisoners and of the guards. At one point I told Gracie to look out the window at the lady in the orange and white striped jumpsuit. This lady was being escorted by guards on both sides. She had a giant brown belt around her waist with some kind of chains from it. Her hands were handcuffed as well as her feet and then she was shackled to the chain hanging from the large brown leather belt. Wow, I thought whatever that lady did had to be pretty damn bad because she looks insane! I actually told Grace to look out the window. When she did, I told her that that was probably like a serial murderer or rapist because of how much security was involved for just her walking down a sidewalk. I commented that orange and white striped must mean yours either on death row or mentally insane. The woman disappeared into an underneath building and I began to think how lucky I was that I was getting to see my Mackenzie, even if behind glass. I felt for a minute like I was being a baby and a bit over dramatic for having such a meltdown because they wouldn't let me have a physical contact visit. The officer that works the desk in the visitation hall came into talk to us. She is such a nice lady that also speaks to us when we visit often. I think she could tell we were getting very worried and anxious because we had been sitting and waiting now for over 45 minutes as everyone else was already visiting with their inmate. The officer told Gracie and I that "Basham" would be coming, they just called her to confirm transporting or something. She told us we could watch out that big window beside us and she would be walking from the center building underneath the tunnel. My mind had a huge relief because she said walking as if she was just like all the other girls walking around out there.

I thanked her and Gracie and I began to watch out the window. Our eyes were glued to that area she pointed to as girl after girls were walking every direction like it was a busy city street in Chicago or something. The sick feeling in my stomach was just twirling and spinning like it was ready to freaking erupt...my nerves were just ready to get this over with already. Just then we see 4 sets of feet coming through the dark tunnel. We could not see their heads but we saw that 2 were guards and 2 were orange and white striped pants.

Gracie and I looked at each other thinking this is scarier than hell because that situation looked dangerous. There was a woman now sitting at the next window waiting for another inmate. We had the front window seat. As we watched the "shuffle" of the shackled inmates in orange and white stripes who appeared to be insane, we could not see their faces because they were shaded from walking through the tunnel.

My heart suddenly felt like it shot out hot blood to every part of my body. My skin began to get warm like a hot flash. My eyes almost seeing blurry because my heart was pounding so fast. I felt almost paralyzed. I had a hollow feeling, kinda like my body was an empty shell and it was a weird scary feeling I had not ever experienced before. I knew those feet "shuffling" towards the large window down below. Then I watched as the legs walked a very familiar walk that I knew. I stood up and said out loud..."that's my daughter". Gracie noticed also as she turned around to take off running to the restroom. I wanted to run after her, I knew baby girl was having a meltdown and she needed me to hug her and tell her we were going to be alright. I couldn't move, I seriously had no feeling in my legs or feet. I never once took my eyes off that inmate in orange and white stripes with the big brown leather belt on and chains hanging from it. I didn't even move my head as I watched the inmate in orange in white stripes "shuffle" from being shackled out of the tunnel onto the sidewalk. My breathing became heavy and my head felt very light. My little girl, my sweet angel. Is this real life right now? I

question my existence and wonder if I'm really standing there....in a prison.... what in the name of Jesus am I doing there? I move closer to the window as I see my child blinking one eye after the other trying to adjust her eyes to the sunlight. The sun was shining beautifully on Wednesday and I didn't even notice it until that moment. I watched my child look to the side, then the other side, then behind her.... repeatedly. It was though there were imaginary people all around her she thought. I watched my child look pale as a ghost as her eyes twitched almost in a nervous tick some people develop. I looked down onto my child who looked insane. She was scarier than the first inmate that we saw who I thought was the scariest thing I had ever seen. I put my hand up to the window as I noticed the guard tell my child that she had a visitor like he was explaining it to a 3-year-old. Mackenzie was getting her eyes focused by then and she looked up and noticed my body in the middle of that large picture window, I read her lips. "That's my Mom", she tells the guards. I started to get hysterical and sat back into my seat. I am not one to show emotion a lot or even ever in public. This was beyond my control. I was sobbing. I hear the voice of a woman say, "Honey are you ok?" I couldn't talk, I didn't have a voice and I could not control the hysterical crying coming out of myself. I shook my head to indicate NO. Next thing I knew this woman sat a chair beside me with her arms around me.
She said, "I think you need a hug sweetheart". I sobbed like a little kid. I didn't even know what this woman looked like. I did not look at her face, couldn't see through my own damn tears. She was comforting. She knew my pain and very few do. I tried to talk and couldn't get it out to be understandable through my crying. She told me it was going to be alright; she was waiting for her daughter too. I try to compose myself. This woman petted my head trying to calm me. I think it worked. I was worried that Gracie would have seen what I just did but she was still in the restroom crying I was sure. I finally was able to speak to this beautiful creature that reached out to comfort a complete stranger. She asks me if I'm ok now. I nod yes and spit out a jumbled "my

daughter....she looks insane". This woman tells me her daughter has been in solitary segregation for a while now. She also tells me that her daughter went into prison at 17 years old for murder or involuntary manslaughter. Oh, my heart feels for her. The lady tells me that her daughter has to serve 11 years....wait a minute, what? How many years for involuntary manslaughter, 11? Ok, now I'm pissed. She asks me how long my daughter is in for and I tell her 14. I can tell by the look on her face she is thinking that my child must have done something far worse than her child has. That's how you register how bad the inmate is honestly. The amount of years a person is serving is how severe the crime is to the common person. The lady asked me what Mackenzie was in for, and I reply. She says in complete surprise, "14 years for burglary charges?" I hear this over and over and have for almost 4 years now. I'll write later, I need a break.

Gracie came back from the restroom red-faced. Bless her little heart, no teenager should have to witness the slow deterioration of their sibling's mental health like this. I remember when my brother's appendix burst as a child. I was so scared and upset because my parents were upset when he had to stay in the hospital. They took me to see him, but I was not allowed at my age, so they wheeled him out onto a balcony where he was able to wave to me. This I remember because I was traumatized...over an appendix surgery! It was the worry for my brother, the worry for my parents, and it was the only thing that had ever "happened" to me as a child. I had a wonderful childhood. My parents are STILL married, in the same house, on the same street. The word "prison" was bad, as well as the word "criminal". They are both still bad, but they relate to my own flesh and blood and that makes me sick. This I know, my children are not sheltered.

Gracie and I wait patiently for our inmate to appear behind our window. Mackenzie had disappeared out of sight of the large window up above. We watch the door at the back of the small room they escorted the inmates into waiting and waiting to see Mackenzie up close. The door opened and in walked my girl. Oh, how I missed that beautiful smile and face. She has always had this cute dimple when she smiled and the prettiest shade of pink rosy lip color ever since she was born. What I saw was a lost girl. She had deep reddish-purple rings around her eyes. Her color of skin was that of a pale-ish gray. Her lips were pale, no color to them. She looked dehydrated, and she looked sick, and she looked pathetic. Her hair was matted all over.

The very worst I can remember Mackenzie was in her mugshot. In that photo she had been up on a roll of drugs and alcohol for over 3 days....this was worse. It was worse because she was sober and the only thing that had made her this way was her own mind. Mackenzie always told me that drugs made her feel comfortable in her own skin and feel "normal", and now it makes sense to me. This is how the mentally ill battle demons. Isolation can drive you insane, she fought battles already. I do not think Mackenzie will recover from this now. She picked up the phone on her side and I picked up the phone on my side. I could not stop the constant flow of my own tears running down my face. I said, "Hi Sis, I've missed you." She said "hi" back. Mackenzie was quiet which is uncommon for her. She told me she was sorry, then got tears in her eyes. I told her how much I love her, and I don't care what she had done or how she looked. Mackenzie told me she has been having conversations with me and laughing about certain times from when she was young. I had not had a conversation with Mackenzie in over 55 days, so I knew her mind was playing tricks on her. I said, "Mackenzie Lee look at mom....I love you so much, and you have all your family back home missing you like crazy. We will not stop loving you even after you come home to us, but you have to come home. You have lost touch with reality honey, and I'm very worried about you." She told me that she had done something bad that is why she had not had any contact with anyone for a while. I asked what she did, but I was honestly scared as hell for her answer. In my mind I pictured her killing another person, that's what the inmate beside her in the phone room did. I think sometimes I try to cope with the very worst that could possibly happen then I can handle anything up to that point. She told me that everything she had was gone.

When she was in 23- hour lockdown for refusing to take her hair out of dreadlocks she got a visit from a woman. She did not know who it was. I think it was the warden. The woman apologized for the guard that had been treating Mackenzie extra harsh because of her race. She said she wanted to apologize on "behalf of the institution". The woman then went on to tell Mack that they had received reports of other inmates he had done this to and that they had "walked the officer out" that day. I myself had also called informing them that if I came to visit and my daughter walked out with a shaved head, they were going to see me, a civil rights attorney, and the Dayton nightly news outside of their prison. Long story short, the officer was let go. Now Mackenzie had told me long ago that you don't ever "rat" on anyone in prison or they will get you from the inside. I get it now. I feel a little responsible for what went down. It was ultimately her actions that placed her in solitary segregation, but I added to it by making the institution look bad in my recent update on the petition I started regarding my child. I am now reaping what I have sewn. Every prisoner has some kind of box that they keep all their belongings in. Mackenzie's box had been "mysteriously" opened and all her clothes, shoes, photos, toiletries, snacks, blankets.... all just gone. Another inmate had passed this on to Mackenzie. The day she was getting out of 23 hour she had just gotten out of the shower and was ready to get dressed out of the big blue jumpsuit attire she had to wear for the past 45 days or something.

Some inmates walk by, waving at her, a smirky "I just effed you over" smile and wave. She was wearing Mackenzie's clothes, and shoes. We are allowed to send ONE clothes box per year. One time to send underwear, sports bra's, t-shirts, sweatpants, a blanket, a fan, one time a year. Mackenzie now has nothing until next year. Family members had pitched in and sent her her clothes box for this year. She treasures anything sent to her like that of gold. When Mackenzie saw the girl wearing her clothes which were brand new never been worn, she just plain and simple snapped. She took off after the inmate and got revenge. "Revenge" what she has now tattooed on her forearm. She told me all she remembered was screaming "My Aunt Bonnie got me this shirt" and then forcibly removing the shirt from the inmate wearing it. Mackenzie tells me over the phone that she did it right in front of the guards, so everyone was on the same page of what happened.

Nothing could be he said/she said, it was seen by all. They are not going to scare the young white girl anymore; she has had enough. Mackenzie was restrained to the ground and maced by numerous different directions as this is their procedure I assume. She told me her body was on fire. She could not see, nor does she remember after that because she was in a different place mentally at that point. She was stripped and thrown in solitary 24 hours a day. No window, no sunlight, no getting out to eat, her food is sent into her. So, there she lays, in an approximately 8x8 room as the hours and the days pass by. She has no contact with family or friends or any other human except the guards who deliver her chow through a small opening on the steel door.

This is why she is having conversations with me and her brother and sisters. I told Mackenzie on the phone that I told her long ago to protect herself in there and that I have no idea what it's like in there. I told her I understand that is what she HAD to do. Now she is paying for it again, and again, and again. Mackenzie tells me she is glad I didn't bring Isiah because she didn't want him to see her like this, I told her I was so sorry, but he was there....in the playroom. She started to cry. I then was finally able to deliver the message I have been dreaming about for about 3 years...I said "Mackenzie look at me.

As of last Tuesday, you now have retained counsel. You only talk to your attorney or his legal team regarding anything about your case. We will no longer discuss anything over the phone or in person, Ok?" The look on her face was priceless. It was as if I had just injected a shot of hope into this lost soul sitting on the other side of the window. She leaned back in her chair and put her shackled hands as close to her face as they would reach. She started to shake her head and sob. I was crying as well as Gracie. She mouthed the words "how" and Gracie and I mouthed back the names of her two guardian angels that made it possible. She just kept crying as I'm sure so many things were going through her head at that moment. Then up walks a little brown bear with a missing bottom tooth. We all straighten up and Gracie puts the phone up to Isiah's ear. He said, "Hi Mommy, why do you have handcuffs on?"

Wow, this kid doesn't miss a thing. Mackenzie told Isiah that she was so sorry he had to see her like that from what I could read of her lips. They talked briefly then Isiah said he wanted to go back and finish his game in the playroom. He said, "I love you Mommy" and put the phone down. Talk about unconditional love, a child's love for a parent is at the top of the list. We talked about small stuff to try to cheer her up, and Gracie was able to make her laugh. I still had a stream of tears throughout the entire visit which was short. I appreciated any amount of time I was allowed that day and so did she.

At one point I got up to go check on Zay and the female officer at the desk approached me. She said to me that she was glad I came but that Isiah told her he was sad. She told me that "Basham" needed to see his face and mine. She told me what I had already observed in that Mackenzie was losing touch with reality being isolated and she needed to be reminded of what she has to live for. I agreed and thanked her. She is doing her job and I get it. I respect her for being human to me and my children and grandchild. We did not run out of things to say to each other and by the end of our visit, Mackenzie was enjoying our real-life conversation. She still looked around her a lot and fidgeted in her chair like at times her mind was at another place.

I noticed a few officers enter the other part of the visitation hall and I knew what that meant. They were there to transport the high-security inmates back to their hole. I felt sick; I didn't want them to take her. I wondered if I begged if they would leave her to sit in that chair? They looked firm and serious and I was intimidated by them. They opened the door to tell my daughter time was up. We all tried to speak into the phone throwing out I love you's over and over. I told Mackenzie that everyone back home loves her, and we are all waiting for the day she is free. I told her she had to stay strong and prepare for life with us and her son. She nodded and cried at the same time while looking down as if too ashamed to even make contact with her own mother. Isiah put his little hand up to the window. Mackenzie tried to put hers up to his, but the chains didn't allow it. Isiah started to cry as well as all of us.

Dear God, why does this little boy deserve this/ He never did anything wrong, why him? Then they were gone. We were escorted out of the hall. At the next set of doors, I could not make eye contact with Isiah or Gracie. I was on the verge of crying hysterically. I showed my stamp to the guards behind the security window and they waved me on almost as if they knew how distraught I was. I wanted to run back in there and rescue my little girl. The very thought of her being put back into that hole was more than I could bear. I didn't want to feel the sunlight because she didn't. I didn't want to eat because she wasn't. I didn't want to talk to anyone because she couldn't.

On the way to the car I actually scared myself, it was if someone had placed duct tape over my mouth. I could not breathe. I had to do one simple thing.... breathing, and I forgot for a minute how to do that. I started to panic. The only other panic attack I have ever had was walking into the courthouse the day of Mackenzie's sentencing, and this was number two! Thank God Gracie and Isiah walked ahead of me to the car. I looked up and asked God to please help me just get home to my house.

I pray for my girl every night and every night I look up at the moon. I say out loud, "the moon is beautiful tonight Mackenzie, I'll tell you about it soon". It's August 7th, 2017....still no contact.

Prison Diaries: August 8, 2017

Mackenzie called!! She is out of the hole after over 60 days. She talked to Isiah. I think we will have a good day today... Thank you, God.

Prison Diaries: August 17, 2017

I am now receiving regular contact from Mackenzie. Ritchie, Isiah and I are leaving to head to Dayton for our second (and last) visit for August. I am confident it will be better than the last, as she is back in regular population. Isiah asked if today would be like the last time and I assured him it would not be.... So help me God it has to be better! I feel stronger when Ritchie is with me. I cannot wait to hug and kiss my girl!

I received this message yesterday from Mack, just a few words but at least she is aware of our visit and hopefully in a healthier mental state.

From: MACKENZIE BASHAM
Date: 8/16/2017 5:09:21 PM
To: Judy Frisby
Attachments:

can't wait to see you guys tomorrow

Prison Diaries: August 18, 2017

Back to the "Normal" visit for us yesterday. It was nothing like our previous visit thank God. This time when we got into the hall Mackenzie was actually sitting there WAITING on us!? That has never been the case before, but I am thankful for every extra minute. As soon as the steel doors buzzed us through, she turned around and the little brown bear stopped and asked me if he had to check in with the officer before he touched his Mommy. I said, "No, you go run to your momma"

.......Isiah did exactly that. Oh, how that warms my heart to see. That little boy loves his mommy no matter what. I think every time a bratty kid gets mad and tells his parent he hates them, they should have to go 30 days in Isiah's footsteps....just 30 days. You appreciate every word from their mouth, every single hug or kiss, and time spent is golden. So yesterday was Isiah's special day because the last month has been tough for him. A long drive to see his mommy for 3 hours was not his choice, but then we went out for dinner and dropped some lines......that was his choice. Fishing has become sort of a saving grace for us. It is Isiah's most favorite thing to do. I can't explain how it felt to put my arms around my child and hold on. I kissed her cheek. I told her I loved her, and I had missed her so bad. Then I hugged her again pushing my luck. I know the "one hug" rule but I needed that second squeeze like a crack head needs their drug. I was willing to take any punishment. The power of a hug is unexplainable. I was comforting my child and protecting her and loving her and letting her know that Momma was there.... just through that extra 3-second embrace.

We had a good talk with Mackenzie. I wanted to her to focus on positive things and help her try to clear her mind of all the horrible dark nasty dirty scary gross things she is engrossed in, in prison. I asked her to start making a game plan for things and goals she wants to do when that day of freedom finally comes. I said let's pretend it's the first day of the rest of your life....what will you do? She was excited to answer, and also very serious. I assume she does not get to that place in her mind often, it seems so far away. In Mackenzie's life, you do not dare let your rainbows and sunshine's take you over because in a split second you will realize you are still living in hell and will be until your 34 years old.

Anyway, I was able to take her to a place of hope by talking about our plans for the future. I told her about the house we bought that we gutted down to the beams. We needed another focus too and downsizing to much cheaper bills was a plus to help with attorney fees for her when we can. I told her about her room and Isiah's room in the home. It is bare. She has to decorate that room and she can do whatever she wants. Mackenzie told me that she is going to live with Ritchie and I the rest of her life. She will never leave our home. She was very serious in telling us both that. We of course laughed, but Mack was serious as a heart attack. She told us she does not want to be around people or interact with other people until she feels like she has made up for lost time with her son. She told us she doesn't know how she will act around people other than family; she doesn't know how to be.

Mackenzie was serious when speaking of her fear of doing something as simple as going to a grocery store. She has a lot of pain and hurt of people. She said that she appreciates so much all of the support and prayers from friends around the community but cannot process having a conversation with another person in the free world in a normal place like Walmart. I cannot imagine that, I talk to people for a living. I can walk up to a complete stranger with complete trust and talk to them or hug them. This is because of my life and surroundings. Let me try to imagine Mackenzie's life and surroundings for a minute.

Just last week she sent me a picture of her face and the chipped tooth in the front. This happened just a few days after she was released out of solitary confinement. She could not tell me over the phone what happened but at our visit, she explained. Another inmate busted her in the mouth with a hard object and it chipped her tooth. Now, I have never in 44 years been hit in the mouth so hard it chipped my tooth yet she has, on just a normal Wednesday afternoon. This is the prison life. Writing these diaries help me to put myself in her shoes or try to imagine her daily routines. I hate it, it turns my stomach to picture my little girl being hit so hard in the mouth her teeth chipping for no relevant reason whatsoever.

Mackenzie said she was tired. Her body was sore and worn down from fighting, like physically battling another human on a daily basis. She told me of the constant altercations that happen in a woman's prison that guards know nothing or DO nothing about. If you look at a certain member of a certain group and they do not like your face, or color of skin, or voice, or shoes, or hair.... you either fight or you are a bitch. You are their bitch. I told Mackenzie that a person like me would not last one hour in that place, and I asked about old women. Are the elderly confronted?

Mackenzie told me of the time in her first few months of being in Marysville when she was just 19 years old. It was shower time and she noticed a pair of shoes with feet in them waiting for her to exit her curtain or whatever. She knew she was not alone in the shower. She told herself it was fight or die and turned around and walked past "the group".

Next thing she knew an inmate was behind her saying into

her ear "well aren't you a little corn-fed white girl". Mackenzie told me this after her body being sore from fighting a woman who had to be over 60 years old. She said you don't think about that you are punching someone's grandma, you are simply trying to live until the next day with a shred of dignity or sleep with both eyes closed instead of with your back to the wall so you're not held down and jumped in your sleep. So now I get it. If lived battling literally on a day to day basis I may not be so trusting and friendly having a normal conversation with Joe Shmoe in the grocery store, Mackenzie trusts no one. Her guard is always up, and she is ready to survive no matter what it takes.

Mackenzie looked healthier as far as skin color and her sense of humor was back. After the isolation, she had told me that she felt very "delusional". I think she was a lot better at our visit. She was more in touch with her surroundings and the physical contact with her Isiah was like a medicine she had so badly needed. He helps heal her wounds mentally. The stand she was taking over her hair being in dreadlocks is not important now. We have a new light, a new focus on her life and that is her freedom. She told us she has until Wednesday, August 23 to have the dreadlocks out of her hair or they are holding her down and taking a clipper guard to her head. That will hurt because the hair is matted. I get her stand. Why can inmates of a different color wear their hair the exact same way and it's not a security issue?

In my world you can win this battle, in prison, you cannot win. I told her hair grows back; of all the things we need to focus on her hair is not at the top. It is not right, but the point has been made and we get it....you are a prisoner. You have no rights the second you are even associated with a crime in this country. You are not innocent until proven guilty. You are guilty if a police officer says you are until you prove yourself innocent. In Mackenzie's case, she was guilty by association and was bullied and scared into saying she was guilty. I myself have trust issues with law enforcement just because of Mackenzie's ordeal. I understand why she trusts no one.

We talked to prepare to see her without hair. She is going to try to cut them out on her own, so she does not have to have the trauma from the clippers being used. It will look horrible and I will cry due to the shock but that is the least of my worries. Mackenzie had beautiful dark hair the day she was born. She was a beautiful baby and her hair added to her beauty. When I see her next, she will be a grown woman with homemade chopped hair or buzzed, in a prison uniform and tattooed arms and hands. That is scary to anyone. She will look hard, or harder. Her "scars" of prison; life tell her story, and this is one of those scars.

What a story we have to tell! I have to believe that sometime, somewhere, someone is going to read our story and it will help them sleep at night. Maybe help to heal a broken heart of a parent who is watching their own flesh and blood battle to survive the next hour because of drugs, or a mistake, or a prison sentence, or their own mental demons.

Isiah has made a new friend that works in the visitation room at the prison...it sounds completely insane that I would let my grandson have a friend that is an inmate. Something about this woman tells me we have met her for a reason. The reason may be selfish, but at this point, I will do ANYTHING to keep my child safe and alive in hell.

From: Judy Frisby
Date: 9/14/2017
To: Angela Outlaw

Hi Outlaw! This is Mackenzie's mom Judy and I'm typing
for Isiah, your buddy! He was very happy to get your
video but very sad he didn't get to play with you in the
visitation playroom. It sure makes the visitation better
when he has friends in there, sometimes he gets sad
going because he knows he'll have to leave his Mommy.

Yesterday he turned 6 years old, so we let him take the day
off from kindergarten and we drove to Dayton for the day.
We took him to Hooters for lunch, haha and he asked the
Hooters girls if they would sing to him! They did and he got
his picture taken. Then we took him to Petland so he could
hold the puppies that were for sale. Then we came to visit
his Momma. We got there at 4:15 and did not get back into
visitation room until 6:30 because of some security issue.
Isiah was about to freak out if he couldn't see his Mommy
so thank God, we even got one hour with her. He missed
you, he said you work on Wednesdays he's so smart. He
did good at his sleep study at Children's Hospital, but we
get test results back in October.

After that, he will have surgery to take out his tonsils at the
children's hospital also. He starts flag football next week so
we will send you some pics of that. Isiah also got elected at
his school to carry the crown across the field at our high
school Homecoming game in 2 weeks. He walks with the
Homecoming King and has to be all dressed up and carry the
crown. We hope you are doing well and stay safe in there,
talk to you later... Isiah your new buddy!

September 24, 2017

I have been able to speak to Mackenzie via jpay email and
limited phone calls for about the past month. Her mind is
healing. It will never be the same and I accept that. One month
ago, our family had a great celebration, a wedding to be exact.
There was a lot of families who attended and a lot at the
wedding, including Isiah Lee. I was so excited to see everyone
and the beautiful dresses and tuxedos and church and
reception hall...I was also so sad that Mackenzie was not going
to be there. If she couldn't be there because she had to work, or
lived out of town, that would have been different.

When Mackenzie misses things because she is sitting
alone in a prison cell, it is a new level of sadness. I was fine
until the Friday after the rehearsal dinner. We had a great
dinner and was full of anticipation for the next days'
activities when we got home. Everyone was in bed and I
lay wide awake at 1:00 am. I knew I needed to be up early
to start the wedding hairdo's, but my mind would not let me
sleep. I went downstairs and decided to look into the bag
that I had picked up from Dayton Correctional Institution
two days before that. It was a gift that Mackenzie had made
for Jordan for her special day. In the bag was a letter, a few
old pictures of her and Jordy, and a light blue crocheted
flower. The flower was for Jordan to tuck away in her
wedding bouquet so that she would feel Mackenzie's spirit
with her all through her special day. I picked up the flower
and I smelled it hoping it would smell like my little girl. It
smelled like nothing and I started to cry. I needed to see
her right then. I needed her to tell me that it was ok to have
fun or eat like a "king" or dance like I used to. I have not
physically been able to enjoy myself since May 2014. I
have stayed in, stayed sober, stayed away from my family
because I feel guilt all over me. It makes me sick to see
people having a good time....don't they know my child is
living in hell right now? She is not dancing, she is not

eating like a "king", she is all alone, and she is missing her beautiful little boy. How was I going to put Mackenzie in the back of my mind and put Jordan's big day first? The next morning, I was at the church bright and early for the festivities. I was too busy to be sad.

At 11:00 that day I had scheduled a video visit with Mackenzie and brought a laptop so that she would be able to see her cousin she grew up so close with in her beautiful gown. I logged on and up on the screen she came. She looked beautiful even with the cement walls surrounding her. She talked to Jordy and a lot of the girls in the wedding. Jordan started to cry, and Mackenzie told her firmly, "Don't cry...this is happy". Then Mackenzie got to see her baby boy and give him the pep talk for being a ring bearer. The sight of a 5-year-old boy staring into a computer screen exchanging his love with his mommy just about breaks your heart. The screen would freeze up and lose connection every few minutes. Isiah would say over and over...Mommy, mommy...oh God bless his little heart. I took a break from curling and spraying hair and got behind Isiah to see Mackenzie's face again. We smiled and talked about all the excitement. Mackenzie then tells Isiah to let her talk to Nana for a second. I got in full view and Mackenzie says to me, "Mom, are you listening?". I tell her she has my full attention. Mackenzie said, "Mom will you do me a big favor? Will you please just have a good time tonight?", How did she know what's going on in my mind? I don't tell her these things, yet it seems like we feel the same emotions sometimes without saying a word to each other. I started to cry, and she was choking back words and desperately trying to have a smile on her face at this point. Isiah looked up at me as I made up something about my coffee making me have to pee yet again. I went to the restroom, sat in a stall and started sobbing. It was a full-on meltdown that I needed to get out of my system.

Sometimes I can talk to Mack about anything because she is such a good listener when you are feeling sad...I miss that the most. She was never a good listener of my parental orders, but she is the most caring and loyal person I know. If you are Mackenzie's family, she has your back for life. The computer shut off when our time ended, and we had to get the show on the road.

When Isiah and Gracie walked down the aisle, I started crying again just feeling Mackenzie's spirit inside of me knowing that she would be so proud of them at that exact moment. The same thing happened when our beautiful bride walked down the aisle. It was a beautiful wedding and a very fun day. I caught myself a few times at the reception wanting to get the kids and go home to my "safe zone", but I owed it to my niece to stay and celebrate with her until it was over. The open bar and the Redds Apple Ale made it a lot easier to stay too.

Isiah started his first day of school and Mackenzie missed yet another milestone. I was not sad that day. I am very thankful that I had my kids young because at 44 and 48 Ritchie and I are very tired of raising this 6-year-old. It is different when you are raising your own children, plus you just have more energy when you're in your 20's. We celebrated Isiah's 6th birthday at the bowling alley with family. He had a blast and while we sang Happy Birthday to him Gracie recorded a short 30- second video for his Mommy. At my age, I know that if nobody remembers my birthday, my mom will. It's that one day that your mom always makes you feel SPECIAL. In my mind, I am thinking about little Isiah and trying to do something "over the top", so that he feels extra special. Isiah has celebrated his last four birthdays with no Mom there, and no Dad there. That kills me. It hurts me for him. He is awesome, why aren't his own damn parents there on HIS special day. I feel I have to overcompensate to make up for his parent's screw-ups. I hope by me doing this it doesn't backfire on me and he becomes a horrible bratty kid, but I am doing the best I possibly can....and so is Ritchie. We always imagined having great times with our grandchildren and spoiling the crap out of them.... then sending them home to our kids. We can't even send Isiah into the other room because he is scared to death to be in a room by himself most the time.

Gracie called me from school two weeks ago and told me she had been voted Homecoming attendant for her class. Then she told me they picked Isiah to be the "crown carrier" for the new Homecoming king this year. Oh, the excitement in our family! We have been busy spending money on earrings, shoes, dresses, ties, dress clothes the past few weeks getting ready for this Friday night. This is my Gracie's special weekend and I am so very proud of her, yet once again sadness. Will this ever go away? I feel like I never get to fully experience a special moment because something is missing, it's Mackenzie. I lay at night and try to picture how proud Mackenzie would have been if she was able to watch her little sister and her little boy walk across that football field under the big lights with the fans, and the football teams, and the excitement. Right now, in our country, everyone is divided over black and white. Divided over Democrat and Republican. Divided over the United States or Foreign lands. I wish everyone could see this real-life story......

It's Friday night lights in a small town in Midwest Ohio. The community gathers for this year's homecoming ceremony. The school is a small school that actually holds k-12 in it. It is primarily a farming community. It is almost all white. It is almost all Republican. There are families that have been going to this school for many many generations. Most people know each other from growing up in that very small community. This Homecoming ceremony you have a lot of names you recognize from their parents, or many other family members that have been on the court in the past. Except for one. This year you have a special little boy. This little boy gets to carry the crown across the field to the new "King" of the school. This little guy just moved to the small town when he was two years old. This little boy's mommy is in prison. This little boy's daddy doesn't come around. This little boy is black, and he is white.

This little boy loves his school and everything about it. He is not a Democrat, and he is not Republican. This little guy loves to stand for the National Anthem and hear his great-gramps tell old Marine stories. This little guy has battles to fight when he grows up that he doesn't even know about, because of the color of his skin...and where his parents are (or aren't). All this little boy knows is that this will be the most exciting day of his little life. He gets to see the big football players up close and see the fans in the bleachers cheer for him, and walk across that giant field on a Friday night...under the lights. Most will not know his "story" and that's not important, but I do. If I could hug every person in this community I would. It brings me to tears that this little guy is accepted, and loved, and treated exactly the same as any other kid out there. I will be sad that his Mommy will miss his big day, but I am very proud of the human race for this night.

From: Mackenzie Basham
Date: 10/1/2017
To: Judy Frisby

Have Zay send emails/videos to outlaw, she got put on lockdown because a c/o touched her inappropriately and she went off on him.... the devil has been weighing heavy here today .... Zay will cheer her up.

From: Judy Frisby
Date:10/1/2017
To: Angela Outlaw

Hi Outlaw! We wanted to cheer you up. Isiah got to carry

the crown at his school homecoming ceremony and Gracie Jo and her boyfriend were elected Junior class homecoming attendants. Isiah had his first football game Saturday and HE SCORED A TOUCHDOWN YAY! We just got back from fishing for a bit, no big ones tonight but getting to bed for school tomorrow. Stay safe and stay strong in there. We'll send a video soon.... your friends, Isiah, and family!

October 17, 2017

Exit 51

It's quiet here. Getting dressed will be a victory, a Tuesday victory. Is this depression? If it is then why do I swallow 150 milligrams of Zoloft a day? I think medicine is a load of crap because it cannot mask the human mind. They could put me in a coma and I would still have this internal need to see my child. When I am home alone, I get sad and I miss Mackenzie. I told Ritchie yesterday that I keep having a feeling of panic. I have been back on my nerve pills daily. I need to see Mackenzie. The last time I saw my daughter was on September 13th. It was a Wednesday. It was Isiah's birthday. Gracie and I made the trip to Dayton, so for the first time since his Mommy went away, he could be with her on his special day. We left early to make sure we could get the entire three hours with her. We arrived at 4:15.

When we arrived there were about six other people seated in the security waiting room. Isiah was trying his best to behave which is pretty hard for him. We sat patiently as the officers sat behind the big desk on and off the phone. I went ahead and signed in our names. I dream of the day I don't have to fill out that visitation form...

Basham-90219 - Judy Frisby, Mother...4:15...
badge number...Basham-90219 - Isiah Simpson,
Son...4:15...Minor…
Basham-90219 - Gracie Frisby, Sister...4:15 -Minor.

I am always worried I will not do something correctly and
be summoned by the guards. They act like I am trying to
pass a civil service test or get in to see the President of
the United States. It's my child, why the hell do I have to fill
out a form to just see my own child? I gave birth to
her...they didn't, who do they think they are? Why were
MY rights taken away? I didn't do anything wrong, yet I
damn near have to go through a strip search to have
physical contact with my own flesh and blood. That place
makes me sick. She doesn't deserve to be in there. It's
filled with nasty people with no morals. Not my Mackenzie,
she is a good person. She knows right from wrong.... she
is clean and normal. I fear the child they will give back to
me when she is finally released. The diseases in that
institution go around like wildfire. They don't care about the
animals in the cages. It was 4:30 and we were still sitting
in the check-in room. We were at the mercy of the
almighty billy club holders. Then it was 5:00 and our name
was not called. I guess it doesn't matter how early I get
there OR if it's a little six-year- old boy's birthday...we will
enter when they say we will. People were getting antsy
and pissed off. An older lady went up and complained, it
got her nowhere. It was now 5:30. The visit is over at 7:30.
How could they do this to this little boy? I hate them. Isiah
was almost in full meltdown mode. He had gone to the
bathroom a hundred times just because it was killing him
to stay seated on the bench in front of the guards. A lady
officer was on the phone asking why she was not allowed
to release us into the other part of the prison. After she
hung up some unmarked cars pulled up in front of the door
we came in and guards got out. They were all hush hush
exchanging keys and talking to each other. The lady guard

that worked the phones at the reception desk finally announces that the entire prison is on lockdown because they have lost power and the backup generator is not powering the barbed wire fences, every person on the grounds is locked down. Um, what in the holy hell? I told the kids it was fine they would get it fixed and we would get to see Mackenzie. It was now 6:00. We have sat almost two hours on a freaking bench in a room with strangers and weird smells......on Isiah's birthday. In my mind, I started to panic. I was in a max security prison...with killers and rapists and child molesters and psychos.... with, my 16-year- old daughter and my 6-year-old grandson and the doors and fences no longer have the power to keep them in! Gracie looks at me and says, "this is like the show Prison Break", then she said she was starting to feel claustrophobic. I told her NO SHE WAS NOT as if I have the power to tell her that. I didn't know what to do. Isiah was saying, Mommy, a hundred times and he was tired, and he was scared and he was over it.

Ok, let me get control of myself for a minute. I was locked in this room, so we were safe. The only thing I could think of was my poor Mackenzie. She was out there...in the trenches.... with the crazies. She is tough, but could she protect herself if a prison break happened? I already know what she would do. I know her. I could feel the anxiety in her at that very minute.

She was worried about us being there being put in a lockdown situation. She was so excited about this visit with her baby on his birthday, she had looked forward to it for months. Now we had just lost two hours of our three hours due to the electricity going out. Oh boy, someone is going to pay! Now I was afraid Mackenzie would snap.

Mackenzie is not mentally capable of rationalizing a situation at this point. She will do whatever it takes to protect her son...and her baby sister, and Mama. I was starting to move around in my seat while trying to create the illusion of calmness to Gracie and Isiah. Is she one of the crazies I am afraid of? Every single prisoner inside those barbed wire fences is someone's daughter, or someone's Mommy, or sister. I'm going to pray now; The God I believe in is going to protect me unless it's my time. I cannot control this situation I am in so I will count on a bigger power. This was how I dealt with it. It was 6:30. The guards came in and used keys to unlock doors around us and the room seemed to relax a bit. They announced we could line up to be scanned and undressed and bear our soul to them so we could be allowed into the visitation hall to see our prisoner finally.

Thank you, Jesus. We got all through security and when we entered the room of tables and chairs everyone had a look of exhaustion and worry on their faces, prisoners, and visitors. We were all humans, all worried about each other being locked in separate rooms in the prison. There she was...red-faced with tears in her eyes and a serious demeanor about her. Isiah ran....and I mean ran to his Mommy. That hug was longer than allowed but it was a beautiful release. We were allowed one hour to have this birthday celebration. Mackenzie told me she was almost ready to lose her mind in panic, she was pacing in her cell and trying to figure out how to get to us to protect us from the violence and destruction if a prison break went down. I knew it, she could care less about running for her freedom...she was going to get to her family in that waiting room before anything could happen to us. That doesn't sound like a hardened criminal to me. My thoughts are confirmed.... she doesn't belong there.

We celebrated for less than an hour with microwave pizza as an entree and we sang "Happy Birthday" to our baby brown bear over a cake made of a honey bun, sweet tarts as a filling, and a zebra cake on top for his birthday cake. It was a birthday he will never forget. If I asked him right now what we did for his birthday this year he would say, "I got to see my Mommy!". That's it, that's all he will remember and that is why I torture myself once a month. It was hard to leave her because we only got an hour together. One hour in the past 35 days is not enough for me. My worry for Mackenzie is overwhelming me lately. I have put in two reservations and both were denied because they were full. I need to take my mom to see her. Mackenzie has only seen her Grandma once this year and hasn't seen her Grandpa since last year. They are getting older and time is not promised for my parents.... it's really not promised for anyone of any age for that matter. My grandparents are all gone and have been for a long time. I remember all of their funerals except a few. I was with family and I had closure and found peace in knowing they knew I loved them.

Mackenzie will not have closure if she loses a grandparent while incarcerated....she will not have peace. She will beat herself up every minute of every day for being gone if something happens to a family member. She will find it hard to live with herself. She will not be just serving a 14-year sentence to the State of Ohio for the crime she has committed, she will be serving a life sentence to her family and herself. This will define Mackenzie and when you look at her it is in her face and in her body and all over her skin, literally. Last week I had to take Isiah to a doctor appointment at Dayton children hospital for a check-up. When his asthma doctor asked what children's hospital, I preferred for his testing I said, Dayton. I only said this because it is where Mackenzie "lives". I was not thinking of the nearest city, or Isiah, or gas money...I was thinking selfishly about myself. It makes me feel closer to her when I take him there. It is so weird.

We drove down for our 11:15 appointment and had his

checkup. He had got sick the day before at school so of course the drive down in the morning he became sicker. It was just Isiah and myself. When they took his temperature, he was running a high fever. He had his checkup and they sent us down to the emergency department because his throat was red and white, and he was just a mess. After 5 hours in emergency, we were told he had a virus. I felt sorry for myself, and for Isiah. We now had a long drive home, he was sick, and I was exhausted. The only time we go to Dayton is to visit Mackenzie. It's exit 51 and I know when I see the highway signs that I'm close to her. Not this time. We passed her exit on our way down and it made me sad, almost like I was hurting her. How could I be so close to her and not go to see her? It was a Tuesday, there are no visitations allowed on Tuesdays.

On our way home I saw exit 51 coming up. I physically could not pass by the exit. I was triggered. Isiah was falling asleep from sickness and exhaustion of our day. I got off at exit 51...Nicholas road. I took it all the way until it dead ends. I was at Dayton Correctional Institution and I didn't have a scheduled visit, but it made me feel close to my daughter. I saw the two rows of barbed wire fences for miles down the road. I turned onto Germantown road and pulled into the parking lot. I was able to see down into the valley where the prison sits. I know I am not allowed to just sit in the parking lot or they will probably think I am a getaway car or something. I just needed to feel like I was with Mackenzie and sitting in this parking lot was all I can do to connect with my child. It's been too long since she has gone away. In my wildest dreams, I never would have thought I would be there...doing this. Am I losing my mind? This is not normal for most people. It was like I was going to visit my kid who lives in a different town as many people do. The only thing about my crazy situation is she doesn't know I'm there...and I don't get to see her or touch her. I sat in my car in a parking lot of a prison and had an imaginary visit with my daughter. Typing this in my diary is making me laugh...because that is insane. I am officially crazy. I have lost my mind, yet I function every day and put on the same "normal" mask Mackenzie puts on inside that giant cage she is kept in. Oh, I just saw some inmates walking through the yard, maybe one of them is my child! I pretend one was so I can put myself at ease and sleep tonight. That damn exit 51 will probably get me every time I pass it for the rest of my life.

Once again I leave and head back on the highway without her. I dream of the day I get to ride in a car with Mackenzie actually in the same car with me.... just going down the highway. That will be such an awesome thing to do. Mackenzie called us that night and it was great to hear her voice. I forget what she sounds like sometimes, so I watch my 30-second videos she has sent via jPay over and over. I told her about Isiah and that he was fine just fighting a virus. She was worried and became very sad because she was not with her baby when he was sick. She told me that the prison had been on lockdown that day because of fog. Apparently, fog means you can escape from prison?

Mackenzie told me they locked them in their cells the entire day and had just let them out to shower so she snuck to the phone room because she had to check up on her baby boy. They had gone through room searches and body cavity searches all day because a pair of gloves had come up missing from the control room. The gloves can touch the barbed wire so it also put the place on lockdown. I asked her what body cavity searches are even though I knew it would be horrific. The guards come in and make them strip clothes off and they check all holes in the woman's body to make sure the gloves aren't stuffed in their.... holes. That makes me sick. They violate my child numerous times a day, and they are allowed to do it because she has no rights. I want to scream. If a person did that to me let's say right outside of those fences it would be rape right...or assault, or molestation?...even though she didn't have anything to do with some pair of gloves?...because it just so happened a correction officer "misplaced" his pair of gloves? So let me get this straight, Mackenzie admitted to a crime in 2014 and because of that it is permitted and ordered for her and 850 other women to be sexually violated multiple times a day on any given day at any given time until the state of Ohio says she is allowed to have her freedom again? What kind of country do I live in? It doesn't matter if you are honest or a liar you will be violated. I'm not sure I could live in a United States prison. Now I understand why the suicide rate is so high in our prison system these days. As a mother, I had to listen to my daughter tell me of this awful day and there was not one thing I could do to help her.

Ironically Mackenzie tells me she is battling severe depression because she misses her son so bad and cannot take care of him when he's sick or needs her........she has no freedom and I have the freedom to do whatever I want, yet we both have the same struggles. I told her of how much I missed her and she told me of how much she missed us too in between sobs. She told me she has to come home soon, she doesn't know how much longer she can take, it's all just become a little too much. I lied to her and told her she has to stay strong and focused because her attorneys have some big game plan. I hope they do; I'm running out of sunshine to throw at her. This struggle is real.

October 23. 2017

My dreams are consuming my nights and days. The dreams I have been having are making me weird. I wake up and go through the motions of the days, but in a little place in my mind, I wonder if certain things really happened or will happen. I keep seeing her, like at the front door or at Isiah's football games, or just lurking in the background watching him. I get so mad at her for escaping because I know that will further her time away. I know she has planned over and over an escape in her mind because Cole said he looks for escape routes when he is there to visit. My fear is...Would she actually do it?

She has no fear of external pain; she has already suffered more than other humans and some animals. She would not survive; she would be shot and then I would be writing in this diary until my last day on earth. She is a ticking time bomb, a cat in a cage my Grandpa Goodwin used to say. She is wearing thin and the last 30 second videos I got, she has a tired and desperate look about her that I have never seen on my child before. Isiah Lee is her only purpose for living. He is the one and the only thing that keeps her from pulling that sheet tight around her throat or running out into the line of fire. Nothing like putting pressure on me to keep him safe!

I often think about my purpose. Four years ago, my purpose was very different then my purpose is now. I was at the top of my game in my career. I was on top of the world...sitting in my own salon, doing what I love every day and being admired for it. In the blink of an eye, I was home in my purple Hawaiian moo moo with a two-year-old watching Bubble Guppies every two hours. It was a Friday morning at the shop, and I was running heavy on iced coffee while mixing color and multi-tasking. I was steadily dialing the Allen County Sheriff's department trying to figure out what exact charges they had arrested Mackenzie on. All I knew at that point was I she didn't show up to pick up Isiah the previous Monday night and I saw her on the six o'clock local news as "woman of interest in a string of burglaries". I got through to the automated line and typed in her name and birthday or something and heard...." Mackenzie Basham, receiving". What the hell was that? I underplayed everything about what I thought it was apparently. The automated message

said she had an arraignment at 1:00 Friday. Oh great, now I
have to find someone to do my afternoon clients to go up there
because of my dumbass kid. I was irate with Mackenzie Lee on
that Friday. Receiving stolen property, really....she knew better! I
was not nervous or upset, I was just mad as hell. I didn't tell
anyone except my close employee who covered my butt so I
could go show my face to my kid who needed to be knocked
down a few notches for the stuff she had been into. My thinking
was there was no need to...she would be given a court date and
sent home with me where then I could rant and rave about how
stupid she was and if she didn't get off the drugs or go into rehab
she was going to end up in prison. I actually called the
courthouse because I had no idea where an "arraignment" would
be held or if I was allowed to even go. It was 12:30 that Friday
as I drove into Lima to go to the Municipal Building. Typing this
is making me have the hot sensation in my body and butterflies
as if I have to do it again. I'm a good girl. I don't go to court. I do
what police officers tell me to do, I abide by most rules that I am
given. I walk in and put my purse through the metal detector.
What the hell? What was this, I would never carry a
weapon...don't they know that by looking at me? I enter the
courtroom and sit in the third isle back. I look around me and
there are a lot of different classes of people throughout both
sides of the courtroom. I felt out of place. I was mad at my
daughter for making me sit in there, take off work, be seen in
that place, period. A few rows back sat Mackenzie's Grandma
and Aunt from her Dad's side. I didn't look at them. I raised
Mackenzie all by myself so when she messed up, it was all my
fault. I should have been so awesome of a parent that
Mackenzie and Cole did not need a father in their lives. We were
told to "All rise" and they announced the honorable judge
presiding that day. We all sat down and I notice the Allen County
Sheriff himself enter the courtroom as well as a deputy and a
detective. Whew, they are intimidating, even I sat up straight in
my seat. Just then off to the right side of the room, a door
opened, and a cop entered followed by three people in black and
white stripes. They were handcuffed at the hands.

Now if I could explain with words the feeling, I had seen that last person sit down at the end of the row, I would. I had not ever in my lifetime seen a real person, in real handcuffs and a striped jumpsuit. Growing up in Bath Township when you saw the people in those outfits on the side of the road picking up trash, my Mom would say, "don't stare at them, they might remember you". What I was staring at across the room was my own child...staring back at me. The look on her face was screaming, Mom help me! Mackenzie was terrified and I knew it. She had gotten into something way over her head, and this time I could not get her out of it. She was blowing on her hands that were handcuffed tightly together. She was fighting back tears. She looked as if she had been on a weekend roll of drugs and alcohol in that she was pale with black eyes. I wanted to raise my hand and tell them I would take her home and "take care of this" because people like us do not belong in that room. Nobody cared who I was.

October 30, 2017

Today is day 47 since I have seen Mackenzie. I'm sure it doesn't seem like a significant number to other people, but when you have a child incarcerated you think differently. I have finally received confirmation that this Wednesday, November 1st, I get to visit Mackenzie. I will be taking Isiah and my Mom. I am very anxious and an unsettled feeling the past few days just not knowing the state of mind Mackenzie will be in.

December 27, 2017

It's been three days since I had a visit with Mackenzie. It was our "new tradition" of going to visit her on Christmas Eve. I hate going there. I hate leaving her behind. If they would tell me I could spend the night with her I would gladly sleep on a steel slab or a concrete floor just to have time with her. I have not spent more than three hours with my own child except once, since 2014. That gave me nightmares and happiness all at the same time. She was doing well.

January 9, 2018

A new year. This year will begin year number five of Mackenzie's incarceration. It seems like she left yesterday. I am not as sad as I was in the past. I was able to actually stomach having "fun" about three times in the past year. In previous years I was not able to do that due to the amount of guilt that consumed my body when I would try to have fun and still know where my sweet Mackenzie is living. When Gracie, Isiah and I went for our fourth annual Christmas Eve visit, we were able to laugh and play games as if we were at home spending a normal holiday together. I thought that this was huge in that we have overcome the obstacles of having our loved one away from us. When we were getting ready to leave and the officer made that horrible statement of "Ladies and Gentleman this visitation session is now over, please say your goodbyes" I was still keeping it together. Then I hugged my sweet girl and kissed her warm cheeks. She was holding back tears and emotion like the robot she has become to survive in the battlefield she lives in. She has no power over me.... I'm her Mama. I told her I loved her so much and I was proud of her for being strong and then I tried to choke out the words "Merry Christmas" but the last few syllables I couldn't get out. It was Christmas Eve! This is not fair, why do I have to leave my little girl in that place again? Then Gracie Jo hugged her sister followed by Isiah. He went back for seconds and thirds. He did not want to leave his Mommy. I tried to just go through the motion without consuming what was happening. It's my defense mechanism. Isiah started to cry. Instantly I brought up "Santa" to snap him out of it while making eye contact with Mack, so she knew what I was trying to do. All I noticed was the shattered eye socket she had told me about that had been healing. He didn't care. You see all the imaginary people in the world and all the presents in the universe does not matter when you want your Mom. This six-year-old little boy just wanted his Mommy for Christmas, and for the fourth year in a row, I had to be the devil. I have to follow the rules that I do not agree with and follow the "terms" of a sentence I do not agree with and follow the laws that are picked and selected for certain people that I do NOT agree with. I had to take this little boy away from his Mommy on Christmas Eve......again. Isiah was crying and I hugged him as I guided him to the steel door we had to exit through. He looks up at me and asks, "Who is my Mommy gonna spend Christmas with?" I was speechless and my heart just re-broke. Do not look back at her I thought to myself, I did not want it to be any harder on her if she saw Isiah's or my face. I was now going to slip into the darkness I have been in since she went away in 2014. I am powerless in my situation. I do not like not having control over my own situation, it makes me angry.

Mackenzie put me in this situation, and her little boy, and her baby sister....should we be angry at her? I cannot look in her eyes and be angry at her, she made a mistake. She put herself in that situation by surrounding herself with the wrong people, but this? I know my child, she never in a million years imagined this. It was her first offense, it is unheard of and it is cruel and unusual punishment but it is written and signed and it is now going to be one-third of her life. It is also going to one-third of her little boy's life and this she did not even think about when she bought some drugs off a few dealers when she was 19. I still to this day have not answered Isiah's question. Our drive home was a quiet one. Everyone in the car was trying to handle their own emotions. We got home and I put on my pajamas and went upstairs to my bed, my safe place. I needed to just lay in silence, no television, no music, I was going to be lucky to stare at a white wall at that point. The kids were exhausted too. We were supposed to go over to a family party which sounded fun the days before. There would be food and family and drinks and laughter and fun.

The question Isiah kept asking me while leaving Mackenzie kept repeating over and over in my mind. Fun was out of the question, laughter and gifts were too. I suppose it could be a temporary fix, but I knew what was going through this six-year old's mind and I thought we better just stay in our safe zone. We ordered a pizza and went to bed early. I would be fine then I would sob and concentrate on "just breathing" for the rest of the night. I become numb to joy and happiness for a while after I leave her there. Sometimes looking forward to the end of a day and the start of a new one is all you have to stay sane. This was one of those days. Those feelings were back, making the vomit in my stomach. I only at this point was thinking of what Mackenzie was eating for Christmas dinner, if she would be getting gifts or sharing laughter with family and friends? I know my answer to well and this is the reason the holidays are brutal for a parent when you are FORCED to be away from your child. It will never be better until she is home for good. I am becoming more and more unable to tolerate people who complain about material things, or who brag about "what" their children have. I get furious and it is my own demons that let it consume my brain. I want to yell at them. I want to say to the little-spoiled brat kids, "what if you had to spend Christmas away from both your parents and not know when the next time you would talk to them again?". Just one time, once, walk in our shoes on Christmas Eve......I guarantee on their next holiday their attitude would be different.

My first meeting with Mack's defense team is approaching. I have hope. One thing I am positive of is that the hiring of these attorneys has saved my child's life....and mine. The past three months I do not have to worry about her taking her own life or getting the "call" I have feared in the past. That in itself is all the Christmas gift I need.

Year Five

Police vs Attorneys

From: Mackenzie Basham
Date: 1/22/2018
To: Judy Frisby

Isiah-

we had a great visit today, and I wish it would have never
ended, we always have good visits though but as you've
gotten older I feel like you can read my mind or think the
same as I do maybe because your just like me, or actually
a part of me but you always come back for one last hug
and kiss and even though I wish I could hug and kiss you
all the time that one more you give me helps me get
through until next time... you're getting older and I love how
close we are and how strong our bond is even when the
distance between us is ALMOST unbearable, the only thing
in this whole world that makes me able to bear this pain in
my heart is your love and the fact that one day our life
won't be like this no more, we won't be separated and we
won't have to wait for another hug or kiss , ... I'm always
with you, don't ever think I've given up trying to get back to
you, I've felt a lot of pain in my life, physically and
emotionally but it's nothing compared to the hurt I feel
when I'm away from you.... your my motivation when I
wake up every morning I know God is telling me I'm one
day closer to being home with you... when I can't sleep, I
lay my pillow on my chest and pretend it's you laying there
sleeping like you use to.... I know it hurts, and it makes you
sad, just hold on a little longer I'll make up for this if it takes
my whole life... all I want is to spend every day with you... I
love you more than steak . can't wait to see you again,
always and forever - momma

January 22, 2018

I'm sitting alone in my bedroom with hot coffee and Sia blaring
on my iTunes thinking about Mackenzie. I had a visit with her
yesterday. I feel so bad for her; she doesn't deserve this. I'm
sure if you talk to the victims of the crimes, they will say
different. I am a mother, my heart hurts for my child. I still sit and
wonder if this is really my life, is this real life right now?
The highway lights and the car rides are killing me. Why would
driving, sitting, then driving again make me exhausted? We had
our big meeting with the attorney last week. It was
overwhelming. I sit and try to process sections of what he said.
He spoke in legal terms and what he said scared me all over
again.... this is why people back down, this is why people just
stop. I was sad after the long drive home. Mackenzie emailed
her Grandma while I was driving us back home and she was
crying and very emotional. Her Grandma started to cry, and I
was there with words to inject hope and sunshine to everyone. I
did not break because I had to be the strong one. I was in front
of people. I thought about the job we had to do, get her home
before her baby turns 18.

My goal is this scenario: The day is here; Mackenzie is being
released from the past that haunts her. She is free, completely
free and her mind is cleansed. Her son is waiting is waiting with
open arms for her to be the mom he has dreamed about all
these years. She gets to be his room mother for the holiday
parties, and she gets to be the voice he hears cheering him on
at his ball games. She is the one that will hold the water bottle
on the sidelines when he needs it. He still needs her because he
still has the innocence of a child. He is not angry because of the
time she has missed. I am once again in the role I am supposed
to be in, which is a grandparent.

My worst-case scenario: Mackenzie serves her time unfairly
given to her. Mackenzie is a 34-year-old woman when released
and she comes home to an 18-year-old Isiah. He is a

man, he is "raised". He loves her but he no longer "needs"
his mommy like that of a child. He is angry at her for never
being there. He resents all those highway lights and drives
and his Mommy in the blue shirt seated in the chair across
from us.
He is embarrassed by the tattoos and the girlfriend she
has and he looks to me and Ritchie as the "only parents
he has ever had". He becomes a statistic. He feels
misunderstood. He gives up and thinks if his parents did
it why can't he. He numbs the pain the same way she
did. I lose this child to the demons that I lost his mother to
at that very age.

I wish I could pick up the phone and call her today. I take
for granted talking to my other kids daily. It is something
you don't think about until you can't. She looks scary to me.
I took her cousin with me on the visit to lift her spirits. Her
cousin said," I'm glad Mackenzie is my family, otherwise I
would be terrified of her". We laughed at that in the prison,
but when alone I know she is tired of being that person.
You can never let your guard down, no weakness. When I
got home from the meeting last week, I had no words. I
couldn't even write what I felt because I didn't know. Our
family has sacrificed so much already.... now a trial? The
attention is horrible. It's not like when I waited up for the 11
o'clock news to see Mackenzie on the sports highlights,
these news clips I dread. The sick feeling in my stomach
seeing it shared hundreds of times on social media, the
comments cutting her down and her "parents". The weight I
feel being the one who raised her and the anger I feel for
the father who didn't. Putting up that protective shield of
armor over Gracie, and Isiah because they cannot handle
the criticism like the older 2 kids. The fake people that will
suddenly give a crap. Feeling the stares whether they are
really there or not. All this will come back like it did in 2014.
At the end of the day, I will cry because this is what I see in
the news....my little girl with a dimple and infectious laugh

and smile. That ornery sweet version of Isiah that everyone loves in him. I will see inside the terrifying person that is tattooed and stern and tough and hard as hell. I see that little girl who fell on the street running to catch the school bus and came back crying for her mommy to make it all go away. I wish I could make it all go away. I wish I could take away her pain, her scars, and broken bones from being beat in prison like that scrape on her little knee when she was little. I know this is how life goes, you can't go back but my God I would do anything to hear my children's laughter again, all together, in the same room, at the same time. That is something I never realized I would cherish at 45. My little brown bear tears if his Mommy doesn't get to come home may just kill me. I keep saying "soon" to him when he asks. He doesn't even know that IF she does come home, people will never allow her to change. She will be labeled, and noticed, and stared at if we stay here. We often talk about going to a new place where nobody knows Mackenzie's story.... a fresh new start her and Isiah could have. The thing that breaks my heart is that I can't go with them and leave who I love here, and I can't stay here and let who I love move away from me. This is my real life, and no matter what, I am not going to win in whatever comes out of the trial. I am the mother of the defendant.

February 14, 2018

I talked to Mackenzie today, she wanted to wish her special Valentine a great big "Happy Valentine's Day" ...and it wasn't me. We were able to pay ten dollars and plan a video visit which was yesterday. Isiah had surgery Monday morning at 9:00 where they removed his tonsils and adenoids. Mackenzie was as nervous as a long-tailed cat in a room full of rockers as my Grandpa used to say. His surgery went fine and hopefully, he can breathe better at night and stop getting sick all the time. I think Mack forgets that this is not my first rodeo, she has stood in the "phone lines" all day to call me three times a day to check

and see how her baby is. I told her, I got this!
She thanks me every phone call for taking such good care of her baby, but this is literally killing her not being here. She told me she has had insomnia so they "medicated" her and the high doses of the anti-psychotic medicine gives her crippling migraines. This morning she told me she tried to just cry herself to sleep because she cannot handle the medication, but she finally slept at 5:00 am. Her worries are playing on her mind 24/7. The funny thing is that I worry about my child just like she does hers. I have not ever missed a visit since 2014, but I missed February 2018 because of Isiah's surgery. I could have taken him but I followed Dr's orders and kept him home to heal. I know she is aching to hold her little boy, but I had to make the decision that the germs and nasty-ness of that place were not what a child healing from surgery needed to be subject too. We are going soon though; I miss Mackenzie as much as she misses Isiah!

March 5, 2018

I haven't seen Mackenzie since January. I had to miss my first month of visiting her since 2014 because of Isiah's surgery.
Ritchie and I are finally able to visit her this past Saturday. I'm worried about Mackenzie. I feel like she is becoming less like my daughter and more like a prisoner. She is broken and wounded from this. I know a lot of people survive this every day, but it does not convince me that she will. I hate when she calls and I hear that tone in her voice.... the tone that there is an empty hollow soul on the other end of the line. We have hope and that's what I prayed for except now I'm being selfish. I want her home. I am angry that she is still in there. She literally could have killed someone in our town, and she would almost have her debt to society all paid up. Enough is enough. I just read that yet another murderer got his charge dropped to involuntary manslaughter and received only 8 years

because they dropped the murder charge in the plea deal. This is what breaks my heart...Mackenzie doesn't even know how unfair she was treated. She has beaten down so small for what mistakes she made. I see a young child sometimes in her demeanor as if she is stuck in the time out chair and just getting comfortable living there which haunts me. She has excepted being treated like an animal, she has no self-pride, she is stripped of all dignity and no human being should ever be ok with the living conditions in that specific prison. I am worried about her health. I am not a medical doctor but it doesn't take a brain surgeon to notice that they keep the inmates drugged to keep them quiet and passive. Mackenzie is forced to take medication or she will suffer the consequences. The ironic thing is that she suffers consequences anyway from the "side effects". Mackenzie was diagnosed as bi-polar and also with severe manic depression......at the age of 17. Now I am not a doctor, but I do not know why she is given injections of the anti-psychotic drug "Haldol". It works by changing the actions of chemicals in your brain. I research everything they pollute my child with.

This drug is also used to CONTROL motor skills and speech tics in people with Tourette's syndrome, which Mackenzie does not have. They also have made her take "Lithium" which is a drug that affects the flow of sodium through nerve and muscle cells in the body. Sodium affects excitation or mania. Lithium is used to treat the manic episodes of bipolar disorder, but some doses can be lethal! The physician at the prison Mackenzie is in was fired for stealing the inmate's medicine....so when MRSA was raging through the prison there was no freaking doctor? Our oldest called the health department in that county and reported it. Mackenzie became very sick last September and kept running fevers etc. Our family has to put money on her books so she can pay to see the doctor, she did and was told she had MRSA in her fingers from using the telephone. She was given antibiotics, but her body rejected them. Mackenzie went through 3 months of antibiotics until it seemed she was clear of the super virus. I visit my daughter every month and get a picture to go with the prison diaries I write. I look at the October visits through last Saturday and it is proof that Mackenzie's health is being jeopardized by whatever medication they are shoving down her throat. They have diagnosed her with so many mental illnesses that it contradicts the very reason she is in there in the first place. Which is it? Is she mentally disturbed from prison or was she mentally disturbed before? The arresting officers said she did not have a drug problem(which she did), they said she had no mental illness(which she did)....so they told the judge she calculated hiding the stolen goods and sold them because she is just a serial criminal. Ok, then why the minute they did a mental exam on Mackenzie in prison, did they put her in mental health and immediately treated her for severe bipolar 1 disorder? It's one or the other. An arrest was NEEDED to put the community at ease, and they made Mackenzie into a poster child of the criminal they needed.

They needed a young punk of a kid that was making a living out of burglarizing people's homes and slipping into the mold of what everyone says about our "lazy youth" who do not know how to work and just live off the government. These people exist probably, but they tagged the wrong person. They made her out to be something she was not and intimidated her into just saying she was everything they NEEDED her to be to make them look like tough guys....badasses who deserve that metal they wear on their sleeve.

April 6, 2018

Yesterday I went to Columbus to be a voice for Mackenzie. I met with her legal team. I had my normal nervous stomach vomit in the morning when I got up. My sister went and drove me to give her recorded statements too, as well as Mackenzie's Uncle from her Dad's side. I felt

supported but out of my element and like I was a small
child trying to play grown up at some point. As the lead
attorney spoke there I sat in his big leather chair, in his
fancy office with beautiful people walking about and I
started to zone out. I was staring at him listening, but as he
talked over the case I became overwhelmed to the point I
could not find words to come out of my mouth that would
make any sense. I only kept thinking, "Is this real life right
now"? Am I really here discussing my child's life? I want to
start over when she was about 10, I'll just know what to
look for and focus on Mackenzie's actions more. Here are
five adults talking about Mackenzie Basham like she is just
someone on the pieces of papers on the desk. I didn't have
any emotion; I was separated from being her mother at that
moment. I was a witness. I gave my statement but not my
opinion. My brain was so full of information that I was
physically nauseated when I got back to my car in Lima. I
am still trying to process yesterday and our plan for the
upcoming months.

When I got home I felt so much better in my comfort zone, and
seeing the kid's faces snapped me directly back to reality.... then
the phone rang. It was Dayton Correctional Institution's number
which meant Mackenzie was calling to hear some "good news". I
froze a second because I was trying to hurry up and fix myself, I
knew that the very first tone in my voice was going to determine
how Mackenzie interpreted what the lawyers are saying. I cannot
crush her hope no matter what they say. It is the thing that is
keeping her tired body and broken soul surviving 24 hours a day,
7 days a week in prison. She has wanted to give up, and I don't
blame her. I have already forgiven her if God forbid she would
take her own life. She is right smack dab in the center of how
she phrased it..." the devil's playground". At 19 Mackenzie was
so impressionable, and to be thrown into a different world at that
age is inconceivable. She has learned things in prison that I fear
cannot be reversed. I know for a fact that she will forever appear
visibly to the outside world as a prisoner. All you have to do is

read her skin, literally. I no longer have my little girl. It is different than when people say they grow up so fast, this is not that. When I say I no longer have her I mean she has been robbed of all innocence, raped of all morals and stripped of all self-worth. I feel so sorry for her when I talk to her on the phone. I hear the animals in the background screaming and fighting as I try to focus on my daughter and the desperate tone in her voice. She is trying and that is why I feel sorry for her. It seems to not matter when you are in prison. They are all classified together as criminals. There is rapists, murderers, child molesters, drug addicts, thieves, raging psychopaths, arsonists, and sadly people who are in there for selling stolen property. Mackenzie should not be in max security, it haunts me every hour of every day. They want everyone to forget about her, but they have underestimated this mother! I ask her what all the screaming in the background is about just to fill the awkward silence in our conversation. Mackenzie tells me that this "nasty bitch" is sobbing and crying and limping around because she and her girlfriend got in a fight and broke up.

Mackenzie then told me that the woman crying over her girlfriend was doing years for killing her OWN baby......

I didn't even know what to say to her. Mackenzie said, "Mom....you gotta get me out of here. These people are sick.

This woman can kill her own child and never cry about that but has a break-up and act like a fool....These women make me sick, I gotta get home, I can't be in here anymore".

What do you say to your child after they say that? Can I google the answer? Can a pastor help me ease my child's pain or a desperate plea for safety....no? My hands felt tied down to the rocking chair I was sitting in. I wanted to put

down the phone and take off running out of my house. I
wanted to run and not stop; nothing would stop me
because my mind would overpower my body and I could
run as fast as I could to exit 51 and run right down
Nicholas Road until it dead ends. I wanted to climb over
those barbed wire fences and feel the pain of them cutting
me, I wanted to see my own blood and not care about the
pain. I wanted to run right past the officers who got in my
way, they couldn't catch me. I wanted to run into that
phone room near the cages the animals live in and yell out
"Mackenzie Lee where are you.....Mama's here......I'm here
sis, and nobody is going to hurt you...your safe, I'm here
now."

All I could say was..." I know honey and I'm doing everything I
can, you just have to hang on and stay positive. You have to trust
me that I'm doing everything I can". The automated
message came across the phone line that we had 60 seconds
left of our phone call. Mackenzie said, "Mom I love you". I told
her I loved her more than chocolate then the phone shut off.
How do you function after that? I wish some smart person would
educate me how to do this because I'm just an average
everyday mother, Nana, and hairdresser and this is killing me.
Who has the answer to this? Usually, I can solve problems, or
take care of things that need to be done. I do put things off that I
don't really want to do, but I get them done when the time is
up.... but this? How can I help my daughter? The answer is I
can't. I am doing everything I can and it's just not enough. When
Gracie goes to Walmart at night I worry about weird people
being in there or in the parking lot....how am I supposed to have
peace in my mind and heart when my other child is sleeping in a
cell with a woman who is capable of killing her own child? I pray
for her safety. I pray for her mind to stay well and sane. I pray
she won't give up because I will not give up. I pray she doesn't
end her own life or that another inmate doesn't end her life
before I can hug my child in the free world. I miss my
Mackenzie. I have to see her soon when I get to touch her and

get that ONE hug and ONE kiss at the beginning of the visit it is like a shot of steroid that makes my entire body feel better for a while. It's like a drug. I am having more and more trouble getting through days, weeks, months, years without that drug. She has just served year four and I pray to God I get her home before year five is served because she is getting further and further away from me while being held in that tiny space, like in a bad dream.

May 19, 2018

It has been almost a week since our Mother's Day visit with Mackenzie. I have spoken of it very little but still feel the visit six days later. It takes days to comprehend the visits for me, and then longer to package them up to set aside and walk away from them. Immediately after leaving my child in that horrible place I have to snap back to MY reality of being a Mom, Nana, and wife. I have to go to work and converse with people as though I am not completely traumatized by our visits each month. I do it well. My pain builds up until it starts to physically cripple me. I remain quite of my emotions until I can write them down so hopefully, they will go away......until the next month. I feel like I have a funeral viewing of someone I love so much every-single-month. I grieve after every visit. I cry at night when I look at the moon for some reason. I try to mentally picture her in front of me, and I talk to her. We are functioning ok, but there is so much "behind the scenes" that the so-called curtain hides. The nightmares I have been having seem real, and they actually could be. I have never in my life had so many thoughts inside my head on a daily basis. My daughter is not the same child that left on May 1st, 2014. My daughter is not the same child from middle school before the drugs either. She is far better....and far worse. The things that she has been through pierce through my veins when I think of them. Mackenzie and I had a good discussion on Mother's Day, as well as Gracie Jo.

Mackenzie is still stuck in time as our world on the outside has kept ticking on. The actual shock of that when she is able to live in the free world is what I fear the most. She was very emotional on Mother's Day. She wants time to stop for us as well. Her baby boy is now a four-foot young boy. He is mature in his speaking. He is not a baby and does not want to be. This is killing her. He has his own personality. He is his own person. I watched as Mackenzie and Isiah talked to each other in that prison visitation room. I felt what each one of them was feeling. I raised her, and she is broken. She is sad and wants her baby to stay little like all of us Mommy's do. I also raise him. He loves life and only sees rainbows and sunshine and can't wait for what the next day brings. On the inside Mackenzie is dark, and Isiah is light. She knows this and it is killing her just as much as her being incarcerated is killing me. What a lesson we are learning. We are being educated in life.

While sitting in that visitation room one of us had brought up Mackenzie getting married and having more kids when she was finally free. Mackenzie began to get quiet and I could tell that something was weighing on her mind. After some small talk, she said to Gracie and I that she wasn't planning on talking about this right now. I had to ask.... but I already knew. I have known for years. Mackenzie told us that she needed us to know that whenever she does get her freedom, she will never be with a man again. There it was! I had not looked forward to this conversation yet I knew this was therapeutic for her. Her lip began to quiver and tears began to roll down her face. I hate this. As a mother, I wanted to just say, "oh don't get upset, whatever it is just don't worry about it". I knew she needed to talk about this and that it had been something she had been battling for years. Mackenzie told us through the shaky voice and tears that after being in prison she hates men. The things that have happened to her and the things she has seen done by the male officers in that hell hole have hardened her. Now I do not think that the entire reason she cannot ever love a man in a spousal way is due only the prison system, but it sure tops the chart. Why does most woman come out of prison homosexual? Well, I have not ever wanted to think of any of my children having sexual relationships of any kind, but I have to be honest with myself. Let's say that Mackenzie has to spend her entire bullshit sentence incarcerated, she will be 35 years old when set free. I do not expect her to not have any desires or feelings of love for 14 years just because she was caught selling stolen property when she was 19. Mack said that for the first time in her life she was finally comfortable in her own skin while being sober. She always felt judged by boys in school, she was always called fat, or lesbo all because she wasn't tiny and petite, or good with a curling iron or makeup. I always thought that she got pregnant on purpose at 16 by a kid she met on MySpace just to get attention from her biological father or to put the "Mackenzie's a lesbian" rumors to rest. She was always a tomboy. Always athletic, and always stereotyped gay. She was never prissy, never played with Barbie dolls, always outstanding at sports and that is the stereotype to a T. It breaks my heart to think that she could have felt like she was different or that something was wrong with her, or that she could not talk to her own mother until she was 24 years old and sitting in a prison visitation room. I was brought up that if you were gay, you were going to hell. I was also brought up that it was wrong to marry, or be in love, or have sex with a person of a different color. I was also raised to think that divorce was wrong. So basically what I was taught was that I had to marry a white man and no matter what he did.... just stay married and conservative and I would go to heaven.

That's probably how my parents were raised also. I did not raise my kids any particular way, I took them to church, taught them in Sunday school and taught them to believe in

Jesus. I guess I just wanted them to be nice to people and for them to respect their elders.... that is important to me.

My children are nice, and they respect their elders, so I guess I win. I never talked about what color or gender or social class the person they fall in love with, I guess I just wanted them to be happy. Mackenzie is finally happy with herself and that is the only feeling of freedom she is going to experience for years. I am happy for her, and if she has found love in a female inside those prison walls, I am just happy that maybe, just maybe it can get her through the days without giving up or giving in to the demons. So many thoughts were running through my head at this point in our conversation. I thought back to that Wednesday in 2013 when I was getting ready to open my new hair salon and I got a call on my cell phone from our doctor. I was told that Mackenzie was being admitted into the hospital because she had taken an entire bottle of pills. A suicide attempt. They would be putting her on the psychiatric floor and she would not have any contact for at least 3 or 4 days.

Honestly, I was pissed off at her. I thought she was just mad because I had been working so hard on my shop that I wasn't paying that much attention to her. I feel like shit just writing that. She had been living with her Grandparents at the time so I assume it happened there. I asked the doctor if it wasn't just the drugs talking because I knew her drug use was getting out of control, I just covered it up to make a pretty picture.

Our doctor for 20 some years told me that she tried to take her own life and did not want to live and that she has serious mental problems that she definitely needed to be in the psychiatric ward to be evaluated. I never told my parents because I thought this was just another phase of Mackenzie's. What if I would have taken this seriously? Could I have helped her get treated and maybe things would have ended up different? I beat myself up over this often, yet it taught me a good lesson with my other kids. Mackenzie has taught me so much, she still does in 2018. The third hour came and the room begins to actually feel like a funeral home. This is when they announce those words we all hate to hear. "Ladies and Gentlemen please say your goodbyes this visitation is now over". Now I'm not feeling sorry for myself, but I don't know many people who have to witness what I witness month after month, year after year on Mother's Day in a woman's prison. The children's caregivers, like myself, have to make these children leave their Mommy's when they don't want to......on freakin Mother's Day. It is heart-wrenching to witness and even more paralyzing when it is your flesh and blood. Then you have to watch these women. The women are criminals, yet they are still human beings, they are Mothers. Some have done horrific things; most have just made some mistakes. I have made mistakes; nobody has ever taken my children from me on Mother's Day after three hours then escorted me to sit the rest of my celebrated holiday in a cage left to think about it. My heart feels for these women. They are Mothers exactly like me. The children are innocent victims. The entire situation is horrible. I cannot put it into words because I hate it, yet I go every single year. I had a wonderful day that day to start out. My son and his girlfriend took me, Gracie and Isiah to breakfast at my favorite place. I'm proud of my son, he has a loving heart. He is compared to his sister on the daily and he fights that battle no one else can imagine.... they can't even come close.

After breakfast, the oldest bought us tickets to my granddaughter's dance recital. It was the absolute cutest thing I have ever seen. I was very emotional and felt so much love when that little girl got up on stage. The civic center was full of beautiful little girls all dressed up looking like they were tiny princesses. It was also full of Mother's.

Mother's that were staring up on that stage with the proudest of eyes and hearts. The tiny dancers felt love and admiration as the crowd cheered and each of their very own Mommy's was so proud of them. I love all the self-confidence that day will give all those beautiful children when they grow up.

Then I looked beside me.

There was little Isiah. He had his head on Amanda's shoulder. He was missing his Mommy. He needed to feel the love from his mom, but he can't. I try to do everything I can so he will have that self-confidence when he grows up but I cannot stop him from feeling this emptiness no matter what I do. We left the recital to head to Dayton Correctional Institution. This was our last leg of our Mother's Day tour. Isiah was so excited to see his Mommy. I dreaded the long drive down, the three hours of sitting in a hard chair, and the hell of leaving her in there. Isiah always goes and writes on the toy chalkboard they have for kids there. He always comes back with chalk on his hands and puts a handprint on his Mommy's pant leg of her state uniform. She used to tell him "NO" in fear of getting in trouble for his prints on her, but the last few visits she wants it left there. Mackenzie actually cut us short by standing up and saying she had to get to the infirmary or something to get her nightly meds and she didn't want to wait in the long line. I said, "Oh ok do you want us to leave?" as we stood up following orders early. She said yes and we had our goodbyes. Isiah instantly became sad. I felt nothing as my body becomes numb and I am only able to focus on getting him out of there without screaming or getting removed by the guards. If the guards ever yelled at us as I am dragging him off his mommy, I'm afraid of what would happen. Mackenzie would lose her shit. She would go to the "Hole" for the rest of her time spent because her son is the only thing she cares about in this life. Nothing else matters. This is the "far worse" I was writing about earlier. I am the end of the visit mediator. I know my job. I hate that job more than life itself. I tried to cheer up the kids by pulling over for some pizza and ice cream. Mackenzie called while we were there. I let Isiah answer and he had her on speaker. Mackenzie was crying. She said she had to go because she was about to start sobbing. She didn't want us to leave. She tried to be hard and not feel the emotion. It came pouring out as she choked the words "I love you so much" out to her little sister and baby boy. Gracie felt it as the water came from her, that is when Isiah asked:" Mommy are you crying?". Gracie yelled at him for asking that, I yelled at Gracie for yelling at him, and Isiah yells out loud..." Did I make her cry? Is it my fault my mommy is crying?". The phone hung up because of an apparent time limit. That's awesome. I got up and just hugged Zay as tight as I could, Gracie cried and we looked like the textbook definition of dysfunctional right there at Casano's on that Sunday night Mother's Day 2018.

The drive home was normal, our normal. As I watched the red taillights on the highway in the quite, I thought about my little Mackenzie. The Mackenzie that brought me home the homemade Mother's Day card from kindergarten that said she loved her mom because I was beautiful and always was nice to her by giving her food. After everyone was in bed for the night I went into the garage in my nightgown and dug through some boxes. I found the potholders. The potholder that has the poem on one side and the tiny hand-painted hand print on the other side. One says Mackenzie and the other says, Cole. I put my hand on those tiny handprints and sobbed. Where did the time go? Where are my babies? As I stood outside looking up at the moon with tears raging down my face, I felt so very close to Mackenzie. I know for a fact that she was looking at that same moon with those same tears thinking of her babies tiny handprints. I have survived another Mother's Day.

May 29, 2018

I emailed Mackenzie's attorney. I am nervous and excited about our filing an appeal. I play it over in my mind almost every night. I have not ever been arrested (until 2016) and have always held the utmost respect for our county and city police departments....until about a year after Mack's arrest.

On our first recorded phone calls, I remember Mackenzie telling me that the guys who did the burglaries were "in with" some cop. She also told me her court-appointed attorney was in with the head Sheriff too. I was mad at her. She had done something wrong, she was abusing drugs, she had put her baby on the back burner.... she did not get the benefit of the doubt from me! I told her this was real life and not "Law and Order". She was a cocky, 19-year-old, trying to fit in with some thugs, girl who was running her mouth. Here is the problem, she still has the same story.

Now she is over 4 years sober and a matured 24 old woman with the same exact story as May 1st, 2014. I believe her. She has told me many things in the past 4 years. She has confessed many mother/daughter confessions as far as things she did growing up that I did not know about. Most are innocent teenage stupidity. The crime in question of receiving stolen property has landed her in prison for 14 years. Currently in our county, if you are a black man, you can walk into a bar with a gun tucked under your belt and draw that gun shooting another human being or two and do LESS than EIGHT years in prison. It happened; it happens a lot here in Allen County. The deals going on between the county prosecutor's office and the county police department are something of that straight out of a Hollywood movie.

Murders get deals for way less time than Mackenzie and almost 90% of them have a prior criminal record.

Mackenzie had no criminal record. This should be looked at. There is so much that needs to come out in a courtroom concerning Mackenzie's case. We should have gone to trial...let a jury of her peers listen to the facts, the truth and decide if she deserves 14 years in prison. From the very moment, we went with the court-appointed attorney Mackenzie was doomed. I wish I had believed her when she told me things, but it is the classic "boy who cried wolf" story. Mackenzie said that her attorney was "buddies" with the then head county Sheriff. I am going to try to journal as much as I can of specifics I remember throughout our legal journey so little Isiah will be able to read my prison diaries when he is a man and knows that his Mommy is not the monster they have made her out to be. He is going to have questions, and I want him to know what I know to be true coming from his Nana...someone he trusts.

June 3, 2018

Mackenzie has been on my mind all day today. I usually can feel it when she is battling something. It may be another inmate, or it may be her own demons but I know. It is a sick feeling in my stomach. It is an unsettled nerve in my brain and it takes over my entire body. Today I slept until around 3:00 pm. I wasn't up late and have not done anything out of the ordinary.... this worry has overcome me. I have a conference call with Mackenzie's attorney tomorrow at noon. His secretary emailed me last week to set it up. I hope it is some positive news on her case. I think when I get consumed with worry my body just shuts down and I am unable to function. I am anxiously awaiting the news coming from this conference call. Her legal team has filed with Allen County and they now know that we as Mackenzie's family are serious about getting her a shorter sentence. I cannot imagine how I am going to handle it if Mackenzie would get an appeal, we are so much praying for. I just have a conference call and I am a nervous wreck.

Anytime I have to talk to an attorney, a prosecutor, a judge, or a cop concerning Mackenzie's case I completely have a panic attack. It stems from being traumatized that horrible day in August 2014. the day I sat in a full courtroom and heard the chains that shackled my little girl clank against her hands and feet as she was escorted into the courtroom like she was a serial murderer. I spoke that day, but I have no recollection of what I even said. I was crying and I was begging the judge to not send her away....I watched my daughter sob and apologize to the victims and to our family. She was such a child; I believe all the way down to my soul that she did not mean to hurt anyone by selling the stolen stuff. She needed money, for what I had no idea. Drugs I'm sure. She was a single mother. Isiah's biological father was arrested at school the day that we brought Isiah home from the hospital. He went to DYS which is a prison for juveniles until Isiah was almost a year old. Then when Isiah was 2 his Mommy went away to prison. Until the day that I die, I will try to smother this little boy with love and attention to make up for what his parents have done to him. He will never understand it all. His parents were 17 when he was born, but that does not give them an excuse. I blame my daughter, but I have forgiven her for leaving him. I still blame his father. He is not in prison and has not seen Isiah since 2017, nor has any of his family. He was there when Isiah was born....and has not been since. My thoughts are these... just because you tattoo your child's name on your hand doesn't make you a father. I wish Isiah didn't have his last name. I often wonder if we should change it. Some think it's not my choice, I beg to differ.

June 17, 2018

Today is Father's Day....today is also Mackenzie's birthday. She is now 24 years old. I went to visit her yesterday and took my mom and Isiah. We had a good visit. My mom was so happy to get to hug and kiss her granddaughter. Mackenzie has always cherished my parents as well as her other grandparents. She has put all four of them through hell, yet she values her grandparent's opinion of her more than anyone else on this planet. Maybe she feels she has to make up for letting them down? I think her battles are what make her unique, or very original in who she is in this world. On my way to pick up my mother up before the visit, I had felt very small. I knew I had to put on my costume on before my mom got in the car. The costume of a strong woman, who is determined and brave, and knows what she is doing that has a plan. Isiah was in the back with headphones on in the world of Netflix. I thought about so many things. I felt like I was crumbling. I literally imagine a rock, a large rock in the shape of my body. Every visit, every drive down the highway, every exit 51 sign, I crack a little bit more. I feel pieces of my strength crumble. I am not the whole person I used to be. My head felt like it was going to explode. My thoughts were racing around and scrambling in my head. I started singing the song I sang to all of my babies when it was just me and them and they were tiny and I was the giant rock they depended on and looked up to...."you are my sunshine, my only sunshine, you make me happy when skies are gray. You'll never know dear; how much I love you...please don't take my sunshine away. The other night dear, as I lay sleeping, I dreamed I held you in my arms. When I awoke dear, I could not find you...so I hung my head and cried...". I was sobbing like the raindrops on my windshield. I had to dry it up because Elva would soon be in the car. I had to reach deep to straighten up this time on Mackenzie's birthday. I did it, just like I always do.

My sympathy goes out to every single mother and father that have to visit their own child in a prison on their birthday and then.... leave them behind. We are a small group compared to numbers of the human race, a group that is looked down upon by many. A group you have to be a bad ass to be in, and a group that I hate being in. This group has made me different. I am different in so many ways. Ironically, I honestly like the person that I am so much better than before this nightmare started, and that doesn't make sense. I would never wish our ordeal on another person because I just don't have that much hate in my heart. I am more awake to connections between myself and other people. I no longer judge, and I am just fine with feeling small and weak. I was not like that before. I look at a person's heart and not the clothes on their back or the car they drove up in. I put myself in other's shoes often, because the shoes that I am in are horrific at times and I know the feeling of what it feels like to be so alone in this world and in those shit shoes. This is why I like the person I am now. I am a better wife and mother because of Mackenzie being incarcerated. I love those better that deserve my love, and those that don't do not get my artificial acts of love.... because its either real or nothing.

That doesn't make sense, but it is weirdly the truth. As most mother's do I was thinking back to the days when I was holding my sweet little Kiki Lee in our rocking chair when she was first born. I had no clue what the hell I was doing with this baby I was holding. I was 21 and she was like a shiny new doll I had just got for Christmas....except this was real life. I just knew she was going to be a star. MY CHILD as I hear so many people say right before they brag about their own kid was going to change the world and most importantly make me proud. She would be the prettiest, and the best at whatever she did. Fast forward 24 years into the future and I am driving down the highway to a maximum security prison to empty my pockets and go through metal detectors to just get to hug her and feel the warmth of her body so that I can sleep at nights knowing she is alive and well. My star. My star came around the corner looking like a mixed martial arts fighter. She looks like she could snap someone's neck with just the strength in her fingers. Same smile, same dimples, same pretty teeth and most importantly as she put her powerful arms around me she sounded the same exact way as she used to...." Hi, Mom...I've missed you". She is still my child, I am still proud as hell of her just like every one of the other kids of mine. I don't care what they do or where they are currently living, I am their number one fan and that will not change.

We have just survived Mackenzie turning 20, 21, 22, 23, and 24 while being incarcerated. I pray to God she will not turn 25 while still in this nightmare.

June 26, 2018

Mommy/Child Day 2018

Today is Saturday, June 30th, 2018 and I still can't write about the Mommy/Child visit.

July 2, 2018

Today my heart is with my son. It was one year ago he and his buddy went out to celebrate the 4th of July at the lake, and later that night there was a horrific automobile accident that took the life of my son's best friend. He was just 21 years old. My son is just now grieving his best friend....and still grieving his sister who is still alive. I worry about my boy but at least he is free, my worries are not as horrific as they are for Mackenzie. A mother always worries and I know that. My son can overcome this, or at least heal in time, I am afraid that Mackenzie will not.

July 4, 2018

Freedom and Independence are celebrated today. I have had a nauseous feeling in the pit of my stomach for the past few days because of the celebrations on or around this day. How in the hell am I supposed to "celebrate" a day of freedoms when my own flesh and blood has no freedom...no independence? If my child was off at war, or even serving our country, she would be honored from all being absent on July 4th celebrations. If my child was gone from me just because she lived in another town or state she could celebrate herself, but she's not. She is paying a very steep price for her mistake, and others also. My child is in a cage. She has no freedom, no independence. She has to be strip searched before and after she uses the bathroom if out of her cell. How can I partake in this holiday? It makes me ill. Mackenzie should not still be in prison. When I think about those who make up prison sentences, I wonder have they ever had their freedom stripped from them? I wonder if the two crooked cops on her case will endure what my child has? Probably not. I know that one day, just one day of being behind bars and having no freedom would weaken me. It would strip me of my sanity and take me to a place in my mind that only fear and panic exist. This makes me think of Mackenzie. She has been incarcerated for over four years now. That is 1527 days. If Mackenzie has to serve out this terrible sentence, she has 3562 more days until she is FREE. I guess I will be able to assume celebrating holidays in 3562 more days. Isiah and I had our Mommy/Child visit over a week ago. It was great and it was horrible. That little boy was so excited to get up at 5:00am and get his blanket and pillow in the back seat for our road trip to visit his mommy. I remember lots of exciting road trips with my parents as a child, I would be so excited I couldn't sleep the night before. My childhood trips were to see Judy Young in Virginia or go to Myrtle Beach, or Aunt Jean's house in Clearwater, or fishing in Tennessee with Kendra and my parents......Isiah's are to a prison to see his Mommy.

We arrived on time and she called us as we were on the highway heading down. She told us to be careful and be cautious of traffic in the morning like it was my first rodeo. Mackenzie had tried to go to bed early so she could get up early and shower and be ready to be the first one into the gymnasium that morning. She told me that she woke up out of a dead sleep at 11:00 pm the night before and couldn't go back to sleep out of excitement. Mackenzie lied awake all night until 6:00 am when she was allowed to start getting dressed. I can't imagine her excitement. On this day that approximately 30-40 inmates are granted, they get to be "Mothers". They get to get up out of their seat without asking permission like they are in grade school. They can hold their children, and hug them, and kiss them....as many times as they want without being stared at or told: "that's enough". We went through our first set of security the same as our monthly visitations. We were then held in a staircase as guards lined up from that point all the way across the prison yard to the gated area where we were going to enjoy our day with Mackenzie. We were told instructions as they allowed us to be released into the inside in groups of ten people at a time. Isiah was his normal energetic self-asking me questions on the long walk back. We were stared at by all of the other inmates. I felt like a celebrity and like a piece of raw meat that a zookeeper holds over a lion's cage at feeding time. Both scenarios made me take short breathes with my arm around my brown bear until we reached our gated area. We walked right next to the barbed wire, as the guards stood between us and the fences. Isiah stops and says, "Ok, I can't do this". Now Mackenzie has been granted one of these days before in 2016. He was four then and not so observant, I think. I asked him what was wrong kind of with a smile on my face so he knew it was ok to feel overwhelmed. Isiah told me that that was real life barbed wire he knows that because he has seen it on his video games and on YouTube. It is a little scary. It actually is really scary being up that close and seeing the layer after layer of that razor sharp fence to walk right beside it.... imagine being six years old. I assured him that we were not going to get hurt we were just going to see Mama in a different room today.

Isiah is old enough that he figured out a lot of things that day, some gave him nightmares. It is times like this that I question my decision I made in 2014 to take him as much as I was allowed so he would keep the bond with his Mommy strong and would realize on his own why she was gone. I just always thought that he needed to know that his Mom has always loved him no matter what and that she did not abandon him as his father did. If she could be with him every day, she would.

We walked into a line of waiting children and grandchildren as we signed our name and inmate we were spending the day with. The looks on these inmates' face as they get to stand up and wave us over to our table they have prepared warmed my heart. For once, those seven hours, those ladies got to be "Mothers". My daughter was so excited it broke my heart. We hugged and sat down as she and Isiah couldn't keep their hands off each other.... hey for once no hug limits! It came to breakfast time and she was on it getting in line to get her boy a pop tart and box of juice. He was still hungry as he always is hungry, and she went to get him another but was told no. It worried her. Mackenzie asked me if when our visit was over, I could get Isiah something more to eat because he was not going to be satisfied at the portions she was allowed to serve him that day. I assured her that he would be fine, he has plenty stored up, neither one of us was going to starve. They opened up the activities, and he was on the go. I did get a little teared up as she got up out of her seat holding hands with Isiah and they walked out of the gym into the fenced in play area. The smiles on both faces could heal a wound. She was so proud of him as most of the moms were of their children.

Mackenzie was very protective of Isiah in there. I imagine it's because she only gets to see him three hours a month, but it still worries me of when she is in the free world and parenting. When you have lost everything and literally stripped of all trust in the human race, you tend to be over-protective of the things that you do still actually have.

Mackenzie has Isiah. She has nothing of that in material possessions, hasn't touched actual money in over four years, no car, no home, no jewelry, no bank account etc.....Mackenzie has Isiah and thank God she does. It was so much fun as fun can be when it's hot as actual hell in a smelly gym inside a prison stuffed full of people. I would sit and look up at the posts of guards looking down on our every move. It made me feel like an inmate as well.

Mackenzie told me of the meeting they had beforehand with the rules of the day. Always keep your hands where the guards could see them and don't even make them think you are putting something in your pocket or taking something from your families hands or your visit is over. At one point Isiah had a Jolly Rancher he had got at the face painting table and he came up and kind of acted like he was putting it in her pocket and she flipped out. She said firmly for him to not ever touch her pockets or she will be in trouble, Isiah was like...Chill out, what's the big deal? Bless her heart she just didn't want this day what she had looked so forward to be taken from her as everything else has been. They announced for us to say our goodbyes around 2:00. Isiah had been complaining of a headache a few times that day. At goodbye time he has on his Mommy's lap and she was rubbing his head...he was exhausted and he knew what was coming. It is such a dark cloud that comes over us when we have to leave her there. He started to cry that he didn't want to leave her and began to hold onto her pretty tight as I tried to pry him off. The line was getting long of our first security check on our way out and it was pouring down rain. We had to walk all the way up to the front check out in the rain, and we had to hurry up. He was now crying "Mommy I don't feel good; can't I stay with you?" as Mackenzie became visibly upset. She looked up at me as if there was something I could do as she held onto him for dear life. She said that he was sick like the guards gave a shit. I had to become the hard-ass. I hate thinking about it. I had to pull them apart and yell at them. I said," Mackenzie I gotta get him out of here!". She knew but she wanted to keep feeling him clinched with her arms around her just a few more seconds. I pulled him off and didn't look back as we headed up the stairs. At the top of the stairs waiting to get dismissed in our group to exit I looked down over the walls that sat up above the gym, we had just been in. I shouldn't have looked down, but I had to see if she was ok. I saw another inmate that had been at the next table standing beside Mackenzie as if to try to comfort her without contact or looking suspicious.

Mackenzie was sobbing. Her face was red as she fell back into ranks of her prison life. Cleaning up tables and chairs and I watched her try to look tough but fail. She could not do it as many, many of the mothers did. After this, I was very sad but didn't cry until Isiah fell asleep thirty minutes down the highway. I imagined her face as I had to take her baby away from her again...this time harder. I was so glad of that decision I made in 2014 to not let their bond be broken, but it just makes this so much harder. This is why I can't wait for her to be free; they need each other. Nothing else matters if the only thing you want in life is to be with your own child, and you are not allowed. Mackenzie will not be celebrating today, and neither will I.

July 6, 2018

I haven't heard from Mack in over a week. It's Friday night. I guess my Friday night is going to consist of trying to keep my mind off of the fact that I'm not going to be able to function properly until I hear Mackenzie's voice. I usually check with her Grandma to see if she has heard from her. If not, I will then start insomnia. The waking up five to six times a night to walk the floor or go outside to try to connect with her by staring at the moon or stars while I twist my hair and smoke cigarettes. I worry too much about my children and grandchildren I know that. I get that from

my mother. It's from a bloodline of having unconditional
love for your child. My worries for Mackenzie are more
severe than my worries for mine who are in the free world.
I do not have to worry about her drinking and driving, or
smoking pot, or getting in an automobile accident, or
someone breaking her heart at a party or nightclub. My
worries for Mackenzie are is she suffering? Is she hungry?
Is she in pain? Is she being raped or beat again? Is she
being injected with those horrific drugs that lock up her jaw
and turn her into a human zombie for days? Are her
demons getting a hold of her mind if she's in isolation? Is
she thinking of suicide again? Is she thinking of homicide?
I usually walk the floor and repeat to myself that as long as
she is alive, I can fix anything else when I get her out of
that hell hole. I know I cannot fix Mackenzie, but I am not
ready to admit out loud that I can't. I still feel like if I just
love her more and more every day she will be alright. I
worry about her coming home. I fight and hope, and wish,
and pray for the day she actually walks into our house....it
makes me smile just to type that but trying to have her
living in our peaceful home is something that makes me
have anxiety. She is not the same child that went away,
she is not a child at all. She has seen and done things that
are going to haunt her right in the next bedroom beside
mine. Will she ever transition back into our world? It's been
way too many days since I have seen her walk down the
street, or ride in a car....way to many years. I am holding
onto anger still. My anger does not show but it sucks life
and blood and peace out of my body every single day. I am
angry at Mackenzie. I am angry at her public defender for
setting her up. I am angry at the Police Department for not
doing their job and not following the procedure in my
daughter's case. I am angry at my family for forgetting
about Mackenzie. I am angry at myself for not doing
something sooner when she was admitted to the
psychiatric floor at St Rita's hospital. I am angry at the two
other co- defendants in her case that did the burglaries. I

am angry at Isiah's father for not being his Dad. I am
holding on to way too much anger. It is eating at my bones
and wearing away the inside of my stomach. I need a
break. Isiah is an up at sunrise, constant, never stop
moving, doesn't give up at night without a fight...job. He
cannot help it, but I am growing tired. I am 45 years old
and I have a 6-year-old. I do not have just any 6 years old;
I have a 6-year-old with baggage. This poor child had two
strikes against him when he came into this world. He had
two seventeen-year-old parents who were just plain
children. He is my child now because I love him the exact
same as I do his mother.

July 9, 2018

I got a phone call!! Boy I sure did need to hear that girls voice.
She sounded good. She got into school and is so very excited to
be taking computer classes. She is now a facilitator in that she
teaches a group of inmates every Sunday about a faith- based
book. Mackenzie is a good person and it breaks my heart that
she will spend the rest of her life trying to prove herself. She
creates a syllabus over a book she has read (usually sent from
Aunt Bonnie) and she has a class of six every Sunday night for
class. They stay in her class for about six weeks as they read
over the book and do the worksheets Mack has made up. She is
so smart and caring, I know her on the inside. Mackenzie wants
to change lives of some of the women in that prison especially
those in for life. If you are given a life sentence you either
choose to go out doing good in that world, or you resent the
place and try to take everyone down with you. Mackenzie's new
attorney went to visit her a few months ago. He was to be
meeting her for the first time.

He looks as if he stepped right out of a movie set of Law
and Order. I can imagine the looks in that visitation room
as he walked into the conference room to meet with
inmate 090219. He is a gorgeous human, and his wife who

is also his secretary is also just as gorgeous. They look the part of big- city lawyers compared to our small-town firms here in Lima.

The attorney and his private investigator met with Mackenzie for over two hours that day. When he left there, he came and met myself and three other family members at a nice little restaurant in Dayton to discuss their meeting. The first words out of his mouth when he arrived at our table in the restaurant was, "Boy she sure don't trust men does she?". He said she was hard, and remained stuck to her story at first. It was when he was trying to crack that mask off of her that he brought up Isiah. That was it.... then she showed emotion. Mackenzie's attorney assured her that he was on her side, and not leaving until she was home with her little boy no matter how long that took. Her family had paid a lot of money for his expertise now she had to let down the wall and let him into her world so he could help her. When asked where she got the stolen goods Mackenzie replied from a crackhead. That was a lie and he knew it because I had already pulled an Erin Brockovich and handed him over the criminal backgrounds of the two co- defendants. I believe this is why the attorney can charge $30,000 to hire him....he simply said, "Look Mackenzie it's either your street creds or you get to see your son grow up". Mackenzie spilled the beans but was worried about protection and the thugs coming for her.... or Isiah, or me, or her brother and sisters.

I went to visit a week or so after her meeting in the conference room and when I walked up to check in, the nice correction officer we deal with every month commented on how "good looking" Basham's attorney is". It was now going to go around that place like when a new kid starts in high school or middle school. They have nothing else to talk about. Basham 090219 has some big shot defense team and she MAY get out of there. Remember those bitter lifers? The ones who blame everyone else because they are going to die there? That night after the lockdown a few inmates mysteriously got into Mackenzie's cell after it was supposed to be locked.

Mackenzie was attacked and cut with a razor blade along the abdomen. She was jumped and held down while beat. She couldn't have even fought back there were too many of them. She was put in the prison infirmary for three days. I knew something was wrong, I don't know how I just did. When I finally got a call from her, she told me this. She told me of a very nice correction officer that knows she's trying to be good in there and lay low. This decent officer had Mackenzie moved up to the third floor in a cell, in hopes that she would stay "safe" being locked up there...Dear God, please keep her safe.

July 19, 2018

Miramar Beach, Florida

The last time I spoke with Mackenzie was this past Saturday. We were staying overnight in a hotel in Alabaster, Alabama on way down to the ocean. When she called, I heard a lot of noise and commotion in the background. Mack was coughing and choking unable to get words out fully without being interrupted by a cough or gag. I started to get panicked as she yelled into the phone that she would call me later because a fight had broken out in her unit and they were all getting sprayed. Pepper sprayed. Sprayed like animals that won't comply. I heard other girls yelling out that they couldn't breathe either, I wonder how many times my child has had that horrible stuff sprayed in her face or eyes? I am 45 years old and I have never experienced anything of the sort. I do know that I had some clients who I cut their hair that was going through the police training here at the local technical school. They were acting all tough because they had to be sprayed once by the pepper spray to complete their training to be a cop. I would talk with them about how horrible that must be, and how brave they must have been......I feel differently now. It was used in the county jail on my daughter by not one, but two correction officers at point-blank range because she got into an altercation with a nasty crack head that Mackenzie didn't want touching her in fear of diseases. The officers thought it was funny. I know this for a fact because about 6 months after Mackenzie was sent to prison I received a phone call from a lady who had been in a nearby cell block of Mack's at the county. The mystery lady tells me when I answered that I didn't know her, but that she was locked up in the county jail with my daughter. She goes on to tell me that she had been in jail for a driving while intoxicated charge and that she felt so sorry for Mackenzie at that time. The lady told me how scared Mackenzie was, and that she was so young at 19 that she felt as if Mackenzie could have been one of her own children.

She told me she had looked out for Mackenzie. I thanked her in return. She then told me that she had made a promise to Mackenzie that when she was released from the county jail she would reach out to me. She told me of how terrified Mackenzie had been in jail, and how much she loved her mom and little boy. I became emotional thinking of that young 19-year-old child in jail with these grown women like who I was talking to. The woman seemed to be in her 40's or 50's. This lady told me that they "did Mackenzie wrong" in that nasty place. Her version of the story was that they set Mack up so that she would look bad when she went in front of the judge for sentencing. Apparently, her behavior was looked at before they sentenced her to a third of her life in prison. Her behavior? I assumed that the crime in question would be the deciding factor in a prison sentence, but I guess I don't know the ropes. The lady goes on to tell me that they had put a "return customer" of the jail who was addicted to crack, in a cell with Mackenzie. They knew it would be toxic. At this time, I admit my daughter was like a fighting pit bull ready to take on her next opponent. She was backed into a corner...and she was terrified...and she could not show her fear or it would make her weak. The crack addict starts an altercation with Mackenzie, and they get into a physical altercation. The lady on the phone told me that she personally went up to a correction officer and told him the addict was starting trouble with Basham and something was going to go down. When the fight broke out other prisoners yelled out "fight" and the lady on the phone said she watched as the correction officer had gone to turned his back on the fight looking the other way. I believe they wanted this to happen. The middle-aged crack addict ended up biting Mackenzie's thumb almost completely off at the end. After a few minutes of letting it go on, finally, two officers come running to "break it up", and they immediately slam Mackenzie to the floor using a lot of force. That was when not one, but two correction officers stand over the top of Mackenzie spraying mace into her face. The other inmate told me that Mackenzie had her hands up in the air as if to mean "I surrender", as well as Mack screaming that she didn't start it and she would stop. The spraying continued.

Now she was choking, couldn't open her eyes, and her thumb was bleeding and in a lot of pain. She was a 19-year-old girl? The lady on the phone told me that the rest of them were cleared out after but she kept her eye on the officer that she had told this was going to happen and he was talking and going on with his back turned just like not one word had been said to him. This is what this lady wanted to inform me of. I thanked her, then I asked her name. She did not have to call me. This must have bothered her enough that she thought I needed to know what had been done to my child. It sickened me. I have only spoken of it twice because the very thought of my daughter laying on her back defenseless with her hands up surrendering while STILL being sprayed in the face out of their pure enjoyment makes my blood boil. I pay taxes. I have worked in this county since I was 17 years old. My hard- earned money pays those sons of bitches wages, and they abused their authority......they abused my daughter and got away with it. To back this story up, I received another phone call from an actual correction officer who works at the county jail. It was the last week of August 2014. I remember it like it was yesterday. I was dropping Isiah off to his Great Grandma who was at the county fair watching the horse show. After answering the phone, a lady on the other end asked if this was Mackenzie's mom, I replied that it was. The lady on the other end simply states that she wanted to inform me that they had just transported my daughter to prison. I didn't really know what to say and was confused at the same time. I replied, "Thank you for telling me". The lady told me that she had promised Mackenzie she would call me so that I wouldn't worry when I didn't hear from her for a few months. I wondered if this was procedure.... but I knew it was not. The lady became very choked up and said that she had taken Mackenzie under her wing in jail because she had been so scared to death and missed her family so awful bad. I thanked her for that. She then continued to tell me that some of the stuff done to Mackenzie while in jail was not "right". Ok now wait a minute.... this is a second person telling me this. What could I do about it? Not one damn thing. Why would a CO call me and tell me they had transferred my kid to prison? Do they call every criminal's mom or dad and tell them that? They do not.

These diaries are actually being written ...like in a book. My cousins have offered me a gift, time away from my reality at their beach house. I packed up Gracie Jo and Isiah and drove to the Gulf of Mexico. The ocean is my favorite thing in the whole world, it is healing. I am sitting and staring at the waves roll in and out. The ocean is so huge- so much bigger than me. It makes me feel safe and comforted for some reason.

Maybe it's the memories I have of always going to the ocean with my parents or taking my children to the ocean. It makes me think that in the big scheme of life my little "situation" is not that big of a deal at all. I think it is the worst anyone ever could endure, but it is not. There are 23 million people right now in prison in the United States. Mackenzie Basham is a statistic, and so is her baby boy. My fear is that Isiah will stay a statistic. When this child was born, he had 2 strikes against him at birth. His parents were 17 years old when he was born. As far as the ocean is big, that's how far I'll go to make sure my little brown bear does not end up a statistic! He is going to be a success story if it kills me, or I will die trying. Ritchie and I are the only chance this little boy has right now, Isiah is right now currently having the time of his life. He is swimming, and playing in the white sand, and fishing off of Okaloosa Island, and floating in the pool at 9:00 am. There are so many mistakes I have made as a parent, he will be my redemption. I refuse to let him fail. I will not let his mother's incarceration be a crutch.... a platform maybe, but not a crutch. I am watching him right now play with children of many different colors and nationalities. They speak all different languages, yet Isiah says they all speak French. It makes no difference to him he doesn't know what French is. My point is that I have raised this child to not see anything on the outside another person. He does not see color, or that anyone is different than him. I wish teaching the world this was as easy.

I almost had a meltdown yesterday and it was my own fault. I was so relaxed in water so clear I was looking down at my own feet, that I almost forgot for one second about my child. Instantly, I thought I should get out and head back up to the condo and cook or clean or do some kind of work. GUILT. How can I be here – do this – while my child is living in an actual hell? Mackenzie told me last week that it was so hot in that prison infested with flies and cockroaches, that she just sat on top her mattress and cried. No air conditioning in the prison just sits on a bare mattress and cry. You cannot move around it's too hot, so you either lay on the concrete floor and battle those cockroaches or sit on the bed and cry. That is what she did.... all day. Dear God, that breaks my heart. I am literally sitting in paradise eating and drinking like a freakin Queen. If I'm not cooling my tanned body off in the crystal- clear water, then I'm in the giant pool. I also go to our luxury condo that sometimes is so cool I go out on the balcony that stares at miles and miles of ocean to warm up. Why do I feel so guilty? It's starting to make me sick. I deserve this. Gracie Jo and Isiah deserve this, why can't I shake this guilt? Now I'm nervous about what to tell Mackenzie when she asks how the trip was. I never know how much to tell her in fear of making her feel bad. Does she want to mentally picture it to escape hell for a while, or does it make her go into the deep dark places in her mind that weaken her spirit? This prison sentence is also mine. I have served over 4 years now, and I still have 10 to go. I am not as tough as my big Mack. I check every day on the county clerk of courts website to see if there is any news of the decision from the courts of the judge concerning the appeal. My dream is that right after her case number it will say appeal granted. That is a whole new worry. The trial, the media, the public's opinion. Social media will eat her alive when they see her. It is not her fault; she has become accustomed to being treated like an animal. She looks wild and broken, and hard, and ice cold, and disturbed, and scary, and I feel so sorry for her. My little girl. She doesn't deserve this. Never in my wildest dreams would I have thought that selling stolen crap to pay off a drug debt would land her in that terrifying place she is sitting in today....never.

This is our last night down here in paradise. I miss my other kids and grandkid, but it sure did warm my heart seeing brown bear forget about his life for a while. I didn't make this possible, my cousins did. Isiah has love from places he doesn't even know about. He is so lucky and rich in that department. That has to be a solid foundation for him to succeed in life. He truly does have his very own village. The percentages are so high of him repeating the pattern of his parents. I will fight that battle every minute of every day to make sure that is not his path. The foundation that has been laid has to carry this child through his life. Mackenzie would never survive a second if one of her immediate family members had to go to prison. She simply would snap.... into her own mind, into that dark place that she blocks to put a smile on her face or converse with a civilian. We have talked about this many times. The reason is she knows, she knows of the terror, the emptiness, the depression, the sexual abuse, the midnight beatings, the rape....she knows because it has all happened to her. This very fact scares her to death that her brother will get caught with weed, or that her son would ever try a joint for the first time as a teenager. Indirectly that led her to here, this point, today. I hope the darkness fades in Mackenzie's mind someday. She battles mental illness and self-worth. Living in a prison cell multiplies those by a hundred. I believe some was born in her, I also believe society failed her. I believe that her biological father and my vicious divorce when she was only 4 years old played a major part in her cracked foundation. We still hate each other and for that very reason, I cannot forgive myself – or him. This is why I have the guilt. At 24 years old Mackenzie Lee wants her father's love and affection so bad it's almost childlike.

The last time Mackenzie saw her father come to her in support was when she had Isiah. She had a child at 17 and got the attention she craved, and that explains a lot. I know that I am on this journey alone with Mackenzie so I must be there enough to carry both parents load. I got this.

August 4, 2018

I am starting to crave writing in this diary. Yesterday as I was driving with the family after working, dealing with clients, the grocery store, unloading groceries, quickly changing clothes, getting the car loaded up for a family cookout, then getting back in the car I was at the point that even a stiff drink and a cigarette couldn't relax me. I block out the noise from my life and look forward to sitting down, and just telling my diary everything. It does not argue with me.... or disagree. My prison diary just simply listens, and it is the only thing I have in my life that does. People ask how Mackenzie is doing, or myself, but when I don't give an answer full of sunshine and rainbows they start to repel. I get it, I wouldn't want to hear the things I know either. I am getting ready to have some time off of work and the kids will be back in school during this time. My plan is to go into the garage and open the box. In 2014 after Mackenzie was sentenced to prison, the county jail called me to pick up her belongings.

When I arrived, I was given the box that contained one pair of her shoes, a sweatsuit she was wearing the day of arrest, and a yellow envelope stuffed full of mail. I have never looked nor read any correspondence she has ever got from other people. I have to do this to see if there are any letters that could help me to get her out sooner.... or help with the appeal. I do not want to read these. I feel like I am invading Mackenzie's privacy and didn't want to do that. I am going to be brought back to a very painful time that I have worked hard to forget or move past. These letters tell a story, but the story is very heartbreaking to me as a mother. I have no idea who all wrote to Mackenzie but I know that I did. My letters in the box are from when she first went away. I was devastated. I was mad at her, and I don't really want to know what I said to her. Mackenzie has already read these letters so the damage is done, but I blocked them out. I need them to help me remember. I surely remember the big details, but I was not listening to my daughter as I do now. She was on drugs, and I did not like her. I have never for a minute stopped loving Mackenzie, but from 2010-2014 I did not like her. She was letting the devil win over her life and she knew it. It is one of the most horrible things to watch, as a mother. My daughter was self-destructing right before my eyes. The good was being taken over by the drugs. She was hanging around people that were bad, but as long as they accepted

Mackenzie she wanted to be in their presence.

I just got a phone call from Mack. She had been sick and is finally feeling better. She has asked for the family to put money on her commissary to recover from her cell being chosen to search. I asked why it was torn apart and she said, "because they can". Out of 100 cells, they chose her and her bunky's and they go in and tear it apart. They took her spices and dumped them on her sheets, tore open all of her packaged food we had bought her, tore down her pictures family had sent, and ruined the ONE sheet she had.

Mackenzie told me she was using her sweatshirt rolled up as a pillow. This breaks my heart. It is like as soon as she attempts to build herself up, the officers know it....and they tear her right back down. I'm going to visit Mackenzie today with Ritchie and Isiah. This child needs to see his Mommy. He is acting out against Gracie and I. He needs his Mother and I am on the other end of the aggression when he cannot be with her. He punched Gracie in the nose last night and told me he hated me. Gracie Jo is a freakin saint. At 17 she is trying to get into college for political science, then into law school.
Gracie has helped raise Isiah, and she was not asked if she wanted to. She has shown more parental guidance then both of Isiah's parents and done a much better job at it.

August 10, 2018

We made the trip to Dayton Correctional Institution yesterday. It was so good to see Mackenzie. We checked in and did everything we were supposed to do to start off our visit, then we waited....and waited, and waited. Ritchie was getting pissed off and Isiah was getting anxious. When we entered the actual prison visitation room, we have to go give our driver's license to the "desk officer" to check in. This just happened to be the same officer that years ago made me change my pants because they looked "too tight", He is a giant douchbag, literally.

This officer stands tall and really loves his authority, which is not much. I know how he tries to make the visitors feel; I can only imagine how he degrades the female inmates inside those prison walls. I wonder if he has a life outside of work? It seems to me that the prison is the only place that caters to his ego. He was talking to one of the female inmates that were working in the visitation hall that day, well they were flirting....it was gross. Ritchie and I were told to sit at table "5". I have visited my daughter every single month except February 2018, and I have not ever been given an assigned table. It was directly underneath a camera mounted on the ceiling and Mackenzie told me that she always runs her hand under the table to see if there are "listening devices" underneath. This seems crazy but it was odd. Anyways, while Hugh Hefner was trying to score with the inmate he did not call Mackenzie's unit to tell her she had a visitor. After we had sat for over 20 minutes, I started getting her food out of the "wheel of death" and her Mountain Dew fix ready. A female officer approached me to tell me that Isiah was getting big and that he was growing so fast. We had a brief conversation and she asked how long we had waited for our inmate. I must have seemed concerned because she offered to call and check on Mackenzie.

The female officer called to Mackenzie's unit and asked if 90219 was there.... turns out she was not even called and told that we were there. They have that power and ole "Hughey" needed us to know that if he wanted to make us sit with a little 6-year-old boy waiting to see his Mama, we would just wait. Ritchie was fuming, but my worry was Mackenzie snapping. She knew we were coming; she counts the very seconds until she gets to see her baby boy. We are supposed to get from 12:30-3:30 but if they want to call her at 2:30 or 3:00 and make us suffer.... they can. That is just how cool they are. I have a meeting with Mackenzie's attorney in Columbus in two weeks, everyone thinks the appeal has been filed and I just found out it has NOT yet....it's been one year since we hired the look- alike" Christian Gray" and we are all tired of waiting on this appeal to get filed. We need to know something soon.... she is slipping away again.

The Outlaw

While at one of our visits in 2017, Isiah would always reference his "friend" from the playroom at the prison. The playroom is a room in the main visitation area where small children can go. The inmate your visiting is not allowed in the playroom nor the visitors. In the playroom, they have one inmate whose job is to get out the worn books, and tattered games, and chalk, and sit at the little table they have in there. I imagine they make the usual prison state pay of $17.00 a month to work in there. Isiah became more and more comfortable going back into the playroom, which was a nice break for Mackenzie and me to be able to discuss things he did not need to hear us discuss. Mackenzie had actually become upset a few visits because I would have to go tell him to come out of the playroom and spend more time with his Mommy. He would call his new friend, "Outlaw" ....which honestly made me very uncomfortable that he was talking to an inmate with the nickname "Outlaw". One time he came out followed by his new friend, he had shown her a new dance move and he wanted us to meet her. My first impression of Outlaw was that she was very intimidating and honestly scared the hell out of me. First impressions are usually only important in an interview or meeting, who knew that they could be important in the prison world. Outlaw is a very, very tall lady with a shaved head and an athletic build. I will just say that she looks like she could whip any man's ass if in a confrontation. I would not ever mess with a woman of her stature, yet Isiah only saw her smile and laugh and kindness towards children. I asked Mack about the Outlaw and she said she only knew that she had been in prison a long time and that she goes by "Outlaw". I was worried that Isiah was having conversations with some mentally sick person, or some criminal that chopped people up and ate their bodies or something...after all, we are in a prison. I was not concerned for his safety in the playroom as the officers monitor it and there is no door it is an open room, I was just creeped out that he could be conversing with some sick human every month.

The next few months Isiah would say that he wanted to go on Wednesdays to visit his Mommy because Outlaw would be there to play with him and she was fun. Now I needed to find out about this "Outlaw" even though a crime is a crime in that place...I needed to know. Mackenzie gave me the impression that nobody messed with the Outlaw and that she would be someone you wanted on your side in that hell hole. I informed Mackenzie that Isiah had asked to send Outlaw a dance video of him through Jpay, she is very protective of her family and this might bother her. Mackenzie said that she didn't know much about her, but that would be alright. I asked her what the woman's real name was honestly because I was being nosy and wanted to research her crime before she talked to my grandson again. Outlaw was not her nickname....it was her actual last name! Later that night I logged onto the Ohio inmate search and found out what this nice lady who talked fishing and baseball and told Isiah to say his prayers was in prison for. Manslaughter? Oh, dear god, what am I doing? I have considered this person kind of my friend now too.... she is a murderer? I need to know more about her case as if I can justify her killing a person. I find out that the Outlaw is my age and has been in prison since 1994...the year Mackenzie was born. She was sentenced to 25 years for involuntary manslaughter. She is kind and caring and hardcore and raised completely in a different culture then my family you can tell. I need to ask her why, but that makes me nervous. She already knows Isiah and that makes me feel unsettled...I need to know why she did it. I feel like I have to give this woman a chance to explain herself because underneath all the hard-tough scary shell she portrays, there is a real person. She is someone's daughter just like my Mackenzie and what if everyone looks at my daughter and turns away? Although the crimes are not the same, the stigma surrounding them is. I felt like I was being selfish in that in the back of my head, I wanted to get protection for my daughter......I thought the Outlaw could get us that. It's a game you play in prison with the inmates, and with the correction officers. This is also my prison sentence and I'm playing the game from the outside. What if Isiah's connection with The Outlaw could keep Mackenzie safe at night in some small way?

One night I could not sleep because this was weighing heavy on me. I decide to write a letter to the Outlaw from one real person to another. The love she had shown for my grandchild made her gain a place in my heart, as a human being, not a murderer. I want to explain that in my diaries I have written about her and ask if she would like to share her story with me.... the story of living inside a prison for 25 years now. I was nervous, and anxious as I was writing because I didn't want her to think I was not sincere...It really does intrigue me. If my daughter has to serve out her sentence of 14 years, she will have become institutionalized, and the Outlaw is institutionalized. I received a letter back from Outlaw explaining that she was thankful that God had brought little Isiah and myself into her life.

August 21, 2018

Isiah is preparing to start the first grade and turn 7 years old. I was able to take my parents to visit Mackenzie last week. It was very emotional, but I was so proud of her. She opened up a little towards the end of our time there. She started to cry and her lip was trembling as she was trying to talk. My mom grabbed her hand and held it as my Mother began to sob. I couldn't make eye contact with my father at that point. I was sitting like the statue I have learned to be in that prison visitation room. You do not allow your emotions to surface, you push them away until you get alone.... then you melt completely down. I can almost be positive that my child does the same when she gets back to her cell. I still cannot believe that my own child sleeps in a cage. That is hard to write. It's 2018 and all the education and money and government official promises have not figured out a different system to rehabilitate a 19-year-old girl that had a minor drug problem. A cage is for an animal, usually a wild one. Something HAS to be done for offenders like my child. The fact that every offender of our criminal justice system is thrown all together makes me question humanity. My daughter never hurt another human being, she sold stolen items and yet she could sleep 4 feet from a woman who cooked her own child in the microwave. If you take a feral animal and cage them with a house dog what do you think will happen? The house dog will get beat down until they have no choice but to act feral to survive....or they will be killed.

Mackenzie was trying to tell us of her fears of coming home. She is afraid of her reaction to people. She gave an example of a family member making a joke about her being in prison.... she became visibly traumatized and emotional. This is when my Mother grabbed her hand as Mackenzie was having trouble getting the next word come out of her mouth. Mackenzie said that prison is not a joke, and the sick things that have been done to her or that she has seen is not a joke either. Her reaction to ignorance of people when she is finally free scares her in that she will let them know immediately. This kind of a reaction will not be socially acceptable and that makes her feel uneasy. Mackenzie told us of her finally feeling comfortable in her own skin away from the outside world. She explained that in prison she doesn't care what anyone thinks leading her to be herself at all times except when playing the game of survival. I promised Mackenzie that she will be safe, in our home from the outside fears she has. It may take years, and that is ok. All she has to do is be Isiah's Mommy. I hope she felt comforted and that she can trust me, and our immediate family when she finally is returned to the free world. Like the feral animal, Mackenzie will seem untamed out in the open freedoms, and she will shy away from people as she told us at the visit. She is hurt by those who made promises they did not keep, and by those she thought she was important to.... but the years have proven differently. The people who stuck by her is less then she can count on her hands. When she finally gets her freedom, those who showed unconditional love for her will be the only ones that she will be able to trust or be in their presence. I understand completely.

People take advantage of their everyday freedoms and those exact freedoms and choices are the very thing that my child is worrying about. I have not ever been stripped of freedom for years upon years, so I cannot even begin to imagine her internal struggles. I have my fill of the human race on a daily basis and I have not been locked in a cage for 5 years. I felt sorry for my little girl at the end of the visit, she doesn't deserve this. My daughter will never be the same, and I accept that now. It is too far fetched to think I will get my daughter back that left, I just want Isiah to get a chance of the joy of having a Mother before he turns 18.

Mackenzie's suffering has exceeded levels I could never even imagine. When I see offenders sentenced every day for crimes that are horrendous, I am at peace knowing that they will suffer from prison....I had no idea how much they would suffer.

September 13, 2018

It is 4:45 and Isiah has been awake for two hours already. It is his 7th birthday!!! He went to bed at his normal 8:00 bedtime, but he couldn't sleep. Ritchie and I are up with him.... we know the drill. Since this boy has been with us his feelings tend to come out in his sleeping patterns. Usually, that means no sleep. He is anxious. At 7 years old now Isiah is still not settled. Will he ever be? Will he ever recover. I was supposed to schedule a video visit with his Momma so he could see her today but I couldn't. I have been out of it since I had surgery last Friday. Having a hysterectomy has allowed me to escape the nightmare for the past six days. That's pretty sad, yet this is my life. I was just sure that the problems I was having resulting in the surgery would be the result of some horrific cancer or illness. I prepare for the worst because I have numbed myself. The amount of stress I endure on a daily basis cannot be normal to a 45-year-old middle aged woman. Stress can kill you, I have seen it before in my family. My mother's twin sister was diagnosed with breast cancer at 45 and died at 48 years old. Her life was a hard one, and nothing ever was easy for Aunty Ellie. My mother's mom was also diagnosed with breast cancer at 45 and died at 48....the pattern is there and I knew of all the woman in the family, I was the most vulnerable one.....the weakest link. Why am I thinking this, maybe it's the narcotics talking? Isiah got a call from his Mommy at 7:00am and he was so happy until the phone call ended. Isiah was getting ready to head to the bus with 24 cupcakes for his class and he had a meltdown, bless his little heart. I couldn't function after all that and he had to go put in a seven-hour school day. It's called resilience and this child is killing it.

While he was in the tub last night Gracie surprised him with a big birthday cake with a giant number "7" on it. We turned out the lights and started singing the Happy birthday song. He loved it. Ritchie told him to make a wish before blowing out his candle and that when our reality hit us all right in the face.

Isiah said very softly...." I wish for my Mommy". Any happiness or joy we were having on that Wednesday night, holding that lit up cake, just came crashing down on us like a piano being dropped off a tall building. We are still in this nightmare. This child has had the same wish for his last five birthdays, what did I ever do to deserve this? He is a gift from God, a pure soul that doesn't deserve these punches from life...why.

Gracie took me to my checkup visit to the Dr on the 14th. The Dr told me that the biopsy's they took so far have all came back to be no cancer!!......I'll be damned, I am one strong woman. I even fought my family genes and won. It's gonna be a good day today.

September 26, 2018

It's Wednesday. I got a call from Mack yesterday that the prison had informed her that she had a visitation reservation for today at 12:30, it was going to be her legal team. I woke up feeling very positive and motivated as ever. This has to be good right? I mean Allen County has made every single request for documents on her case become a giant mountain to climb. Why don't they want her new attorney to obtain all of the information from her case? When asked for the log sheet from when Mackenzie was in the county jail, her attorney was told that they were not willing to give them that information.

They told us that a subpoena had to be obtained. Why would that information be so "top secret"? I mean.... so don't share it with just anyone, but this is her legal counsel representing her now....why the resistance? Maybe her court-appointed attorney who was BFF'S with the "good crooked sheriff" did not do his job, just maybe he let my child get sent down the river for some things she didn't do to fulfill a deal he had to make right with a few police officers who have been indicted. He didn't care, he was paid from the county auditor his money for taking the job. Her former attorney was sick, dying of cancer to be exact. He died 10 months after Mackenzie went to prison, and after that horrific day in August, we were of never to heard from him again.

It is now 10:24 at night, not one word from Mackenzie as of right now. I am letting my nerves get a hold of me. I am playing out each scenario in my head so that I am prepared for the news in the upcoming days. I have built her up with so much hope. I had to, I do not regret that. Mackenzie had hit a point mentally where if we would not have come through with a private attorney, she would have taken her own life, or have been killed in prison. She was like an empty shell walking around with no touch of reality and no cares for herself or others. Her thinking was if she wasn't going to get to be with her baby boy until he was 17, then why live? I tell her what she needs to hear, not what is happening. Shoot me, I just want to see my daughter alive in the free world someday. The attorney is very honest in his speaking and will not sugar coat anything to her as I do. I 'm not there to ease the punches so to speak. I'm hoping it was positive information from filing a motion to withdraw her guilty plea. She had no idea what she was pleading guilty to, she was 19, and never been arrested before. I had no idea either. The sad thing is that when she was asked if she wanted to take the deal or go to trial, her reply was..." ask my mom what she wants me to do". She had absolutely no idea what to do. I didn't either, so I asked her court-appointed attorney. He already had it all worked out...." Judy, she has to take the deal. If we go to trial, they are gonna give her 64 years in prison." My decision for my daughter's life was 14 years, or 64 years.... of course, I told her to just say what the attorney told her to say. Now 5 years later when I find out that she plead guilty to crimes that weren't even committed I get sick to my stomach. Mackenzie pleads guilty to NINE felony 2 burglaries.

A felony 2 burglary is one in which you enter a home when someone is inside with the intent to harm or kill. She did not do that, that didn't even happen to the homes in question. All of the victims whose homes were broken into said in a victim statement and out loud in the courtroom that none of them were home? They all said they got home and discovered that their homes had been disrupted.... but not by Mackenzie. There were no eyewitnesses, and no person that could personally put Mackenzie in those homes or on the properties....yet she was pinned with the entire crime spree. She had the stuff. Damnit, why did she do that? Mackenzie told me one time that nothing that I had done as a mother had put us in this situation. She owed money for drugs; she sold her soul to the devil. The devil is who broke into those homes and set her up....he knew exactly what he was doing to the stupid young white girl. She had no clue what nightmare storing that stuff could place her in. Her drug fused and alcohol stemmed decision five years ago has made my life a living hell. We could not have known that the bad guys were connected to the good guys and she was just a tiny little pawn in their game. It disgusts me, yet I sit writing my frustrations in my diary because even after hiring a highly recognized legal team the bad guys are gonna win.

It's Thursday morning, Mackenzie called at 7:00 am. I could tell from the very first word that came out of her mouth it was not good. "Mom" was the word. That word I love to hear coming through the phone paralyzed my body for a minute. We had a brief silence because she knew that I knew the news was not what we were hoping for. While listening to my incarcerated child tell me of her crushed hopes to be home by her baby sister's graduation, I was pouring a bowl of Apple Jacks for brown bear acting like nothing was wrong. That is what sucks. I can't even process my own emotions in fear of upsetting Gracie or Isiah. So I act....I deserve a fucking Oscar. I want to get into bed and pull the covers up so only my mouth is out. I want to sit in silence. I want to stare at a wall, I mean just really stare for hours at nothing. The attorney has been working for over a year on ways to get Mackenzie to be heard in a courtroom in our county. Yesterday, Mackenzie had the "meeting" she had been waiting for...over 400 days for just a tiny shred of hope that she may be able to be a free woman before she is 35 years old. It doesn't look good. How did we not know how damaging it would be for her to just plead guilty? I thought that if you apologized to the courts and admitted your mistakes and well, told the truth, that things would work out for you. The criminals that broke into the homes are hugging their families, or spending Christmas together, or sharing birthdays with family, and I'm still sitting at my computer crying. I want Isiah to wake up for school by his Mommy. I want Isiah to be on that football field, or ball diamond and look over to his Mommy cheering him on. Is this too much to ask? Now we wait for what is next. We spend another holiday season inside a nasty institution's visiting area with my child on the other side of the table. No opening gifts, no turkey dinner, no church on Christmas Eve....only snacks from the wheel of death and one hug when the time is up. I feel as if Mackenzie is starting to accept her "place" inside that prison cell. A human can only endure so much time in a cage. Her spirit is shattered. I do not imagine I will get any emails or phone calls because she is going to go into a deep depression. This was a hard hit, and it may have been my fault for letting her believe that justice will come out. I lost my grip on reality for a while. I am so damn tired of my mind being consumed with panic and not feeling complete without my firstborn. Are my entire middle-aged years going to be full of heartache and grieving a child who is still alive? I need to talk to God today. There is no one else that can fathom my feelings right now, no one that can even have a clue. I felt so close to happiness; I was so excited to give good news to a little 7-year-old boy. It's not going to happen anytime soon. My fear is that Mack will give up. I am now back to the fear of getting a phone call from Dayton Correctional Institution saying that they have bad news. I have slipped back into the living hell I am starting to become so comfortable with.

October 5, 2018

Isolation has become my best friend. I think I slip into this darkness every time the holidays are approaching. I never imagined in my wildest dreams that I would be spending 5 Thanksgiving's or 5 Christmas's without her being here. They do not get easier. I hear people say that the holidays are stressful because of the financial part of it, or the busyness of it all, that makes me want to punch them in the teeth. Try waking up on Christmas to a little 7-year-old boy that you could give him a million dollars and all he would want is for his Mommy to be in the same house that he is. Hell, I would even be happy if his biological father would give him a phone call on Christmas day. It crushes my heart that this small human so full of love for his parents has to be without the presence of the very people that brought him into this world. It's not his choice by no means. I know other children live life without parents in their lives, or with shitty parents, but not many I know. This just blows my mind. I have had my parents for 45 years and I am so selfish that I am in no way ready to spend one day without them. If I want to call them, I can. If I am feeling scared, or overwhelmed with life, I just go to their house. It makes me feel safe. I feel like the outside world cannot touch me when I'm in my parent's house. I was probably babied as a child too much, but can you really love a child too much? When Mackenzie says she has to make up for so many years with Isiah, I know now what she means.

She wants more than anything for him to feel safe and comfortable and loved by her, and right now he feels loved by her but that's about it. When he is sick, he doesn't want his Mommy and that would kill her if she knew. He wants me, and his Papa. I love that, but it kills me that she cannot feel that from her only child. I cherish the need my kids have for me. As I sit here in my nightgown pouring my fears and heartaches into a computer screen, I am wondering what Mackenzie is doing. I missed a call from her yesterday and the email system is down so no letters coming in. I also haven't heard from our friend the Outlaw in a bit. Do not get me wrong that I think these girls can take "care" of themselves in prison but referring to other inmates or the day to day drama. When a correction officer has the devil inside him or her, these girls are at their mercy. I see the intimidation the correction officers in that specific prison put on the inmates. I know about the secret beatings, the "off camera" sex, or drug exchanges. One time when Mack was in the first prison straight from the county jail, she told me of an incident that gives me nightmares to this day. There was a female correction officer that was a complete dick. My daughter was a child in an adult's world. She needed to appear tough and hard and crazy to survive. This was not a church camp. The officer thought it would make her cool to take Mackenzie's food tray and drop it on the floor. When Mack bent down to pick it up, the officer said: "No, No, No... eat it down there". While the entire nasty prison cafeteria laughed at the super cool lady officer, my child was hungry. The officer knew that. If she was that hungry, she was supposed to eat her slop off of the floor. Mackenzie had to stand up for herself or she would be eating off that filthy floor every day from there on out. Mackenzie turned to the officer and said, "I am not a dog...I'm not eating off that floor". The officer told Mackenzie that she would eat that food or she could go to the hole. If I reread that sentence as a mother it makes me lose my shit. My child had to choose between eating or being humiliated in a room full of adult officers and adult criminals at the age of 19 years old. It was many weeks after that incident that I heard from my daughter, she was in solitary confinement. They had taught her a lesson real quick, a sick twisted lesson on how some of our American prisons operate.

I sometimes grab an extra sandwich for the local homeless people that stand by the intersections in our town. I would never, ever, put the food on the ground for them to eat it.

These people are being paid by my tax dollars and they can treat fellow human beings like this. This is wrong on many different levels. It is a job, a badge these officers get after a two-week training...not a license from Satan himself to do whatever they want. Who do they think they are? She is my child, my little sweet girl. For the last five years every time I don't hear from my child, this is the worry.

Still, I sit here with my hands tied. How am I supposed to function in society with this in my brain?

October 9,2018

Today baby girl received a letter of acceptance to Ohio Northern University to major in political science. This girl is living the nightmare with her big
sister and if anyone can get prison reform....it's Gracie Jo. I am so proud of her resilience I could do cartwheels...I probably shouldn't, but I could.

October 15, 2018
From: Mackenzie Basham
To: Judy Frisby

The love between a mother and daughter is forever.

The love between a mother and daughter is the bond of the strongest kind.

It is a love of the present, interwoven with the memories of the past and dreams of the future.

It is strengthened by overcoming obstacles and facing fears and challenges together.

It is having pride in each other and knowing that our love can withstand anything

It is wanting only the best for each other and wanting to help anytime there is a need

It is making time to be together and knowing just what to say It

is an unconditional forever and ever kind of love....

Mom,

This card speaks everything I wanted to say to you. I am so proud to have you as my mother as we have grown together during a time when most people would fall apart. You have yet to give up on me and Isiah, and I am so very thankful for that. My biggest fear was to be forgotten when I came here, but you wouldn't let that happen. You have been a strong woman and you have raised us kids to be the same. Our bonds are unbreakable, our love could never fade.

I love you more than steak, thank you...Mac

October 22, 2018

As I click on Google my history searches come up. For the past 447 days, I have clicked on the County Clerk of Courts website. I search the last name Basham and enter the first name of Mackenzie. It takes me to two sets of numbers and one is when Mackenzie tried to appeal the case herself, the other is her case number for what she is currently serving time in prison for. I always click on the case number and look at the docket to see if anything "new" has been entered in the case since we have hired her legal team. Every day the same thing, no change......but not today. Today is a Monday...October 22, 2018, and today it said: "Motion to withdraw plea filed". I have looked every day for 447 days to see those words. This may not mean anything to anyone else, but to me and Mackenzie it means hope. Hope that maybe she will be home before her baby boy is 17 years old. Hope that everyone will know Mackenzie's side of the story. Hope that just because you have a badge, you can make mistakes and have to admit those mistakes. I took a giant deep breath and felt a small victory. Four years....it has taken four long, excruciating years to just get this tiny sliver of hope for my child. I spoke with Mackenzie and when I told her she said she had to go to the bathroom and get off the phone. I asked if she was ok, and she replied...." when you just said that, my stomach just instantly became sick".

I can't imagine how Mackenzie feels right now. I know how I feel and I am not living in a cage most of my day like she is. I am nervous about her spirit if the trial court Judge turns it down immediately. I have built her up saying this chance of freedom was coming, and now it's here and I cannot promise her anything else to keep her hanging on. This has been a very good tool to "talk her off the ledge" many many times in the past four years. Dear God, let me be strong for her.

If the motion is denied, we can file an appeal with the third district court of appeals in Ohio. I will not stop trying to get her sentence reduced. I cannot sleep at night if I do. It goes back to the feelings of guilt I have as a mother having freedom, while my child does not.

October 28, 2018

I woke up Saturday morning to Mackenzie being on the front page of the local newspaper. It was titled "Lima woman seeks new trial". Mackenzie was pictured above the article. The news got it from her latest prison identification photo. The photo seems to be under scrutiny because she has a partly shaved head and a big neck tattoo as well as putting on a lot of weight. The comments on social media are cruel. They are very critical of Mackenzie...and me for supporting her. I want to find each and every person who is saying those horrible things about my child.

I went to my family doctor on Thursday to get medication for the panic attacks I was going to be having. How do I know these are coming? At least I could prepare for this backlash, unlike back in 2014. I was blindsided then. It is never ever easy reading and hearing people you have not met speak horrible things about your little girl. The ignorance of some people amazes me. It is like they want to get social media attention by cutting down another human being, even if they don't know her...or me. This is gut-wrenching not fighting back at the comments. I want to tell them all the true story that I know. I have to keep my cool or they win.

My circle just got smaller again. I did not work yesterday. I was afraid that I would be standing in the salon, doing my job, and hear a comment about Mackenzie from a customer or a co- worker. I became very sick Friday night, like psychically ill. My resistance is down and my nerves are punching me all over my body. I have become severely paranoid now. Ritchie and I took the grandchildren out for dinner on Saturday. I could not eat because I was constantly looking around as if people were staring at me. My mind was playing tricks on me. At one point I even thought the manager of the restaurant was whispering to an employee and looking at me. In my mind, the police are going to come storming in and arrest me right in front of my grandkids, all because Mackenzie's petition was in the newspaper. I actually told the owner of my shop to call someone if I go missing. I keep my prison diaries loaded on a flash drive and carry that with me all the time I am so paranoid now. This is the truth I know and I am afraid it is going to be stolen from me. I am experiencing the same paranoia I had back in 2014. I have worked so hard to shake this feeling, and I just brought it on to myself again. I cannot imagine what Mackenzie has to battle in her own head. When she feels someone is out to get her, they really are in prison. That place is a violent living hell.

November 4, 2018

It's been a week since the local newspaper ran the article

on Mackenzie filing a motion to withdraw her guilty plea. The backlash has quieted down and now I am just left with the waiting. The state has filed their response to Mackenzie's motion, now the decision is up to the trial court judge. I was told by the detective that worked on Mack's case that the trial court judge would be retiring in six years, as well as himself. That was when he carried Mackenzie's stuff to my car and asked me if I wanted to have a cigarette with him? What a weird and inappropriate thing that was that day. He actually said..." she can be out in six years" ....then just stood there leaning on the door of my car. I didn't say one word. I wanted to ask him how that would be if I had sex with him or something? What kind of police detective does this? Not one person had ever said anything about six years, now this guy comes up with six years. I imagine if I would have gone into the bar we were in the parking lot of with Mr. Big detective and had that cigarette and drinks and whatever followed, my daughter would be home. Then again maybe that's his "pick up line". Yea...blue lives do matter, except slime ball corrupt ego fused douchebags like this. I have spoken with an employee of the county department and asked if this was "policy" to carry the stuff from the evidence room to the family members car and have a casual smoke and convo with the person. It is not. I knew what he meant. I will do anything to get my daughter home with her son, except that. I was afraid to tell Mr. Frisby about my encounter with the "good detective". Well, I wasn't afraid, I just did not have any bail money to get him out. This was just one more thing that left a bad taste in my mouth so to speak about my dealings with our local department back then. That cop knew he had ruined my life and Mackenzie's at 19. Days before he had been in that courtroom and watched me stand up to the court and beg for mercy for my little girl who had just made a mistake. She didn't hurt anyone, or kill anyone, or rape anyone, and he was bound and determined to make sure the state went for this 14- year plea deal or 64 years if we went to trial. Now, this guy wants to be friends? Share a cigarette and just chat out in the parking lot beside a bar across from the courthouse? Is this real life right now? I couldn't even speak, I just nodded my head and remained silent. This had to be processed. Is this an everyday thing with police? I have actually never in my life talked to a police detective in a one on one conversation, so maybe this is the norm. It's invasive and made me feel gross and confused.

The decision of the trial court judge to give Mackenzie a hearing is consuming me. I went with Gracie Jo to her college preview day yesterday from 9:00 to 1:00 then went to work from 1:30 to 8:30 yesterday and when I got home I was at the point of exhaustion where I didn't have the strength to even sit at my computer and write in my prison diary. Friday night about 10:30 I got a call from the prison which was very odd. It was Mackenzie, and she had a desperation in her voice. She does not usually call that late knowing that Isiah is in bed. I immediately asked what was wrong. Mackenzie said she just needed to hear the sound of my voice, then asked if any chance of Isiah being awake. I told her no, he is never up that late. I repeated myself in asking what was wrong. Mackenzie just said that she was very depressed and needed to hear my voice and then I heard an officer say something in the background. Mackenzie quickly said she had to go but that she loved me and to tell her baby she loved him as well as to tell Ritchie and Gracie Jo she loved them too. Then she hung up. That was not a normal call. Now I just worry. My mind is playing every scenario that could be wrong and it's my own personal torture. After the long day the next day it wasn't until I got home after 12 hours that I started to think about Mackenzie again. I had to try to think positive. She had to be fine, just the depression. I needed silence. Real silence to only hear my own breathing and focus on that. I had to stop my mind from playing out the horrible things that could be happening to Mackenzie in that prison, or why she sounded panicked. I ran a very hot bath and loaded it with eucalyptus bath salts. This is the only way I can truly get silence. I put my fingers in my ears while on my back. I submerge myself in the water until everything is under water except a small circle around my eyes, nose, and mouth. I hear nothing. I concentrate on my breathing and it calms me. I stare at the white ceiling. I just lay there until the busyness in my head goes away. When will this ever be over? Where did my life take this turn that my joy and excitement of life are literally drowning the world out and pretending I am invisible? It is the only way to escape my life right now. I dream of escaping for real.

November 12, 2018

Motion denied.

Now, I prepare how I'm going to tell my little girl right before the holidays that she will not have a chance to tell her story.... the real story. One more Christmas in a cage, for all of us.
This is going to be hard. I

I'm angry. I am angry.

I am angry because I have had to work so hard for over 4 years to get my daughter justice

I am angry because my country has let me down

I am angry because no one hears me

I am angry because my children are looked down upon

I am angry because I don't make enough money

I am angry because Isiah is treated differently

I am angry because I am sad every single day

I am angry because Mackenzie's family forgot her

I am angry at people for not caring the same way I
do I am angry I don't care about myself anymore

I am angry I look this way

I am angry I have nobody to talk to I am angry children are
suffering

I am angry that Isiah doesn't have his mother or his
father I am angry that I didn't go to college

I am angry that my child turned to drugs

I am angry that my dreams were shattered I am angry my
daughter is not normal.

I am angry that my family will never forget her
past I am angry I cannot show my emotions

I am angry I do not like many people

I am angry I have to go to that prison every month

I am angry that I have to watch Mackenzie cry every
month I am angry that people hurt Isiah's feelings

I am angry that people I love talk negative about my child to
other people

I am angry that nobody really has my back

I am angry I have to break my daughter's heart again

I am angry I have to plan my child's funeral in my head just in case

I am angry people were mean to her

I am angry people are mean to themselves

I am angry about what has been done to my beautiful daughter in prison

I am angry she will never be the same

I am angry she is scared to death

I am angry for what Mackenzie has seen

I am angry that I questioned God

I am angry that I have to say I'm sorry every night when I pray

I am angry my beautiful sweet Mother don't remember

I am angry my strong Dad looks weak

I am angry I have to struggle

I am angry I can't buy more shoes

I am angry I am not a better Mother

I am angry I don't look like other women

I am angry I want to hurt someone

I am angry because the only thing that listens is a computer I am angry that people ask me questions

I am angry that I don't want to talk to anyone
anymore I hate carrying around all this anger
I hate that I use the word hate

I am going to be OK, but I am angry.

November 18, 2018

Today is Sunday. I am taking my Mother and Isiah down to
Dayton Correctional Institution to visit Mackenzie. We are
allowed to arrive at 4:30 pm and are made to leave at 7:30
pm. I cannot wait to kiss her chubby cheeks and hug her
sweet face! She will never be to me what others see in
Mackenzie. She is my child and I love her no matter what.
At the sight of me and my mother, Mackenzie turns
instantly from a hardcore inmate that is halfway
institutionalized into a silly girl that giggles and makes
jokes and cuddles her baby boy.

Isiah is the same way in that he loves his Momma no
matter what. The reason I started The Isiah's Hope Project
is that I see that child/mother love every single month at
these prison visits. Those female inmates have done some
pretty horrific unforgivable things, and some just sold stolen
items...but when they are buzzed in through those big steel
doors it all goes away and the room fills up with love. Pure
love for that person you are there to visit. More people
should have this unconditional love for one another, this
world would change. It is too easy to give into social
stigmas, or not exercising your love for something being
afraid of what people will say. When I walk into that prison, I
am judged immediately, the very second I enter that
institution. I was not confident at first, and I let the looks
make me feel small.... but not anymore. I am as proud to
walk in there as if I was walking into a sporting event to
watch my kid play on some field. No other human can

break my spirit at that disgusting place. You can overpower sadness by putting your energy and positivity into something. Mind over matter. I tried a yoga class and it really does make you feel empowered. Gracie told me she loves it, and it is giving her confidence in herself. The meditation was remarkable and healing to my wounds for sure. I had nothing to lose, I was being consumed by hatred and anger and sadness. Have you ever been to the point where something had to give or your head would literally explode? I have lived that since April 29, 2014. It is horrible and self-destructive. I still feel sorry for myself a lot, but I am working on allowing it to happen....then moving forward. If I went the other way I would be getting comfortable on a mat, inside a cage just like Mackenzie. My anger tends to be the fuel that was driving me insane. I work a full-time job trying to remain calm, and function on a daily basis. Why me? I have no idea, but I am a badass of a person and I know that. I am tough on the outside, and I am resilient as hell. My life is not for the weak, or the conceded. Some think they are better than me because of where my child is, or what my children have done. I embrace their ignorance and hope they never ever have to live one day in my size 8.5 size shoes. I am going to have a good day today, I get to hug and kiss my child in prison. Writing this makes me smile. I know that I will be in a very sad place tonight when my day is over and I will be back to missing her like crazy.... then comes the Holidays.....and the roller coaster keeps moving along...

November 21, 2018

"Uncle Mike"

Tuesday, November 20, 2018 heaven gained an angel. Everyone says this when they have a loved one die, but I have not ever said this. When I say things, I mean them. I am not a beat around the bush kind of gal, or sugar coat type of person. Yesterday when I say heaven gained an angel, I mean that literally, a person who was a guardian angel right here on earth...passed away.

Mackenzie had always written back and forth with my Uncle and Aunt since the time she entered the prison system. They used to drive down to Ohio to watch Mack play softball in her prime years. Through Mackenzie's "troubled years" they were still supportive of all my children, yet noticed the battles Mackenzie faced internally. My Uncle lived in another state, so we spent many holidays apart, but when they made the trip down to Ohio it was always a big deal as a child. He is my Dad's little brother, and all three of the brothers are like cookie cutters of each other in a lot of ways. They are strong men; they demand respect and they get it. The family traditions of the Shepherds are something of which has been handed down for years. They are simple men, and the love of family runs deep in their blood. When I say that love is no matter what, this is where I get it from. We get mad, we back away on occasions, but this bond of family is no matter what. It has built a foundation in me of which I have taught my own children to stay connected to those that share your blood.

In 2017 Mackenzie got jumped by four inmates in the yard. They beat her. They broke her nose and busted her eye sockets leaving both eyes swollen and blackened. One inmate had a razor blade hidden and used it to cut my child on the one side of her body leaving her scarred.... literally. When Mackenzie was found she would not snitch on the ones who had brutalized her, she was placed on suicide watch for over 14 days. She was placed naked in a room with nothing but a mat to lay on. There were a toilet and a sink in her cell. No toilet paper, no clothing, no blankets, no pillow in fear she would harm herself. She stayed on suicide watch until her wounds healed or she snitched, whichever came first. When my Uncle heard this he was beside himself. He called and wrote emails demanding that we did something to get Mackenzie out of the hell she is living in. I was doing everything within my power to get an attorney but financially falling short with the day to day expenses of raising another child and my own. It came down to this...Mackenzie would not ever have a chance in hell unless we hired a private legal team to tell her story. My Aunt and Uncle wanted to help Mackenzie and I knew that. I was too proud to receive any because she is my responsibility and it was my problem. In the summer of 2017, Mackenzie was in solitary confinement for almost 65 days. I had scheduled a visit to bring her little boy and little sister to see her. She had been isolated so long that her grip with reality was distorted. She battles a mental illness anyway and when isolation is added to that, the mix was scary. When I watched my child in stripes and shackles shuffle while being escorted by a guard on each side to the visit hall, I knew I had to forget my pride from there on out. She looked like a wild animal and her eyes were blackened with rage and pain. She was submitting to her insanity. I was going to lose her to prison violence or suicide and I had come to terms with it. I had to get help. The help I needed for my daughter would be to give her hope that she would not have to rot in that prison for the next 11 years. Mackenzie could not see the future in those walls, all she saw was darkness. I answered a message from my Aunt and Uncle after being traumatized by seeing my child that way. My Uncle wanted to help pay for an attorney. Now I was on a mission to find someone who would represent Mackenzie legally. This was the hope that would save her life.

My Uncle said that he didn't care if he had to put up his house for collateral, or what it cost...an attorney had to be found. He knew that if Mackenzie did not have hope soon, she was going to give up. I did not even have to tell him this was my fear now.... he just knew. I found an attorney that would just listen to Mackenzie's story, I did not ask any price of anything. Five hundred dollars is a lot of money to me, but I thought if that was a retainer...I could swing it. I went to Columbus and met with the attorney that was nationally recognized. I was nervous I was out of my element and there was no way in hell I could afford his services. The attorneys said they had not ever read such a botched-up case or unjust sentence in all their years. They believed Mackenzie's story. At the end of the meeting, we had to talk financials. They told me what I had to have to retain them, and what the entire case would cost. I sunk a little into my fancy leather chair in that conference room that day. There was no way in hell I could hire them. I would have to have two years' salary or a winning lottery ticket to afford this. My Aunt had told me to just meet with them and call while still there to see what I thought of the attorneys. I called my Aunt and Uncle from the big shot attorney's office lobby. They asked what I thought and I honestly have a good feeling about this law firm. That's it, a good feeling. I am a hairstylist, I know hair. I know nothing about the law, but I know my daughter needs a voice and she needs hope and she needs it right now. I began the drive home when my Aunt and Uncle called me. They had called the attorneys office and retained his legal services for Mackenzie. Just like that.... they saved my daughter's life. I cried all the way home. I could never repay them and neither could Mackenzie. They knew this, and they did it anyway. A family is about love.... it's no matter what.

I scheduled a visit with Mackenzie the next week. There is no doubt in my mind that at that moment in that prison, on that day, when I was able to say the words...."Mackenzie listen to me, you now have legal representation....you now have hope" that it saved my daughter's life. She now has light in her eyes. She helps others in that awful place who are stuck in the dark place she was for so very long. She is motivated to become a better person, and mother, and daughter, and niece. She smiles now when I see her. She has the will to live. This is because of my Uncle Mike. He was the guardian angel that came in and wrapped his arms around me and my child and literally saved us. I will forever be in debt to my Uncle for his unconditional love for me and my children. I know he is in heaven with Jesus and doing things angels do. He already knew how to save people because he did it already here on earth. The day will come when Mackenzie walks through the doors of those prison walls into the free world. Mackenzie will look up into the sky and feel her Uncle Mike's warm wings wrapped around her again just like when she was a little girl, and he will be smiling down.... because he is an angel now just like he was here on earth.

Rest in Peace Uncle Mike

December 4, 2018

Mackenzie called me about 5:30. She was quiet and spoke very low. I know the voice, she's depressed. I knew this would happen because of the overruling of the appeal and the holidays. She has such a huge heart and her hopes were way too high that she may be coming home soon, I think I am at fault for that. I am trying to save her life and save her name. I cannot stop fighting for her. I still miss her like I did the very first week she went away. This has not gotten any easier like people said. They are full of shit; I want my daughter back.

Mackenzie told me she had broken her hand and she was in pain. They had set it and gave her generic Tylenol and she was being casted tomorrow. The meds she had been taking since 2017 were now restricted in all Ohio prisons she informed me. She told me of how she lay on her floor in her cell the past five days and just wished she was not alive. Now that the new medicine is not in her system she is having suicidal thoughts. She needs me, she needs her Mama to hold her and tell her she is going to be alright. They have control of her for the next 10 years.... control of her mind, control of her body, control of the outcome of all of our lives.....

Federal Court here we come......#justiceformackenzie

January 4, 2019

I cannot believe it's another year passed and my Mackenzie is still in prison. I really thought if I did not stop fighting for her freedom that she would be home by now. Am I a fool? One time I was doing a customer's hair and they of course were talking about Mackenzie's situation. The person said something I will never forget, they said, "you'll never be able to get her out of there...you know that right?". That statement plays in my head all hours of the day, especially at night. You see, this customer said that with such confidence that it made my skin crawl. I have not done this customer again. I have so much to say now to them in rebuttal. Why would you say that to a mother who you know is missing her child so desperately? Why would you say that to anyone? I am becoming enraged just thinking of that day. The customer had a spouse that was a retired correctional officer. It was said to me with the attitude of that they felt sorry for poor pitiful Judy....... it's really cute that you keep fighting but in the end you stupid lady, your daughter is going to rot in that prison and there is nothing you can ever do about it. Typing that haunts me to think that people think that. I am not powerless. I am a mother. I look defeated right now, but I am rebuilding. What the hell do I have to lose if I keep fighting for justice? If I can get one day or one hour before April 29, 2028....then it is worth the fight. I had another woman who apparently is

"Mother of the Year" send me a message telling me that and I quote "I am fighting the wrong battle". She seems to have life all figured out I guess. You see, she said that my other children need my attention and that I should not worry about Mackenzie so much. Well thank you Miss Lady....thank you for figuring out my life! I feel so complete now just because of the advice of the 2000's -mom and dad's club- perfect little house and kids- never walked a footstep inside a prison in her life- 30-year-old know everything- mom. I needed that guidance, shew, now I can move on.

One thing I have learned on this journey with Mackenzie is that before you say something to someone, make sure it is important and useful to mankind. I choose to encourage people; it makes me feel good. I like to build people up, especially when they are down. I have no right to kick someone when they are down because I am not God. I do not make judgments anymore of anyone...that is not my job either. I am glad this horrible nightmare has taught me lessons. I needed those lessons I will admit. I was not always kind to people before. I can honestly say that now I have a love for mankind that I did not have before. You have no idea what a human being is going through behind that smile or frown...or Face book picture. Mackenzie went into a severe depression right before Christmas. I didn't hear from her for over a week. It was right after the denial of her motion from the trial court. I could have almost called this episode, but it was justified in my book. I went through the same funk, only not while living alone in a prison cell. The antidepressant Mackenzie was taking in high doses was simply banned from the prison. It was banned from all prisons to be exact. Not replaced, just not given to her. There is approximately 950 women in that prison, and the dangers of stopping those kind of medications are dangerous. I knew this was going to be rough until she was given another one (2 weeks later). It was a Thursday when she called finally. As I said my first "Hello" after they tell me I am being recorded and monitored....I knew she was in a dark place. I could tell the weakness in her voice and the pain. I knew she wanted to hear our voices, but didn't want to speak to us. I asked if she was doing alright. Mackenzie broke down into a sob. She told me that she didn't want to live anymore in that hell. She said that the very thought of knowing she was going to wake up in there, made her want to throw up. She sounded shaky and unstable and very very suicidal. She sounded wounded, but not firm in her thoughts. I told her I did not blame her for wanting to take her own life, she has lived there much longer than I would have been able to. It got deep when she asked if it really mattered to Isiah if she stuck it out until he was possibly 17. He will have been already grown, raised by Ritchie and I. What can she possibly do to be a good mother to her son if she could not return to his life until he was 17 years old, she asked? I had to think, I needed to give a response quickly so that I sounded confident in my answer.

Honestly, I did not know what to say. I would be the one to suffer the most if she committed suicide. As horrible as it is to write this, Isiah would not be affected like I would. He only knows his Mommy to see her for three hours in a prison uniform, sitting in a chair, once a month. Isiah does not speak of his father, and he has seen him before...in the free world. Children only know routines and the feelings of comfort and safety. Neither Mackenzie, nor Isiah's other parent have provided any of those things for him in the short seven years he has been on this earth. I told Mackenzie that she was being very selfish for considering leaving Isiah, and the rest of her family. I probably didn't sound convincing because I did not mean that. She has suffered so much for her mistake. She has withstood the unthinkable at such a young age. She deserves to be free. Free from pain, free from depression, free from being terrified, free from being alone, and free from hate. I do not want to think of her battles inside that prison, with her own mind, and literal battles with prisoners out to kill. The suicide rate in female prisons is much

higher than in a male prison. There are many "natural
causes" deaths every year. I am sure it is more from
Mothers feeling like my child is than from actual "natural
causes". I continued to talk her off the ledge by reminding
her of the holiday dinner that upcoming Sunday that the
prison was having. Isiah and I were really counting on it,
he was so excited to spend a few hours with her for
Christmas. She could not stop sobbing. Mackenzie told
me that she had laid on the floor of her cell for the past
five days straight. She had not showered because the hot
water did not work at that time. She had not went and
taught any of her classes she usually does on Sundays,
nor had she worked her third shift fire watch duty. What
was the point? She had not one single care left in the
world at that point. All I felt was hopeless. I could not think
of any reason I had not said before to keep her motivated
to live out this sentence. That sounds sick. I myself have
prepared for the news of her taking her own life. I have
accepted it. I know of the songs she will want played at
her funeral. I already know what and who to thank for
constantly supporting Mackenzie through this nightmare.
Writing that without emotion means that some of my feelings are
dead. I have to be able to face the absolute worst. My body
physically cannot take another punch so to speak. My heart is
getting worn out from worry and fear, and sadness. I'm positive
my forty-five-year-old heart is weaker than most sixty-year-old.
There is no amount of money, or material items, or love that can
replace the wounds I have sustained......every single day for five
years now. I wonder if the ever-perfect PTA mom who was
concerned about which battle I am fighting, knows what it is like
to be a soldier like Mackenzie? I wonder if that woman thanks
God every night for keeping her daughter alive and safe, and
prays for God to protect her just one more day? There is
absolutely nothing else I am capable of doing to get my child
free, except believing in a higher power. I believe in the battle I
am fighting, and that is all that really matters at the end of the
day. Now we prepare for year five and thank God that I still have

Mackenzie.

February 25, 2019

15 Minute Phone Call

I spoke with Mack yesterday. Afterward, I began to become
consumed with how our phone call ended. The maximum
amount of time we are allowed to speak is 15 minutes. It
shuts off, no matter what. I began thinking what if everyone
only had 15 minutes to speak to someone you loved?
Imagine this.... you have no idea when you will speak to
your loved one...or child again, or if you even will....15
minutes. Did I want to say the words that I said? I was tired,
I had worked all day... and Isiah does not let you forget that
he is a child for one minute of the day. I hate to talk on the
phone. I try to think of every excuse that I can to avoid
phone conversations, except Mackenzie's. Since
Mackenzie has went away, I have begun to not tolerate
small talk. It is irrelevant. If something needs said, you
have to say it. This lesson has just smacked my family in
the face. At the end of the day, you have to rest your head
at night on a pillow of no regrets. It makes you love people
with a deeper and more forgiving heart, and it makes you
more comfortable with speaking your mind and the truth
also. My cousin just left this world at way to young of an
age. We were buddies, and we would casually shout out
the ole' "Love you guys" at the end of some late-night
phone conversations, but this was with every intention of
seeing them in a few months. Life just happened. I will not
ever get to talk or not talk to him again. Did my cousin
know everything he needed to know from me? He did not.
This I will live with for the rest of my life. I whispered to him
how much I loved him as he lay peaceful in his casket. We
have to find comfort in our own minds that he knew this just
as we assume all of our loved ones know this. At the end of

the day I will always make sure I talk and listen to everything Mackenzie has to say.... even if I hate talking on the phone. I have to go to bed at night knowing that she knows I love her and I always will. Nothing else matters. I can be tired later, or sleep later, or be irritated later, but for those 15 minutes when my child is allowed to call her Mom....I will be there. What if you knew a single phone call would be the very last time you ever talked to another human being again? Pretend there was a stamp on all of us that had our last day on this earth, kind of like our expiration date. All conversations would be different, they just would. When you tell someone you are going to do something, you need to do it. I have made so many empty promises in my life , all with the best of intentions. This lesson I have been taught at 45 years old, and I want to teach my children and grandchildren this.

March 24, 2019

The last entry for now; not the last chapter.......

I am beginning to live in fear. I am beginning to think I should stop pushing for justice for my child. It very well may be my mind playing tricks on me, then again it may be that my life is playing out to be a true story motion picture. I think back to August 2014. I was sitting in the filthy county jail waiting for my 19-year-old to come to her side of the glass. We would pick up our phones and try to attempt to talk like any normal mother and daughter. That moment feels like it was yesterday, not five years ago. I wish I would have believed my daughter back then when she told me that her attorney was "in" with the sheriff at that time. I was mad at her. Her story seemed like that of a movie.... now everything she told me back then has came out. I have been arrested, my son's house has been raided, my husband has been pulled over and harassed, we have been followed, and I thought it was just "coincidence".

This is real life, and it is scary. The cop that tore down her pictures of Isiah and was yelling in her face calling her "sticky fingers", now is serving a ten-year sentence in an Ohio private prison. He indeed was a thief and was a crooked cop....just like Mackenzie said in 2014. The head sheriff at the time of Mack's arrest was also indicted of extortion, bribery, and providing false statements to the FBI. He just plead guilty to the charges and faces up to 12 years or so. This makes me feel vindicated. I can get some sense of peace knowing that at some point Mackenzie stopped lying to me and told me the truth. This is the real reason why I cannot let it go. I know. I know I can trust her. At one point when she was drug fueled I would sleep with my valuables under my pillow at night and she don't even know that. This is why I had to find out the truth, I had to be able to believe her, and finally....I do. My sweet , loving Kiki would never do the things so many are saying she did. I know what she did do, and I can live with that. She committed a crime, but not the crimes those dirty cops said she did. She was vulnerable and young and stupid and high and a very easy target for grown men with a badge. It will forever haunt me that I didn't believe her in 2014. I told her to shut her mouth and just plead guilty to everything...and she did. I trusted her court appointed attorney more than my own child. Why did I do that? I didn't even know that man very well, yet I told her that if she didn't do what he said that I was done with her. I guess because he had a law degree? That is horrible for a mother to do to her child. I will spend the rest of my life not believing every word my children say but believing IN my children. There is a difference, and I have been taught this from Mackenzie. This past year my son battled an addiction and I acted like it wasn't happening. I didn't believe he could survive it. You see, he is not as strong mentally as his sister. She is a powerful presence, and he is a sweet, loving, handsome, kind, soft warmhearted presence. I was just certain that I was going to bury him.

We have four children and I was going to be left with number one and number four in the free world. The middle two are from the same genes. Is this a coincidence? I have not ever craved drugs, never felt any desire to put anything in my body that altered my reality other than a few drinks. Why would my children crave this feeling? Since 2014 I have been consumed by Mackenzie being locked in a prison cell. It navigates my every waking moment and would not allow other things to enter my mind.

My son's situation needed my full attention, and I couldn't even focus on it because I was consumed. It was the point when I heard myself praying at night for Jesus to please keep my Coley alive until the next day that I finally woke up! Dear God, I haven't noticed this kid in five years. He was in his sister's shadow and he was ok with that. He was in pain, and just because he wasn't sitting in a prison cell, I felt he was fine. I decided to start going over to his house a lot, calling him every day. My presence needed to be in his life more, even though he never said a word, he needed his mother. He would never ask for it, because he is a "grown ass man" .....I know him, he needed his Mama. I only have thought about myself missing a child. I have been very selfish in only thinking about myself. I did not ever think about how my other children are coping with Mackenzie being gone. How do they feel about Ritchie and I having to raise Isiah as our own? This never crossed my mind, their feelings on our situation. It is like my other kids can't complain about one thing because their sister is living in hell and facing horrific things. Kinda like if you are not trying to avoid getting your ass beat every day or not getting raped in the shower your problems don't matter. That's not fair. I really just realized this is how my mind has worked for the past few years. Since my son knows he has my full attention, he has become different. He is a different man, he is living a new life with a woman he loves, and a great job he loves, and goals in life that he is reaching. It was not me that did this, but there is no doubt in my mind that as soon as he knew I was not giving up on him.... he had a new self- confidence and self-esteem about him that was noticeable. He does not try to escape reality anymore; he can stomach feeling how he feels mentally...and that is important.

Everyone has a story, and every story matters...especially to that person. I should not make another situation seem minor just because it is not like the life I am living. That would be like asking someone to pick one, sleeping in a prison cell for 14 years or have cancer. I know which one I would choose.

These are thoughts that should not run through my head. I have taken a step back. I am re-focusing on the things that are important to my soul. My husband deserves a more loving wife, and that I cannot be. My children, all of them, deserve their Mom. It does not mean that I love Mackenzie any less if I don't sit and grieve her 24 hours a day. I used to feel like I was not being loyal to my sweet girl, like I had to make it up to her that I didn't believe IN her back then. I did not think I could live without Mackenzie in my life every day, and I have. I miss her so much that it physically makes my chest ache when I stare at her pictures to pretend like she is in the room. I am stronger than I thought I was. My faith in God is at an all-time high right now. The path I am on is the path I am meant to be on....it is a very rough path, but there is a reason for this. I can take it, and I can walk with my head held high no matter what others say about me or my children. I am no longer intimidated by that bully from 7th grade study hall. The same adult man that happens to be the county prosecutor. The same man that would yell out for kids to move their desks so I could fit through the isle.... actually he yelled "ox" every time I came into study hall. After I sat, that kid would point at me if my face twitched while I was writing my homework, well it still twitches! The very sight of him back then made me cower down in embarrassment and shame so that he wouldn't notice me and make fun. That same man grew up and went

to law school, coincidentally he signed the search warrant
for the sheriff to search my daughter's house and car back
in 2014. Small town luck I guess. I have had nightmares of
my middle school bully walking into the court room if
Mackenzie ever gets her appeal granted. This will be a
battle inside myself that nobody around me will even know
I'm dealing with. I will do anything for my children, even
overcome this fear after 32 years of avoiding this bully.
Some would wish that his very own children would get
bullied like he used to make fun of kids in school, but not
me. I love any child, and always want a child's innocence
protected from the cruelty of the real world. I can defend my
children with knowledge, and without ignorance. This is
also how I raised my children. I can make other parents feel
all nice and cozy at night knowing their kid is not in the
situation my kid is in. I can live with this. What I cannot do
is enjoy my life to the fullest yet or think about myself and
that I will continue to work on. Hopefully someday, maybe
when I am cuddled up on the couch watching movies and
having a movie party with all of my children beside me, I
can finally have fun. That will be the ultimate sense of
comfort as a mother.

I will never be complete, and my heart will not ever be whole
until I have Mackenzie home. Until the day I stand outside those
barbed wire fences and watch my child walk through the exit
gate into my arms, I can then start to heal. I dream of this day
quite often. She is smiling from ear to ear, all while those
beautiful dimples appear. Her baby boy will scream "Mommy"
while he runs into her arms. I hope my parents will be there.
All her sisters and little brother will be waiting with tears and joy
and open arms for her to fall into. Nothing in the world will
matter when this happens. Nothing can hurt us anymore. We
will have our girl back safe. I can actually feel the warmth of her
body and warm chubby cheeks as I get to hug and kiss her as
she enters the free world. I know how she smells, that clean
smell of prison soap. The smell I always use three or four times

on my hands at visitation, so it will last the rest of the day. I smell my hands the entire night at home after visits. I smell my shirt because sometimes if I'm lucky it will have her scent on it from our hug that day. I smell Isiah, because he smells like her scent after she gets to hug and kiss him at visitation. It's been five years and I still crave her presence this bad. Maybe Mackenzie is the drug that I crave? It has control over me, I just don't actually swallow or snort it into my body. It is there, and it is still to this day crippling to my body. There is so much more to Mackenzie's story, and mine. Our next chapter in our prison diaries will be hopefully the day Mackenzie gets her day in court to tell her real story. I will not stop fighting for this day. I will get a little more peace no matter the outcome, but just knowing she is heard. That's all.... just heard.

Our diaries have taught me many good lessons. They have broke my heart, made me angry, played tricks on my mind, made my circle smaller, and made me realize who the real people are. Our diaries have shown me into the inside of somewhere I have never been.... they have also introduced me to my adult child who I did not know. The child who left I missed, the grown woman I know now, I miss even more. She is an amazing person and I'm so glad she's my daughter. Our diaries have ended some relationships, and they have brought new ones. They have shown the importance of certain relationships I have in my life and made some friendships irreplaceable to me, and also to Mackenzie. They have also shown us both what relationships we need to let go of and move on. It is the end and the beginning.

I just put in for a reservation for a visit for next week to see Mackenzie. The petition just hit 2,500 supporters. I miss her so bad. There cannot be a final chapter in "The Real Prison Diaries" until I no longer have to make a reservation to see my own child........ I have to get her out of there.